Pliny the Younger, Constantine E. Prichard

Selected Letters of Pliny

Pliny the Younger, Constantine E. Prichard

Selected Letters of Pliny

ISBN/EAN: 9783337017408

Printed in Europe, USA, Canada, Australia, Japan

Cover: Foto ©Thomas Meinert / pixelio.de

More available books at **www.hansebooks.com**

Clarendon Press Series

PLINY

SELECTED LETTERS

PRICHARD AND BERNARD

A

HENRY FROWDE, M.A.

PUBLISHER TO THE UNIVERSITY OF OXFORD

LONDON, EDINBURGH, GLASGOW
AND NEW YORK

OF

PLINY

WITH NOTES FOR THE USE OF SCHOOLS

BY THE LATE

CONSTANTINE E. PRICHARD, M.A.

Formerly Fellow of Balliol College

AND

EDWARD R. BERNARD, M.A.

Formerly Fellow of Magdalen College

NEW EDITION

PART I. — TEXT

Oxford

AT THE CLARENDON PRESS

M DCCC XCVI

Oxford

PRINTED AT THE CLARENDON PRESS

BY HORACE HART, PRINTER TO THE UNIVERSITY

PREFACE.

THE text of this selection of Pliny's letters is that of Keil
(Leipsic, 1870). Keil has prefixed to this (his second
edition) an admirable account of the materials extant for
a critical edition of the works of the author, and an
estimate of their comparative authority. He distinguishes
three families of extant MSS. The first is represented by
the Medicean and Vatican MSS. Of these the Vatican,
though perhaps the more ancient, contains only the first
four books. The Medicean, containing all the letters
except those to and from Trajan, must therefore hold the
first place in importance.

The second family is best represented by the Florentine
MS., and contains only one hundred letters.

The third family is of a much later date, and consists
of a great number of MSS. of the fifteenth century, which
are also all imperfect, as they omit the eighth book, put the
ninth in its place, and disarrange the order of the letters in
the fifth and the ninth books. Keil considers the Codex
Dresdensis the most valuable of this class of MSS.

The letters to and from Trajan (formerly called the tenth
book), stand on a different footing. We have no MS.
authority for their text, and depend entirely on printed

editions of the early part of the sixteenth century. About the beginning of that century a very ancient MS. was found in France containing the whole of the works of the younger Pliny, and among them, the letters to and from Trajan, hitherto unknown. Aldus in his complete edition (1508) speaks of his access to this MS. It is no longer extant. If it were, Keil thinks it would probably take precedence of the Medicean (mentioned above) in respect of the nine books of letters, as well as being the sole authority for the tenth. Keil's text of the letters to and from Trajan is therefore founded on the editions of Avantius (ed. pr.) and Aldus.

Nine books of Pliny's letters are mentioned by Sidonius Apollinaris as known to him in the fifth century. After that date they seemed to have shared the general oblivion which befel classical literature, and there is no notice of them till the thirteenth century, when Vincent of Beauvais found a MS. of the 'second family,' and made extracts from it.

The letters were first printed by Valdarferus at Venice in 1471.

All explanatory editions of Pliny's letters are much indebted to that of Catanaeus (Milan, 1506). His notes form the foundation on which subsequent commentaries have been built up. The edition of Cortius and Longolius (Amsterdam, 1734) gives copious illustrations from other authors, and some variety of notes by other critics, but contains little that is original and distinct in the way of explanation of difficulties. Cortius' critical observations on the text, which occupy much space, have been antiquated by modern investigation. The edition derives value from Masson's learned Life of Pliny, which he allowed to be reprinted with it, and from the very copious indices which are appended to the book.

Gierig's edition (Leipsic, 1800) with Latin notes is a thoroughly good book. A great part of the notes to this selection were prepared without consulting Gierig, but on comparison they will often be found to coincide.

The letters in this selection are not arranged chronologically, but printed in the order in which they stand in the ordinary arrangement. The lines of each letter have been numbered in the text to facilitate reference to the notes. Reference in the notes to a passage contained in this selection is made thus, Ep. 2. 1, the first figure referring to the number of the letter in this selection, and the second figure to the line in the text. References to letters not in this selection are preceded by the abbreviation Bk., thus, Bk. 3. 9. In these cases, the first figure gives the number of the Book according to the usual arrangement of the letters, and the second figure the number of the letter. Book 10 is referred to by the abbreviation Trai., thus Trai. 20. Frequent references have been made to Madvig's Latin Grammar (as Madv.), which, with other references, and some of the notes themselves, are addressed rather to the teacher than to the pupil.

ADVERTISEMENT TO THE
THIRD EDITION.

THIS edition differs from the second by the addition of a Life of Pliny, a table of the Letters included in the selection, and an index of the names which occur in them. The Text and Notes are reprinted without change from the second edition. The additions are the work of Mr. L. Huxley.

LIFE OF PLINY.

C. PLINIUS CAECILIUS SECUNDUS, son of L. Caecilius Cilo and his wife Plinia, was born at Novum Comum in the latter half of 61 or the beginning of 62 A.D. Both the Caecilii and the Plinii were families of good position ; both belonged to the municipal nobility, and the elder Pliny at least was of equestrian rank. Cilo himself died too young to reach any higher eminence than the municipal aedileship ; but the family had been established so long in Como that young Pliny could not be described as a *parvenu* on entering public life at Rome. Catullus (35) mentions the Caecilii as established at Como in Caesar's time, and Pliny himself (Ep. viii. 10. 3) speaks of leaving to the son he hoped for *non subitas imagines.*

On his father's death in 76, Pliny, still a minor, was left to the care of his uncle, after whom he had been named Secundus, and of Verginius Rufus. Though Pliny was impressed by the simple kindness and indefatigable activity of his uncle (Ep. 43), the richer and more varied nature of Verginius stirred him with the warmest love and veneration, and it was doubtless to Verginius that Pliny owed the full development of the gentler side of his nature. In the year 79, however, the elder Pliny perished in the eruption of Vesuvius which overwhelmed Pompeii, and by his will adopted his nephew as his son and heir. It is to this testamentary adoption that the younger Pliny owes his name as we know it. From P. Caecilius L. f. Secundus he became C. Plinius L. f. Caecilius Secundus, not, as in republican times, C. Plinius C. r. Caecilianus Secundus. The usage at this period, when the strict gentile system of society was breaking up, stood half way between that of the republic and that of the later empire, when the adoptive father's names were added bodily to the heir's.

The addition of his uncle's fortune to the estates inherited from his father and mother near Lake Larius or Como, and at Tifernum, made Pliny a man of great wealth. His Etrurian estates alone brought him in 400,000 HS. (Ad Tr. 8. 4). Accordingly he resolved to pursue the regular high road to fortune and ambition, the senatorial career. With a natural gift of speech, and trained in oratory by Nicetes Sacerdos and the famous Quintilian (viii. 14. 4) he began speaking at the bar in his nineteenth year (v. 8. 8), not without success (Ep. 12. l. 15). Before entering the senate as quaestor, he held various minor offices, such as decemvir stlitibus iudicandis, tribunus militum of the Legio III Gallica, and sevir of the Roman knights. The same course, it may be remembered, was followed fifteen years later by Hadrian, who also was not of senatorial rank.

As to Pliny's military career, a formal period of service, six months, or a year at most, was still required of a candidate for public life, but it was generally service without campaigning. The *tribunus militum honores petiturus* was almost a supernumerary, and was usually very young ; Hadrian held the position for the second time when only twenty-one, while Pliny describes himself as *adulescentulus* (Ep. 6. l. 4) and found time to attend the lectures of the leading philosophers in Syria, where his legion was quartered, and to live in the closest intercourse with Euphrates and Artemidorus, the son-in-law of a more famous philosopher, Musonius (Ep. 28).

Pliny was elected quaestor in 89, tribune 91, and praetor 93. As quaestor his financial power gained him the favour of Domitian, and he was named *quaestor imperatoris*. Possibly the '*pessimus imperator*' hoped to gain another willing agent in the easy and unassuming young Italian. The latter, however, was of steady principle, and indeed still clung with a certain youthful affectation to the last shadows of republican usage. While tribune, he abstained from pleading in the centumviral court, for fear that the sacred dignity of his office might be impaired in the collisions and rebuffs of legal practice (Ep. 15). The chief act of his praetorship was the prosecution of Baebius Massa for extortion in Baetica. According to his account in

Ep. 69 Pliny and his colleague Senecio distinguished themselves by the courage with which they continued their attack
on this creature of Domitian's, though Senecio paid for it with
his life before the year was out (Ep. 28), and Pliny himself
was finally denounced by the informer Carus, and only saved
by the timely death of Domitian, in whose desk the signed
information was afterwards found (Ep. 68). As praetor,
too, he celebrated public games, but with the same *modestia*
(Pan. 95) which had marked the games given by Agricola
(Tac. Agr. 6).

Up to this point his advancement had been very rapid. He
had been made tribune as soon after his quaestorship as the
leges annales permitted ; then a year of the legal interval
between the tribunate and praetorship was remitted by the
Emperor (vii. 16), as if he were qualified by Augustus' ius
liberorum, whereby a year of the necessary age was remitted
for each child. Thus Pliny laid down the tribunate on Dec.
10th, 92, and assumed the praetorship 1st Jan. 93.

After this his advancement was slower. He could not be
consul before 95 at least, and considering the number of candidates, it would be no slight to be passed over for two or three
years further. As far as imperial favour went, he might have
intrigued for advancement *extra ordinem*, but this would have
been to place himself on a level with such men as Carus and
Messalinus : he chose rather to wait.

In the interval he was appointed one of the three *praefecti
aerarii militaris* in 94 or 95, for the usual term of three years,
and here showed such financial skill, that in 98, soon after
Nerva's accession, he was promoted to the State Treasury, as
praefectus aerarii Saturni. This is the only case known in
which one man held both offices in succession. He had
cleared the way for this advancement by prosecuting Publicius
Certus, one of the last holders of the office, at the end of
97, with the result that Certus was removed from the Treasury
and passed over in the list of consuls for the next year
(Ep. 77). According to custom his colleague, Vettius Proculus, left the Treasury at the same time ; the two places
were filled by Pliny and Cornutus for the succeeding term

of four years, including therefore the year of their joint consulate, 100.

At this period the consulate was no longer confined to two colleagues, for the year. Office was held for two or four months only, and pairs of *suffecti* were appointed during the rest of the year. Thus Pliny was consul suffectus in Sept. and Oct. 100, and his instalment in office was the occasion on which he delivered the Panegyric, an account of his own career and an ornate glorification of Trajan, his intimate friend as well as his emperor.

He was made augur in 103 or 104, and *curator alvei Tiberis et riparum et cloacarum urbis* from 105 to 107, a post always given to a consular as that of *praefectus aerarii* was always given to a praetorian. The Emperor also often summoned him to assist at his private council (Ep. 13. l. 51). His last and most important post was that of legate to the province of Pontus and Bithynia, in 111-12, or 112-13. This was a consular and senatorial province, into which, as so often happened, various abuses had crept. The proconsuls, chosen from the senate by lot, were generally inefficient or oppressive. Their tenure of office was too short, their responsibility too slight, for good administration. Government by legates selected by the Emperor, and directly responsible to him, was so far preferable that provincials sometimes went so far as to petition for an exchange to the latter.

It was a high mark of confidence in Pliny that he was chosen as the Emperor's representative in such a matter. Trajan writes (Ad Tr. 113) '*ego ideo prudentiam tuam elegi, ut formandis istius provinciae moribus ipse moderareris et ea constitueres quae ad perpetuam eius provinciae quietem essent profutura.*' To invest the reforming legate with a dignity equal in name to that of the senatorial governors, he was given the somewhat contradictory title of *legatus propraetore consulari potestate.* (Mommsen compares with this the Emperor's election as consul when he already possessed the proconsular power.) Among the abuses which needed reform were the doings of the clubs and secret societies, which included the meetings of the Christians, the relaxation of administrative control due to the yearly change

of governors, and the consequent disorder of the municipal
government and the treasury. Yet it may be inferred from
the tone of the many administrative questions with which he
plies the Emperor in his correspondence, that Pliny was not
so well skilled in civil law as in finance. The misgovernment
of the province seems to have continued after Pliny's departure,
for Cornutus appears to have occupied the same post later, and
a third legate was sent out by Hadrian. Finally Pontus was
made an imperial province in exchange for Lycia and Pam-
phylia.

As to Pliny's return from Bithynia, the Letters contain no
mention even of preparation for it. His death must have taken
place abroad or very soon after his return, probably in 114.

In addition to his imperial offices, Pliny was *flamen divi
Titi Augusti*, just as his connection Fabatus was *flamen divi
Augusti*. This was probably a priesthood at Como, for the
corresponding priest at Rome, as Mommsen points out, was
called *flamen Augustalis*. But this was not the only way in
which he kept up his connection with Como. His great wealth
enabled him to display on a magnificent scale all an Italian's
love for his native town. The importance of universal education
was beginning to be felt. Vespasian had endowed public professors ; Domitian stimulated literature by the prizes of the
Alban and Capitoline games, and now even private individuals
began to endow education (Ep. iv. 3. 5). One of the most
munificent of these was Pliny. In the lifetime of Domitian
(Ep. v. 7) he presented Como with a library worth a million
sesterces and a fund of as much more to maintain and to
enlarge it. He contributed one third of the support of a school,
when the people of Como were compelled to send their children
to Milan for education (Ep. 39). Again in Ep. 66 (where see
note 7) he speaks of having given half a million sesterces to the
bringing up of boys and girls at Como, and explains to a friend
who has similar intentions his method of securing the income
by a perpetual rent-charge upon an estate. This clear-sighted
arrangement, which provided against loss of income by bad
management of the lands, is another testimony to Pliny's
financial powers.

Besides these benefactions during his lifetime, Pliny provided by will for the building and maintenance of public baths or thermae, while another legacy of a million and three quarters was devoted to the support of a hundred of his freedmen. After their death, it was to provide an annual feast for the people of Como in commemoration of their benefactor.

We read also of a temple with statues of the *divi* which Pliny erected at Tifernum, a town which had chosen him as patron (Ep. iv. 1). Ep. 84 tells how he enlarged this with a portico, and Ep. 26 how he gave a valuable statue to another temple at Como rather than keep it in his own house.

But Pliny's generosity was not reserved for public actions. His kindness and equity to dependents (Epp. 38, 50, 70, 73, 79), his interest in his friends (Epp. 9, 18, 19, 46, 48, 49), even when his own life was endangered by the aid he offered, for example, to Artemidorus in Domitian's persecution of the philosophers (Ep. 28), his appreciation of what is best in every character (Epp. 6, 14, 16, 24), his loyalty to old friendships (Ep. 40), his generous dealings (Ep. 54 and 70), his deep affection for his wife (Epp. 41, 54, 56), all unite in showing a very fine and loveable side of his character. So far does this *mollitia animi* (iv. 21) carry him, that, with two exceptions only, he never fails to speak well of every one still living and not in exile. The two exceptions are Iavolenus and Regulus : the one for a breach of good manners towards an old friend of Pliny's, the other for his infamous success in delation, against which Pliny could not restrain his indignation. This excess of graciousness may be explained by the exigencies of publication during the life of the correspondents : but even Pliny's friends found him too catholic in his indulgence, and in Ep. vii. 28 he has to defend himself against the charge of praising his own circle in season and out of season. No doubt there was a good deal of 'log-rolling' in the literary coteries of the day, and Pliny himself was slightly touched by it, for all that he declares (Ep. 8) that he attends recitations solely for the advantage of literature. Such mutual admiration was common to all but the strongest characters, and Pliny's was weakened by a certain vanity of aspiration, and a too easy self-complacence in success. Yet he was firm enough to resist the advances of Domitian and his courtiers ; he came of the pure and upright stock of North Italy (Ep. 9. note 20) and filled with reverence for the life and teaching of such men as Verginius and Euphrates, could honestly write 'mihi autem egregium in primis videtur, ut foris ita domi, ut in magnis ita in parvis, ut in alienis ita in suis, agitare iustitiam' (Ep. 70. l. 5).

Pliny has often been compared to Cicero. With smaller gifts and fewer opportunities, he was more fortunate, but less eminent. The influences of the time even conspired to accentuate his like failing. The moral oppression and instability of fortune under the worst emperors tended to exaggerate the importance of every struggle for right and freedom, and to make every action an appeal from the wrongs of the present to the judgment of the future. Men of position, debarred from influence in the State, turned to oratory and literature for an occupation and a pastime, seeking piquancy of expression rather than real solidity. A wide-spread growth of self-consciousness and the feeling of the worthlessness of the present are to a great extent responsible for the feverish desire so often met with in the Letters to survive oblivion in the remembrance of posterity (Epp. 18, 27, fin.) Pliny puts the alternative of life very shortly in Ep. 74 ; men should either consider, he says, the immortality of fame, and work for it, or the shortness of life, and enjoy it. And so, comforted by the reflection that the name of Pliny is known wherever the love of letters exists (Ep. 8), he is able to moralise over the cheap diversions and unprofitable pursuits of the many (Epp. 5, 75).

A similar restless tone is perceptible in the correspondence with Trajan, which contrasts with the business-like simplicity of the Emperor's replies. Indeed Pliny lays himself open to a general indictment of posing before the public. The letters were arranged by himself and published in his lifetime. We have seen what effect this had on his praise of others : it had no less on the praise of himself. All the letters appear to have been written with a view to publication and immortality. A selection from these could not fail to be a most partial autobiography ; while the elaboration bestowed on the letters has often been at

the cost of their spontaneity and simplicity. Yet even here he
unmasks himself. His vanity is too simple and harmless to
conceal itself, too free from any touch of that saving humour
which perceives its own incongruities and disproportions. He
naively tells us it was to bring himself into notice that he prose-
cuted Certus, and to enhance his own impartiality that he waited
until the first wave of indignation against the lesser crowd of
informers had spent itself (Ep. 77). He praises himself
that his friend may have the same pleasure as he himself had
felt in his good deed (Ep. 44). Tacitus may have the laugh
of him for waiting by the coverts, a spear in one hand, a pencil
in the other, ready to secure the flying game or a fugitive thought ;
still, these trifles go to the making of immortality (Ep. 4).
We are offended by his adulation of Trajan ; but must remember
the contrast between Trajan and Domitian. If Pliny is fond of
celebrating his own praise, he is still modest enough not merely to
tell of his own modesty, for example, that he keeps no precious
bronzes at home (Ep. 26), but openly to admit his inferiority
to Tacitus as a writer of prose, to Arrius as a writer of verse
(Epp. viii. 7, v. 15). He is unfeignedly pleased at being coupled
with Tacitus as a leader of literature (Ep. 80).

A collection of letters is always peculiarly valuable for the
intimate views it gives of social life. Pliny, with his wholesome
and gentle life, was not stirred to pour unmeasured satire on the
worst excesses of his time. His nature led him to look on the
brighter side of society, to move in the purest atmosphere he
could find. His letters, reflecting what was best in Roman life,
are therefore a necessary corrective to the writings of the great
satirists. Those times could not be utterly bad in which we meet
with the record of such a circle as Pliny's ; so much fortitude
under suffering, such devotion to right among its earlier mem-
bers ; such delicacy of feeling, such generous affection, such
wide humanity seeming natural to those who survived to enjoy
the repose of Trajan's reign. If the life of action had narrowed,
the life of sentiment had vastly widened. It was not to unre-
sponsive listeners that Pliny spoke of the beauties of nature
(Ep. 72), or called his slaves not servi but sui (Epp. 50, 79),
or told the unselfish delight he took in the pleasures of others

(Ep. 6, fin.). We see that his was a happy life; the vein of serious purpose that sometimes made itself ridiculous in seeking an opportunity for self-improvement in the most incongruous circumstances, preserved him from all ruinous excess or extravagance, and in the industrious leisure of the country (Ep. 82), to which he retreats from the busy idleness of the town (Ep. 5), he was able to devote himself to those works which should preserve his fame to posterity. His greatest grief was, that though, after Trajan's accession, he married a second, perhaps a third wife, in Calpurnia (see Ep. 86, note 10) no children survived to bear his name.

Pliny's claim to literary eminence now rests upon the Letters and the Panegyric; more correctly, perhaps, upon the Letters. His other writings, published speeches and verses, have not come down to us. Like most other Romans, Pliny began his career by oratory (cp. what is said of Tacitus, Ep. 16). His especial arena (Ep. vi. 22) was the Centumviral Court (Ep. 12, note 9), where he delivered, for instance, the speeches in favour of Attia Viriola (Ep. 62) and of Corellia (Ep. 40); but his fame as an orator rested chiefly upon the five great causes he undertook at the request of the Senate (Ep. vi. 29). Those against Baebius Massa and Julius Bassus are described in Epp. 69 and 39 respectively. Pliny attached great value to these speeches; he composed them with care, and still more carefully revised and enlarged them before publication (Ep. 78). 'Egi magnas et graves causas; has ... destino retractare, ne tantus ille labor meus—mecum pariter intercidat' (Ep. v. 8. 6). In Ep. 62 he writes of revising his speech for Attia Viriola, which he considers his masterpiece; in Ep. 32 he has enlarged the Panegyric to such an extent that two days did not suffice for its recitation to a select body of friends before it was given to the world. But it was not only thus that speeches were arranged for mere literary effect. The very pleadings of the lawyers were intended for nothing but display, and the law-court became the scene of a fashionable recitation (Ep. 20). If such serious matters were profaned by the dilettanti, it is no wonder that every aspirant to fame was bound to try his hand at poetry of all kinds. 'Magnum proventum poetarum annus hic attulit,' writes Pliny in Ep. 8. Who can wonder that their recitations were sparsely attended ? Pliny himself had done as others did : 'Variis me studiorum generibus, nulli satis confisus, experior' (Ep. ix. 2. 9. 1), and in

> 'the spirit of a youth
> That means to be of note, began betimes'

with a Greek tragedy (!) at the age of fourteen (Ep. vii. 4).

We hear of elegiacs on the Island of Icaria while he was weather-bound on his way back from Syria, of Latin iambics, in which he says he was 'facilitate corruptus ;' later he published a collection of hendecasyllables, which achieved some popularity (Ep. iv. 24) ; 'lusus et ineptiae' hardly fitting the ideal senator, for they appear to have been of the usual personal and abusive character. In Epp. iv. 18 and v. 15 he speaks of translating three Greek epigrams by Arrius Antoninus, and these translations are perhaps preserved in the Anthologia Latina 710 R.

But though his verses were a failure and his orations laboured, Pliny possessed enough sympathy and discernment to be, not a poet or a historian, but a letter-writer. His sensibilities were easily moved by humanity or by nature ; he instinctively saw the brighter side of men and things, and writing of them was picturesque without malice and sympathetic without mawkishness. His own nature reproduces itself in his way of looking at the world, grouping things too often as harmless vanity directed, yet requiring no little of its own sympathy and honour from all its circle. The affectations in the Letters belong to the training of the age ; rhetorical trappings weighing down the subject-matter ; endless metaphors, due to the wide study of epic and lyric poetry, diversifying the whole language, as in modern times.

The collection of letters displays much skill in its arrangement. With rare exceptions, each letter gains in artistic completeness by treating of one subject alone ; while the reader finds a pleasant variety of theme in the succession of felicitation and condolence, anecdote and description, sketches of men and things, and slight essays suggested by passing events. They were probably intended from the first for publication ; no less care is spent over the diction than over the arrangement : witness the choice mentioned in the dedicatory letter (Ep. 1) of 'epistulas si quas paulo curatius scripsissem,' and the advice to a friend in Ep. vii. 9, 'volo epistulam diligentius scribas . . . pressus sermo purusque ex epistulis petitur.' Thus it comes that so many of them but for the address, seem to be no more than models of style for any given subject.

Like the works of Martial and Statius, the histories of Tacitus and the biographies of Fannius (Ep. 46), Pliny's letters appear to have been published in successive volumes, one or possibly three books at a time. As far as the dates can be verified, the letters in the first three books range from the year 97 to 104, the first possible date, therefore, of publication: i. 7 and i. 17 belonging probably to 101, and ii. 13 to 104 at earliest. Nothing, then, was published during Domitian's reign, though ii. 20, with its stories about Regulus the fortune-hunter, was written then. Book IV. contains letters of 103 to 106, with a few of earlier date, while Book V., though belonging chiefly to 106, has one letter which cannot be dated before 108, if, as is likely, Julius and Junius Avitus (Epp. v. 21 and viii. 23) are to be identified : and Book VI. belongs to 106 and 107. While a fairly long interval separates the publication of Book III. from the next book or group of books, we know from a reference in ix. 19 that vi. 10 was already published, thus making it not unlikely, from the quick succession of the later books, that all the nine books were published in groups of three, Book VII. affording dates of 107, VIII. of 108, and IX. of 109.

Pliny's statement in his dedicatory letter (Ep. 1) that the letters are not in strict chronological order, and that some older ones might find a place in later books, is borne out by the fact that Book II. contains the earliest letter of all, and others, such as IV. and V. contain letters written before the publication of the preceding group. [See Asbach's Examination of Mommsen's chronology in the Rheinisches Museum, xxxvi. 1.]

The correspondence with Trajan constitutes a tenth book. It consists of enquiries from Pliny upon questions of law and administration connected with his province, and Trajan's replies to these. The care and judgment of the emperor are as conspicuous as Pliny's conscientious desire to administer the law

with perfect equity.   These letters, dictated by necessity, show
perhaps somewhat more spontaneity on Pliny's part than do the
rest ; the emperor, seeing clearly what he wishes to have done
and with no fear of publication before his eyes, is delightfully
lucid and direct.   Two excellent examples of the contrast between
the emperor and his legate are given in this selection, the question of dealing with the foundlings (Epp. 87, 88) and with the
Christians (Epp. 90, 91), both interesting as throwing light on
provincial life.

Note.—For a detailed discussion of the facts of Pliny's life see
Mommsen's Essay in Hermes, iii. pp. 31 ff.

L. H.

LIST OF PLINY'S LETTERS CONTAINED IN THIS VOLUME.

A

SELECTION FROM THE LETTERS

OF

C. PLINIUS CAECILIUS
SECUNDUS.

1. (BOOK I. I.)

Pliny sends his letters to Septicius, who had encouraged him to collect them.

C. PLINIUS SEPTICIO SUO S.

Frequenter hortatus es ut epistulas, siquas paulo curatius scripsissem, colligerem publicaremque. Collegi non servato temporis ordine (neque enim historiam conponebam), sed ut quaeque in manus venerat. Superest ut nec te consilii nec me paeniteat obsequii. Ita enim fiet ut eas quae adhuc neglectae iacent requiram, et siquas addidero, non supprimam. Vale.

2. (BOOK I. 2.)

Pliny sends a speech to his friend Arrianus for correction by him.

C. PLINIUS ARRIANO SUO S.

Quia tardiorem adventum tuum prospicio, librum quem prioribus epistulis promiseram exhibeo. Hunc rogo ex

c

consuetudine tua et legas et emendes, eo magis, quod nihil
umquam peraeque eodem ζήλῳ scripsisse videor. Temptavi
enim imitari Demosthenen semper tuum, Calvum nuper 5
meum, dumtaxat figuris orationis : nam vim tantorum virorum
'pauci quos aequus amavit' adsequi possunt. Nec materia
ipsa huic, vereor ne inprobe dicam, aemulationi repugnavit :
erat enim prope tota in contentione dicendi. Quod me
longae desidiae indormientem excitavit, si modo is sum 10
ego qui excitari possim. Non tamen omnino Marci nostri
ληκύθους fugimus, quotiens paulum itinere decedere non
intempestivis amoenitatibus admonebamur : acres enim esse,
non tristes volebamus. Nec est quod putes me sub hac
exceptione veniam postulare. Nam quo magis intendam 15
limam tuam, confitebor et ipsum me et contubernales ab
editione non abhorrere, si modo tu fortasse errori nostro
album calculum adieceris. Est enim plane aliquid edendum,
atque utinam hoc potissimum quod paratum est! (audis
desidiae votum ?) edendum autem ex pluribus causis, 20
maxime quod libelli quos emisimus dicuntur in manibus
esse, quamvis iam gratiam novitatis exuerint ; nisi tamen
auribus nostris bibliopolae blandiuntur. Sed sane blandi-
antur, dum per hoc mendacium nobis studia nostra com-
mendent. Vale.

3. (BOOK 1. 3.)

Pliny counsels Caninius to employ his delightful retirement at Comum
in authorship.

C. PLINIUS CANINIO RUFO SUO S.

Quid agit Comum, tuae meaeque deliciae ? quid suburbanum amoenissimum ? quid illa porticus verna semper ? quid
platanon opacissimus ? quid euripus viridis et gemmeus ?
quid subiectus et serviens lacus ? quid illa mollis et tamen
solida gestatio ? quid balineum illud, quod plurimus sol 5

implet et circumit? quid triclinia illa popularia, illa paucorum? quid cubicula diurna nocturna? possident te et per
vices partiuntur? an, ut solebas, intentione rei familiaris
obeundae crebris excursionibus avocaris? Si te possident,
10 felix beatusque es; si minus, unus ex multis. Quin tu
(tempus est enim) humiles et sordidas curas aliis mandas et
ipse te in alto isto pinguique secessu studiis adseris? hoc sit
negotium tuum, hoc otium, hic labor, haec quies: in his
vigilia, in his etiam somnus reponatur. Effinge aliquid et
15 exclude, quod sit perpetuo tuum. Nam reliqua rerum
tuarum post te alium atque alium dominum sortientur, hoc
numquam tuum desinet esse, si semel coeperit. Scio quem
animum, quod horter ingenium. Tu modo enitere ut tibi
ipse sis tanti, quanti videberis aliis, si tibi fueris. Vale.

4. (BOOK 1. 6.)

The sportsman need not leave his studies at home.

C. PLINIUS CORNELIO TACITO SUO S.

Ridebis, et licet rideas. Ego ille quem nosti apros tres
et quidem pulcherrimos cepi. Ipse? inquis. Ipse; non
tamen ut omnino ab inertia mea et quiete discederem. Ad
retia sedebam: erat in proximo non venabulum aut lancea,
5 sed stilus et pugillares: meditabar aliquid enotabamque, ut,
si manus vacuas, plenas tamen ceras reportarem. Non est
quod contemnas hoc studendi genus: mirum est ut animus
agitatione motuque corporis excitetur. Iam undique silvae
et solitudo ipsumque illud silentium, quod venationi datur,
10 magna cogitationis incitamenta sunt. Proinde cum venabere,
licebit auctore me ut panarium et lagunculam sic etiam
pugillares feras: experieris non Dianam magis montibus
quam Minervam inerrare. Vale.

5.   (BOOK 1. 9.)

*The industrious leisure of the country is delightful, compared with the
busy idleness of the town.*

C. PLINIUS MINUCIO FUNDANO SUO S.

Mirum est quam singulis diebus in urbe ratio aut constet
aut constare videatur, pluribus iunctisque non constet. Nam
siquem interroges 'hodie quid egisti?' respondeat 'officio
togae virilis interfui, sponsalia aut nuptias frequentavi, ille
me ad signandum testamentum, ille in advocationem, ille in 5
consilium rogavit.' Haec quo die feceris necessaria, eadem,
si cotidie fecisse te reputes, inania videntur, multo magis,
cum secesseris. Tunc enim subit recordatio 'quot dies quam
frigidis rebus absumpsi!' quod evenit mihi, postquam in
Laurentino meo aut lego aliquid aut scribo aut etiam corpori 10
vaco, cuius fulturis animus sustinetur. Nihil audio quod
audisse, nihil dico quod dixisse paeniteat: nemo apud me
quemquam sinistris sermonibus carpit, neminem ipse repre-
hendo, nisi tamen me, cum parum commode scribo; nulla
spe, nullo timore sollicitor, nullis rumoribus inquietor: me- 15
cum tantum et cum libellis loquor. O rectam sinceramque
vitam, O dulce otium honestumque ac paene omni negotio
pulchrius! O mare, O litus, verum secretumque μουσεῖον,
quam multa invenitis, quam multa dictatis! Proinde tu quoque strepitum istum inanemque discursum et multum ineptos 20
labores, ut primum fuerit occasio, relinque teque studiis vel
otio trade. Satius est enim, ut Atilius noster eruditissime simul
et facetissime dixit, otiosum esse quam nihil agere.   Vale.

6.   (BOOK 1. 10.)

*Pliny describes the pleasure and profit which he derives from the
teaching and example of the excellent Euphrates.*

C. PLINIUS ATTIO CLEMENTI SUO S.

Siquando urbs nostra liberalibus studiis floruit, nunc

maxime floret. Multa claraque exempla sunt; sufficeret unum, Euphrates philosophus. Hunc ego in Syria, cum adulescentulus militarem, penitus et domi inspexi amarique
5 ab eo laboravi, etsi non erat laborandum. Est enim obvius et expositus plenusque humanitate, quam praecipit. Atque utinam sic ipse quam spem tunc ille de me concepit implev- erim, ut ille multum virtutibus suis addidit! aut ego nunc illas magis miror, quia magis intellego. Quamquam ne nunc
10 quidem satis intellego. Ut enim de pictore scalptore fictore nisi artifex iudicare, ita nisi sapiens non potest perspicere sapientem. Quantum tamen mihi cernere datur, multa in Euphrate sic eminent et elucent, ut mediocriter quoque doc- tos advertant et adficiant. Disputat subtiliter graviter ornate,
15 frequenter etiam Platonicam illam sublimitatem et latitudinem effingit. Sermo est copiosus et varius, dulcis in primis, et qui repugnantes quoque ducat inpellat. Ad hoc proceritas cor- poris, decora facies, demissus capillus, ingens et cana barba; quae licet fortuita et inania putentur, illi tamen plurimum ven-
20 erationis adquirunt. Nullus horror in cultu, nulla tristitia, mul- tum severitatis: reverearis occursum, non reformides. Vitae sanctitas summa, comitas par: insectatur vitia, non homines, nec castigat errantes, sed emendat. Sequaris monentem attentus et pendens et persuaderi tibi, etiam cum persuaserit,
25 cupias. Iam vero liberi tres, duo mares, quos diligentissime instituit. Socer Pompeius Iulianus, cum cetera vita tum vel hoc uno magnus et clarus, quod ipse provinciae princeps inter altissimas condiciones generum non honoribus princi- pem, sed sapientia elegit. Quamquam quid ego plura de
30 viro, quo mihi frui non licet? an ut magis angar, quod non licet? Nam distringor officio ut maximo sic molestissimo: sedeo pro tribunali, subnoto libellos, conficio tabulas, scribo plurimas, sed inlitteratissimas litteras. Soleo non numquam (nam id ipsum quando contingit!) de his occupationibus
35 apud Euphraten queri. Ille me consolatur, adfirmat etiam

esse hanc philosophiae et quidem pulcherrimam partem,
agere negotium publicum, cognoscere, iudicare, promere et
exercere iustitiam, quaeque ipsi doceant in usu habere.
Mihi tamen hoc unum non persuadet, satius esse ista facere
quam cum illo dies totos audiendo discendoque consumere. 40
Quo magis te, cui vacat, hortor, cum in urbem proxime
veneris (venias autem ob hoc maturius), illi te expoliendum
limandumque permittas.   Neque enim ego, ut multi, invideo
aliis bono quo ipse careo. sed contra sensum quendam
voluptatemque percipio, si ea quae mihi denegantur amicis 45
video superesse.   Vale.

7. (BOOK 1. 12.)

Pliny laments the loss and admires the fortitude of Corellius Rufus,
who had ended his sufferings by abstinence from food.

C. PLINIUS CALESTRIO TIRONI SUO S.

Iacturam gravissimam feci, si iactura dicenda est tanti viri
amissio : decessit Corellius Rufus, et quidem sponte, quod
dolorem meum exulcerat.   Est enim luctuosissimum genus
mortis quae non ex natura nec fatalis videtur.   Nam utcumque in illis qui morbo finiuntur magnum ex ipsa 5
necessitate solacium est, in iis vero quos arcessita mors
aufert hic insanabilis dolor est, quod creduntur potuisse
diu vivere.   Corellium quidem summa ratio, quae sapien-
tibus pro necessitate est, ad hoc consilium compulit,
quamquam plurimas vivendi causas habentem, optimam 10
conscientiam, optimam famam, maximam auctoritatem,
praeterea filiam uxorem nepotem sorores, interque tot
pignora veros amicos.   Sed tam longa, tam iniqua valetudine conflictabatur, ut haec tanta pretia vivendi mortis
rationibus vincerentur.   Tertio et tricensimo anno, ut ipsum 15
audiebam, pedum dolore correptus est.   Patrius hic illi:
nam plerumque morbi quoque per successiones quasdam

ut alia, traduntur. Hunc abstinentia sanctitate. quoad viridis
aetas, vicit et fregit; novissime cum senectute ingravescentem
20 viribus animi sustinebat, cum quidem incredibiles cruciatus
et indignissima tormenta pateretur. Iam enim dolor non
pedibus solis, ut prius, insidebat, sed omnia membra pervaga-
batur. Veni ad eum Domitiani temporibus in suburbano
iacentem. Servi e cubiculo recesserunt: habebat hoc moris,
25 quotiens intrasset fidelior amicus; quin etiam uxor, quamquam omnis secreti capacissima, digrediebatur. Circumtulit
oculos et 'cur' inquit 'me putas hos tantos dolores tam diu
sustinere? ut scilicet isti latroni vel uno die supersim.'
Dedisses huic animo par corpus, fecisset quod optabat.
30 Adfuit tamen deus voto, cuius ille compos, ut iam securus
liberque moriturus, multa illa vitae, sed minora retinacula
abrupit. Increverat valetudo, quam temperantia mitigare
temptavit, perseverantem constantia fugit. Iam dies alter
tertius quartus: abstinebat cibo. Misit ad me uxor eius
35 Hispulla communem amicum C. Geminium cum tristissimo
nuntio, destinasse Corellium mori nec aut suis aut filiae
precibus flecti, solum superesse me, a quo revocari posset
ad vitam. Cucurri: perveneram in proximum, cum mihi
ab eadem Hispulla Iulius Atticus nuntiat nihil iam ne me
40 quidem inpetraturum, tam obstinate magis ac magis indu-
ruisse. Dixerat sane medico admoventi cibum κέκρικα, quae
vox quantum admirationis in animo meo tantum desiderii
reliquit. Cogito quo amico, quo viro caream. Implevit
quidem annum septimum et sexagensimum, quae aetas
45 etiam robustissimis satis longa est: scio. Evasit perpetuam
valetudinem: scio. Decessit superstitibus suis, florente re
publica, quae illi omnibus suis carior erat: et hoc scio.
Ego tamen tamquam et iuvenis et firmissimi mortem doleo,
doleo autem (licet me inbecillum putes) meo nomine.
50 Amisi enim, amisi vitae meae testem rectorem magistrum:
in summa dicam quod recenti dolore contubernali meo

Calvisio dixi, 'vereor ne neglegentius vivam.' Proinde
adhibe solacia mihi, non haec 'senex erat, infirmus erat'
(haec enim novi), sed nova aliqua, sed magna, quae audierim
numquam, legerim numquam. Nam quae audivi, quae legi, 55
sponte succurrunt, sed tanto dolore superantur. Vale.

8. (BOOK I. 13.)

Pliny complains that the activity of poetical literature is ill requited
by the general unwillingness to attend the public recitations.

C. PLINIUS SOSIO SENECIONI SUO S.

Magnum proventum poetarum annus hic attulit: toto
mense Aprili nullus fere dies, quo non recitaret aliquis.
Iuvat me quod vigent studia, proferunt se ingenia hominum
et ostentant, tametsi ad audiendum pigre coitur. Plerique
in stationibus sedent tempusque audiendi fabulis conterunt 5
ac subinde sibi nuntiari iubent, an iam recitator intraverit,
an dixerit praefationem, an ex magna parte evolverit librum:
tunc demum ac tunc quoque lente cunctanterque veniunt:
nec tamen permanent, sed ante finem recedunt, alii dissimu-
lanter et furtim, alii simpliciter et libere. At hercule 10
memoria parentum Claudium Caesarem ferunt, cum in
palatio spatiaretur audissetque clamorem, causam requisisse,
cumque dictum esset recitare Nonianum, subitum recitanti
inopinatumque venisse. Nunc otiosissimus quisque multo
ante rogatus et identidem admonitus aut non venit aut, si 15
venit, queritur se diem, quia non perdiderit, perdidisse.
Sed tanto magis laudandi probandique sunt quos a scribendi
recitandique studio haec auditorum vel desidia vel superbia
non retardat. Equidem prope nemini defui. Erant sane
plerique amici: neque enim est fere quisquam qui studia, ut 20
non simul et nos amet. His ex causis longius, quam
destinaveram, tempus in urbe consumpsi. Possum iam
repetere secessum et scribere aliquid quod non recitem, ne

videar, quorum recitationibus adfui, non auditor fuisse, sed
25 creditor. Nam ut in ceteris rebus ita in audiendi officio
perit gratia, si reposcatur. Vale.

9. (BOOK I. 14.)

Pliny having been asked by Mauricus to look out for a husband for
his niece, the orphan daughter of Rusticus, can confidently recommend
Minicius Acilianus on the ground of his education, his connections, his
personal appearance, and his circumstances.

C. PLINIUS IUNIO MAURICO SUO S.

Petis ut fratris tui filiae prospiciam maritum ; quod merito
mihi potissimum iniungis. Scis enim quanto opere summum
illum virum suspexerim dilexerimque, quibus ille adulescen-
tiam meam exhortationibus foverit, quibus etiam laudibus
5 ut laudandus viderer effecerit. Nihil est quod a te mandari
mihi aut maius aut gratius, nihil quod honestius a me
suscipi possit, quam ut eligam iuvenem, ex quo nasci
nepotes Aruleno Rustico deceat. Qui quidem diu quae-
rendus fuisset, nisi paratus et quasi provisus esset Minicius
10 Acilianus, qui me ut iuvenis iuvenem (est enim minor
pauculis annis) familiarissime diligit, reveretur ut senem.
Nam ita formari a me et institui cupit, ut ego a vobis
solebam. Patria est ei Brixia ex illa nostra Italia, quae
multum adhuc verecundiae, frugalitatis atque etiam rustici-
15 tatis antiquae retinet ac servat. Pater Minicius Macrinus,
equestris ordinis princeps, quia nihil altius voluit: adlectus
enim a divo Vespasiano inter praetorios honestam quietem
huic nostrae ambitioni dicam an dignitati constantissime
praetulit. Habet aviam maternam Serranam Proculam e
20 municipio Patavino. Nosti loci mores: Serrana tamen
Patavinis quoque severitatis exemplum est. Contigit et
avunculus ei P. Acilius, gravitate prudentia fide prope
singulari. In summa nihil erit in domo tota, quod non

tibi tamquam in tua placeat. Aciliano vero ipsi plurimum
vigoris industriae, quamquam in maxima verecundia. Quae- 25
sturam tribunatum praeturam honestissime percucurrit ac
iam pro se tibi necessitatem ambiendi remisit.   Est illi
facies liberalis multo sanguine, multo rubore suffusa, est
ingenua totius corporis pulchritudo et quidam senatorius
decor.   Quae ego nequaquam arbitror neglegenda: debet 30
enim hoc castitati puellarum quasi praemium dari.   Nescio
an adiciam esse patri eius amplas facultates.   Nam cum
imaginor vos, quibus quaerimus generum, silendum de
facultatibus puto: cum publicos mores atque etiam leges
civitatis intueor, quae vel in primis census hominum 35
spectandos arbitrantur, ne id quidem praetereundum vi-
detur. | Et sane de posteris et his pluribus cogitanti hic
quoque in condicionibus deligendis ponendus est calculus.
Tu fortasse me putes indulsisse amori meo supraque ista,
quam res patitur, sustulisse.   At ego fide mea spondeo 40
futurum ut omnia longe ampliora, quam a me praedi-
cantur, invenias.   Diligo quidem adulescentem ardentissime,
sicut meretur; sed hoc ipsum amantis est, non onerare
cum laudibus.   Vale.

10.   (BOOK I. 15.)

Pliny rallies Septicius on having broken his engagement to dine
with him, and tells him it was his own loss.

C. PLINIUS SEPTICIO CLARO SUO S.

Heus tu promittis ad cenam nec venis!   Dicitur ius: ad
assem inpendium reddes, nec id modicum.   Paratae erant
lactucae singulae, cochleae ternae, ova bina, alica cum
mulso et nive (nam hanc quoque computabis, immo hanc
in primis, quae periit in ferculo), olivae, betacei, cucurbitae, 5
bulbi, alia mille non minus lauta.   Audisses comoedos vel

lectorem vel lyristen vel, quae mea liberalitas, omnes. At
tu apud nescio quem ostrea, vulvas, echinos, Gaditanas
maluisti. Dabis poenas, non dico quas. Dure fecisti:
10 invidisti, nescio an tibi, certe mihi, sed tamen et tibi.
Quantum nos lusissemus, risissemus, studuissemus! potes
apparatius cenare apud multos, nusquam hilarius simplicius
incautius. In summa experire, et nisi postea te aliis potius
excusaveris, mihi semper excusa. Vale.

11. (BOOK 1. 16.)

Pliny wishes to make his friend Erucius aware of the varied literary
gifts of Saturninus.

C. PLINIUS ERUCIO SUO S.

Amabam Pompeium Saturninum, hunc dico nostrum, lauda-
bamque eius ingenium, etiam antequam scirem quam varium,
quam flexibile, quam multiplex esset; nunc vero totum me
tenet, habet, possidet. Audivi causas agentem acriter et
5 ardenter nec minus polite et ornate, sive meditata sive subita
proferret. Adsunt aptae crebraeque sententiae, gravis et
decora constructio, sonantia verba et antiqua. Omnia haec
mire placent, cum impetu quodam et flumine pervehuntur,
placent, si retractentur. Senties quod ego, cum orationes
10 eius in manus sumpseris, quas facile cuilibet veterum,
quorum est aemulus, comparabis. Idem tamen in historia
magis satisfaciet vel brevitate vel luce vel suavitate vel
splendore etiam et sublimitate narrandi. Nam in contionibus idem qui in orationibus est, pressior tamen et
15 circumscriptior et adductior. Praeterea facit versus, quales
Catullus aut Calvus, re vera quales Catullus aut Calvus.
Quantum illis leporis, dulcedinis, amaritudinis, amoris!
inserit sane, sed data opera, mollibus levibusque duriusculos
quosdam, et hoc quasi Catullus aut Calvus. Legit mihi
20 nuper epistulas; uxoris esse dicebat: Plautum vel Terentium

metro solutum legi credidi. Quae sive uxoris sunt, ut
adfirmat, sive ipsius, ut negat, pari gloria dignus qui aut illa
componat aut uxorem, quam virginem accepit, tam doctam
politamque reddiderit. Est ergo mecum per diem totum :
eundem antequam scribam, eundem cum scripsi, eundem 25
etiam cum remittor, non tamquam eundem lego. Quod te
quoque ut facias et hortor et moneo. Neque enim debet
operibus eius obesse quod vivit. An si inter eos quos
numquam vidimus floruisset, non solum libros eius verum
etiam imagines conquireremus; eiusdem nunc honor prae- 30
sentis et gratia quasi satietate languescit? At hoc pravum
malignumque est, non admirari hominem admiratione dig-
nissimum, quia videre, adloqui, audire, complecti, nec laudare
tantum verum etiam amare contigit. Vale.

12. (BOOK 1. 18.)

Pliny endeavours to reassure Suetonius' anxiety about his dream, by
relating an experience of his own; but if Suetonius still desires a post-
ponement of the case, he will contrive to obtain it for him.

C. PLINIUS SUETONIO TRANQUILLO SUO S.

Scribis te perterritum somnio vereri ne quid adversi in
actione patiaris, rogas ut dilationem petam et pauculos dies,
certe proximum, excusem. Difficile est, sed experiar: καὶ
γάρ τ᾽ ὄναρ ἐκ Διός ἐστιν. Refert tamen, eventura soleas an
contraria somniare. Mihi reputanti somnium meum, istud 5
quod times tu egregiam actionem portendere videtur.
Susceperam causam Iuni Pastoris, cum mihi quiescenti
visa est socrus mea advoluta genibus ne agerem obsecrare.
Et eram acturus adulescentulus adhuc, eram in quadruplici
iudicio, eram contra potentissimos civitatis atque etiam 10
Caesaris amicos; quae singula excutere mentem mihi post
tam triste somnium poterant. Egi tamen λογισάμενος illud

εἰς οἰωνὸς ἄριστος, ἀμύνεσθαι περὶ πάτρης.

nam mihi patria, et siquid carius patria, fides videbatur.
15 Prospere cessit, atque adeo illa actio mihi aures hominum,
illa ianuam famae patefecit. Proinde dispice, an tu quoque
sub hoc exemplo somnium istud in bonum vertas: aut si
tutius putas illud cautissimi cuiusque praeceptum, 'quod
dubites ne feceris', id ipsum rescribe. Ego aliquam
20 stropham inveniam agamque causam tuam, ut istam agere
tu, cum voles, possis. Est enim sane alia ratio tua, alia mea
fuit. Nam iudicium centumvirale differri nullo modo, istud
aegre quidem, sed tamen potest. Vale.

13. (BOOK i. 20.)

Pliny asks the opinion of Tacitus on a controversy in which he had
been engaged with a friend of his, namely, whether a long speech or a
short one is the more effective in judicial pleading.

C. PLINIUS CORNELIO TACITO SUO S.

Frequens mihi disputatio est cum quodam docto homine
et perito, cui nihil aeque in causis agendis ut brevitas
placet. Quam ego custodiendam esse confiteor, si causa
permittat: alioqui praevaricatio est transire dicenda, prae-
5 varicatio etiam cursim et breviter attingere quae sunt incul-
canda, infigenda, repetenda. Nam plerisque longiore tractatu
vis quaedam et pondus accedit, utque corpori ferrum, sic
oratio animo non ictu magis quam mora imprimitur. Hic
ille mecum auctoritatibus agit ac mihi ex graecis orationes
10 Lysiae ostentat, ex nostris Gracchorum Catonisque, quorum
sane plurimae sunt circumcisae et breves: ego Lysiae
Demosthenen, Aeschinen, Hyperiden multosque praeterea,
Gracchis et Catoni Pollionem, Caesarem, Caelium, in primis
M. Tullium oppono, cuius oratio optima fertur esse quae
15 maxima. Et hercule ut aliae bonae res ita bonus liber
melior est quisque, quo maior. Vides ut statuas, signa,

picturas, hominum denique multorumque animalium formas, arborum etiam, si modo sint decorae, nihil magis quam amplitudo commendet. Idem orationibus evenit; quin etiam voluminibus ipsis auctoritatem quandam et pulchritu- 20 dinem adicit magnitudo. Haec ille multaque alia, quae a me in eandem sententiam solent dici, ut est in disputando inconprehensibilis et lubricus, ita eludit, ut contendat hos ipsos, quorum orationibus nitar, pauciora dixisse, quam ediderint. Ego contra puto: testes sunt multae 25 multorum orationes et Ciceronis pro Murena, pro Vareno, in quibus brevis et nuda quasi subscriptio quorundam criminum solis titulis indicatur: ex his apparet illum permulta dixisse, cum ederet, omisisse. Idem pro Cluentio ait se totam causam vetere instituto solum perorasse et 30 pro C. Cornelio quadriduo egisse; ne dubitare possimus quae per plures dies, ut necesse erat, latius dixerit postea recisa ac repurgata in unum librum, grandem quidem, unum tamen, coartasse. At aliud est actio bona, aliud oratio. Scio non nullis ita videri. Sed ego, forsitan fallar, per- 35 suasum habeo posse fieri ut sit actio bona quae non sit bona oratio, non posse non bonam actionem esse quae sit bona oratio. Est enim oratio actionis exemplar et quasi ἀρχέτυπον. Ideo in optima quaque mille figuras extemporales invenimus, in iis etiam quas tantum editas 40 scimus, ut in Verrem, 'artificem quem? quemnam? recte admones: Polyclitum esse dicebant.' Sequitur ergo ut actio sit absolutissima quae maxime orationis similitudinem expresserit, si modo iustum et debitum tempus accipiat: quod si negetur, nulla oratoris, maxima iudicis culpa est. 45 Adsunt huic opinioni meae leges, quae longissima tempora largiuntur nec brevitatem dicentibus, sed copiam, hoc est diligentiam, suadent; quam praestare nisi in angustissimis causis non potest brevitas. Adiciam quod me docuit usus, magister egregius. Frequenter egi, frequenter iudi- 50

cavi, frequenter in consilio fui: aliud alios movet, ac
pierumque parvae res maximas trahunt. Varia sunt hominum iudicia, variae voluntates: inde qui eandem causam
simul audierunt, saepe diversum, interdum idem, sed ex
55 diversis animi motibus sentiunt. Praeterea suae quisque
inventioni favet et quasi fortissimum amplectitur, cum ab
alio dictum est quod ipse praevidit. Omnibus ergo dandum
est aliquid quod teneant, quod agnoscant. Dixit aliquando
mihi Regulus, cum simul adessemus, 'tu omnia quae sunt
60 in causa putas exequenda, ego iugulum statim video, hunc
premo:' premit sane quod elegit, sed in eligendo frequenter
errat. Respondi posse fieri ut genu esset aut talus, ubi
ille iugulum putaret: 'at ego' inquam, 'qui iugulum perspicere non possum, omnia pertempto, omnia experior,
65 πάντα denique λίθον κινῶ, utque in cultura agri non vineas
tantum verum etiam arbusta, nec arbusta tantum verum
etiam campos curo et exerceo, utque in ipsis campis non
far aut siliginem solam sed hordeum, fabam ceteraque
legumina sero, sic in actione plura quasi semina latius
70 spargo, ut quae provenerint colligam. Neque enim minus
inperspicua, incerta, fallacia sunt iudicum ingenia quam
tempestatum terrarumque. Nec me praeterit summum
oratorem Periclen sic a comico Eupolide laudari,

πρὸς δέ γ' αὐτοῦ τῷ τάχει
75   πειθώ τις ἐπεκάθητο τοῖσι χείλεσιν.
οὕτως ἐκήλει καὶ μόνος τῶν ῥητόρων
τὸ κέντρον ἐγκατέλειπε τοῖς ἀκροωμένοις.

verum huic ipsi Pericli nec illa πειθώ nec illud ἐκήλει brevitate
vel velocitate vel utraque (differunt enim) sine facultate
80 summa contigisset. Nam delectare persuadere copiam
dicendi spatiumque desiderat; relinquere vero aculeum
in audientium animis is demum potest, qui non pungit,
sed infigit. Adde quae de eodem Pericle comicus alter,

ἤστραπτ', ἐβρόντα, συνεκύκα τὴν Ἑλλάδα.

Non enim amputata oratio et abscisa, sed lata et magnifica 85
et excelsa tonat, fulgurat, omnia denique perturbat ac
miscet.   Optimus tamen modus est.   Quis negat? sed
non minus non servat modum qui infra rem quam qui
supra, qui adstrictius quam qui effusius dicit.   Itaque
audis frequenter ut illud 'immodice et redundanter,' ita 90
hoc 'ieiune et infirme.' Alius excessisse materiam, alius
dicitur non inplesse. Aeque uterque, sed ille inbecillitate,
hic viribus peccat; quod certe, etsi non limatioris, maioris
tamen ingenii vitium est.   Nec vero, cum haec dico,
illum Homericum *ἀμετροεπῆ* probo, sed hunc,   95

καὶ ἔπεα νιφάδεσσιν ἐοικότα χειμερίῃσιν·

non quia non et ille mihi validissime placeat,

παῦρα μέν, ἀλλὰ μάλα λιγέως·

si tamen detur electio, illam orationem similem nivibus
hibernis, id est crebram et adsiduam et largam, postremo 100
divinam et caelestem, volo.   At est gratior multis actio
brevis.   Est, sed inertibus, quorum delicias desidiamque
quasi iudicium respicere ridiculum est.   Nam si hos in
consilio habeas, non solum satius est breviter dicere, sed
omnino non dicere.   Haec est adhuc sententia mea, quam 105
mutabo, si dissenseris tu; sed plane cur dissentias explices
rogo.   Quamvis enim cedere auctoritati debeam tuae,
rectius tamen arbitror in tanta re ratione quam auctoritate
superari.   Proinde si non errare videor, id ipsum quam
voles brevi epistula, sed tamen scribe (confirmabis enim 110
iudicium meum); si errare, longissimam para.   Num
corrupi te, qui tibi, si mihi accederes, brevis epistulae
necessitatem, si dissentires, longissimae inposui? Vale.

14. (BOOK I. 22.)

A delightful picture of the virtues of T. Aristo, whose serious illness detains Pliny in Rome.

C. PLINIUS CATILIO SEVERO SUO S.

Diu iam in urbe haereo, et quidem attonitus. Perturbat me longa et pertinax valetudo Titi Aristonis, quem singulariter et miror et diligo. Nihil est enim illo gravius, sanctius, doctius, ut mihi non unus homo, sed litterae ipsae
5 omnesque bonae artes in uno homine summum periculum adire videantur. Quam peritus ille et privati iuris et publici! quantum rerum, quantum exemplorum, quantum antiquitatis tenet! Nihil est quod discere velis, quod ille docere non possit. Mihi certe, quotiens aliquid abditum
10 quaero, ille thesaurus est. Iam quanta sermonibus eius fides, quanta auctoritas, quam pressa et decora cunctatio! quid est quod non statim sciat? et tamen plerumque haesitat, dubitat diversitate rationum, quas acri magnoque iudicio ab origine causisque primis repetit, discernit,
15 expendit. Ad hoc quam parcus in victu, quam modicus in cultu! Soleo ipsum cubiculum eius ipsumque lectum ut imaginem quandam priscae frugalitatis aspicere. Ornat haec magnitudo animi, quae nihil ad ostentationem, omnia ad conscientiam refert, recteque facti non ex populi sermone
20 mercedem, sed ex facto petit. In summa non facile quemquam ex istis qui sapientiae studium habitu corporis praeferunt huic viro comparabis. Non quidem gymnasia sectatur aut porticus nec disputationibus longis aliorum otium suumque delectat, sed in toga negotiisque versatur, multos
25 advocatione, plures consilio iuvat. Nemini tamen istorum castitate, pietate, iustitia, fortitudine etiam primo loco cesserit. Mirareris, si interesses, quae patientia hanc ipsam valetudinem toleret, ut dolori resistat, ut sitim differat, ut incredibilem febrium ardorem inmotus opertusque

D

transmittat. Nuper me paucosque mecum, quos maxime 30
diligit, advocavit rogavitque ut medicos consuleremus de
summa valetudinis, ut, si esset insuperabilis, sponte exiret
e vita, si tantum difficilis et longa, resisteret maneretque :
dandum enim precibus uxoris, dandum filiae lacrimis,
dandum etiam nobis amicis ne spes nostras, si modo 35
non essent inanes, voluntaria morte desereret. Id ego
arduum in primis et praecipua laude dignum puto. Nam
impetu quodam et instinctu procurrere ad mortem commune cum multis, deliberare vero et causas eius expendere,
utque suaserit ratio, vitae mortisque consilium vel suscipere 40
vel ponere ingentis est animi. Et medici quidem secunda
nobis pollicentur : superest ut promissis deus adnuat tan-
demque me hac sollicitudine exsolvat ; qua liberatus Laurentinum meum, hoc est libellos et pugillares studiosumque
otium, repetam. Nunc enim nihil legere, nihil scribere 45
aut adsidenti vacat aut anxio libet. Habes quid timeam,
quid optem, quid etiam in posterum destinem : tu quid
egeris, quid agas, quid velis agere, invicem nobis, sed
laetioribus epistulis scribe. Erit confusioni meae non medi-
ocre solacium, si tu nihil quereris. Vale.   50

15. (BOOK I. 23.)

Pliny tells Falco that he did not think it suitable in his own case to
plead at the bar, when he was tribune; but Falco may reasonably
entertain a different view of the importance and obligations of the
office.

C. PLINIUS POMPEIO FALCONI SUO S.

Consulis, an existimem te in tribunatu causas agere
debere. Plurimum refert, quid esse tribunatum putes,
inanem umbram et sine honore nomen, an potestatem
sacrosanctam et quam in ordinem cogi ut a nullo ita ne
a se quidem deceat. Ipse cum tribunus essem, erraverim 5
fortasse, qui me aliquid putavi, sed tamquam essem, abstinui
causis agendis : primum quod deforme arbitrabar, cui ad-

surgere, cui loco cedere omnes oporteret, hunc omnibus
sedentibus stare ; et qui iubere posset tacere quemcumque,
10 huic silentium clepsydra indici; et quem interfari nefas
esset, hunc etiam convicia audire, et si inulta pateretur,
inertem, si ulcisceretur, insolentem videri. Erat hic quoque
aestus ante oculos, si forte me appellasset vel ille cui ades-
sem vel ille quem contra, intercederem et auxilium ferrem,
15 an quiescerem sileremque et quasi eiurato magistratu pri-
vatum ipse me facerem. His rationibus motus malui me
tribunum omnibus exhibere, quam paucis advocatum. Sed
tu, iterum dicam, plurimum interest, quid esse tribunatum
putes, quam personam tibi inponas, quae sapienti viro ita
20 aptanda est, ut perferatur. Vale.

16. (BOOK 2. 1.)

A sketch of the life and character of Verginius.

C. PLINIUS ROMANO SUO S.

Post aliquot annos insigne atque etiam memorabile
populi Romani oculis spectaculum exhibuit publicum funus
Vergini Rufi, maximi et clarissimi civis, perinde felicis.
Triginta annis gloriae suae supervixit : legit scripta de se
5 carmina, legit historias et posteritati suae interfuit. Per-
functus est tertio consulatu, ut summum fastigium privati
hominis impleret, cum principis noluisset. Caesares quibus
suspectus atque etiam invisus virtutibus fuerat evasit, reliquit
incolumem optimum atque amicissimum, tamquam ad hunc
10 ipsum honorem publici funeris reservatus. Annum tertium
et octogensimum excessit in altissima tranquillitate, pari
veneratione. Usus est firma valetudine, nisi quod solebant
ei manus tremere, citra dolorem tamen. Aditus tantum
mortis durior longiorque, sed hic ipse laudabilis. Nam cum
15 vocem praepararet acturus in consulatu principi gratias,
liber, quem forte acceperat grandiorem, et seni et stanti
ipso pondere elapsus est. Hunc dum sequitur colligitque,

per leve et lubricum pavimentum fallente vestigio cecidit
coxamque fregit, quae parum apte collocata reluctante aetate
male coiit. Huius viri exequiae magnum ornamentum 20
principi, magnum saeculo, magnum etiam foro et rostris
attulerunt. Laudatus est a consule Cornelio Tacito: nam
hic supremus felicitati eius cumulus accessit, laudator
eloquentissimus. Et ille quidem plenus annis abiit, plenus
honoribus, illis etiam quos recusavit: nobis tamen quae- 25
rendus ac desiderandus est ut exemplar aevi prioris, mihi
vero praecipue, qui illum non solum publice quantum
admirabar tantum diligebam; primum quod utrique eadem
regio, municipia finitima, agri etiam possessionesque con-
iunctae, praeterea quod ille mihi tutor relictus adfectum 30
parentis exhibuit. Sic candidatum me suffragio ornavit,
sic ad omnes honores meos ex secessibus accucurrit, cum
iam pridem eius modi officiis renuntiasset, sic illo die, quo
sacerdotes solent nominare quos dignissimos sacerdotio
iudicant, me semper nominabat. Quin etiam in hac novis- 35
sima valetudine veritus ne forte inter quinqueviros crearetur,
qui minuendis publicis sumptibus iudicio senatus consti-
tuebantur, cum illi tot amici senes consularesque super-
essent, me huius aetatis per quem excusaretur elegit, his
quidem verbis, 'etiam si filium haberem, tibi mandarem.' 40
Quibus ex causis necesse est tamquam inmaturam mortem
eius in sinu tuo defleam; si tamen fas est aut flere aut
omnino mortem vocare, qua tanti viri mortalitas magis
finita quam vita est. Vivit enim vivetque semper atque etiam
latius in memoria hominum et sermone versabitur, postquam 45
ab oculis recessit. Volui tibi multa alia scribere, sed totus
animus in hac una contemplatione defixus est: Verginium
cogito, Verginium video, Verginium iam vanis imaginibus,
recentibus tamen, audio, adloquor, teneo. Cui fortasse cives
aliquos virtutibus pares et habemus et habebimus, gloria 50
neminem. Vale.

17. (BOOK 2. 6.)

Pliny cautions Avitus against the mean economy, which he had witnessed, of making distinctions between guests of the same table in the quality of the entertainment provided for them.

C. PLINIUS AVITO SUO S.

Longum est altius repetere, nec refert quem ad modum acciderit ut homo minime familiaris cenarem apud quendam, ut sibi videbatur, lautum et diligentem, ut mihi, sordidum simul et sumptuosum. Nam sibi et paucis opima quaedam, 5 ceteris vilia et minuta ponebat. Vinum etiam parvulis lagunculis in tria genera discripserat, non ut potestas eligendi, sed ne ius esset recusandi, aliud sibi et nobis, aliud minoribus amicis (nam gradatim amicos habet), aliud suis nostrisque libertis. Animadvertit qui mihi proximus recum-10 bebat et an probarem interrogavit. Negavi. 'Tu ergo' inquit 'quam consuetudinem sequeris'? 'Eadem omnibus pono: ad cenam enim, non ad notam invito cunctisque rebus exaequo, quos mensa et toro aequavi'. 'Etiamne libertos'? 'Etiam: convictores enim tunc, non libertos puto'. 15 Et ille 'magno tibi constat'. 'Minime'. 'Qui fieri potest'? 'Quia scilicet liberti mei non idem quod ego bibunt, sed idem ego quod liberti.' Et hercule si gulae temperes, non est onerosum quo utaris ipse communicare cum pluribus. Illa ergo reprimenda, illa quasi in ordinem redigenda est, si 20 sumptibus parcas, quibus aliquanto rectius tua continentia quam aliena contumelia consulas. Quorsus haec? Ne tibi, optimae indolis iuveni, quorundam in mensa luxuria specie frugalitatis imponat. Convenit autem amori in te meo, quotiens tale aliquid inciderit, sub exemplo praemonere, 25 quid debeas fugere. Igitur memento nihil magis esse vitandum, quam istam luxuriae et sordium novam societatem; quae cum sint turpissima discreta ac separata, turpius iunguntur. Vale.

18. (BOOK 2. 10.)

Pliny begs Octavius Rufus to collect and publish, or at any rate to recite,
his poems.

C. PLINIUS OCTAVIO SUO S.

Hominem te patientem vel potius durum ac paene crude-
lem, qui tam insignes libros tam diu teneas! Quousque et
tibi et nobis invidebis, tibi maxima laude, nobis voluptate?
Sine per ora hominum ferantur isdemque quibus lingua
Romana spatiis pervagentur. Magna et iam longa expecta- 5
tio est, quam frustrari adhuc et differre non debes. Enot-
uerunt quidam tui versus et invito te claustra sua refregerunt.
Hos nisi retrahis in corpus, quandoque ut errones aliquem
cuius dicantur invenient. Habe ante oculos mortalitatem, a
qua adserere te hoc uno monimento potes: nam cetera 10
fragilia et caduca non minus quam ipsi homines occidunt
desinuntque. Dices, ut soles, 'amici mei viderint'. Opto
equidem amicos tibi tam fideles, tam eruditos, tam laboriosos,
ut tantum curae intentionisque suscipere et possint et velint.
Sed dispice ne sit parum providum sperare ex aliis quod tibi 15
ipse non praestes. Et de editione quidem interim ut voles:
recita saltem, quo magis libeat emittere, utque tandem perci-
pias gaudium, quod ego olim pro te non temere praesumo.
Imaginor enim qui concursus, quae admiratio te, qui clamor,
quod etiam silentium maneat; quo ego, cum dico vel recito, 20
non minus quam clamore delector, sit modo silentium acre
et intentum et cupidum ulteriora audiendi. Hoc fructu
tanto, tam parato desine studia tua infinita ista cuncta-
tione fraudare; quae cum modum excedit, verendum
est ne inertiae et desidiae vel etiam timiditatis nomen 25
accipiat. Vale.

19. (BOOK 2. 13.)

Pliny recommends to Priscus for promotion Voconius Romanus, his
intimate and accomplished friend.

C. PLINIUS PRISCO SUO S.

Et tu occasiones obligandi me avidissime amplecteris, et
ego nemini libentius debeo. Duabus ergo de causis a te
potissimum petere constitui, quod inpetratum maxime cupio.
Regis exercitum amplissimum; hinc tibi beneficiorum larga
5 materia: longum praeterea tempus, quo amicos tuos ex-
ornare potuisti. Converte te ad nostros, nec hos multos.
Malles tu quidem multos; sed meae verecundiae sufficit unus
aut alter, ac potius unus. Is erit Voconius Romanus. Pater
ei in equestri gradu clarus, clarior vitricus, immo pater alius:
10 nam huic quoque nomini pietate successit. Mater e primis
citerioris Hispaniae: scis quod iudicium provinciae illius,
quanta sit gravitas. Ipse flamen proxime fuit. Hunc ego,
cum simul studeremus, arte familiariterque dilexi: ille meus
in urbe, ille in secessu contubernalis, cum hoc seria, cum hoc
15 iocos miscui. Quid enim illo aut fidelius amico aut sodale
iucundius? mira in sermone, mira etiam in ore ipso vultuque
suavitas. Ad hoc ingenium excelsum, subtile, dulce, facile,
eruditum in causis agendis: epistulas quidem scribit, ut Musas
ipsas latine loqui credas. Amatur a me plurimum nec tamen
20 vincitur. Equidem iuvenis statim iuveni quantum potui per
aetatem avidissime contuli et nuper ab optimo principe trium
liberorum ius impetravi, quod quamquam parce et cum
delectu daret, mihi tamen, tamquam eligeret, indulsit. Haec
beneficia mea tueri nullo modo melius, quam ut augeam,
25 possum, praesertim cum ipse illa tam grate interpretetur, ut,
dum priora accipit, posteriora mereatur. Habes qualis,
quam probatus carusque sit nobis, quem rogo pro ingenio,
pro fortuna tua exornes. In primis ama hominem: nam

licet tribuas ei quantum amplissimum potes, nihil tamen
amplius potes amicitia tua; cuius esse cum usque ad 30
intimam familiaritatem capacem quo magis scires, breviter
tibi studia, mores, omnem denique vitam eius expressi.
Extenderem preces, nisi et tu rogari diu nolles, et ego tota
hoc epistula fecissem: rogat enim, et quidem efficacissime,
qui reddit causas rogandi. Vale.   35

20. (BOOK 2. 14.)

Pliny complains that the centumviral court, in which his practice lies,
is being rapidly deteriorated by the audacity of the younger pleaders,
and the paid applause of their audience.

C. PLINIUS MAXIMO SUO S.

Verum opinaris: distringor centumviralibus causis, quae
me exercent magis quam delectant. Sunt enim pleraeque
parvae et exiles: raro incidit vel personarum claritate vel
negotii magnitudine insignis. Ad hoc pauci cum quibus
iuvet dicere: ceteri audaces atque etiam magna ex parte 5
adulescentuli obscuri ad declamandum huc transierunt, tam
inreverenter et temere, ut mihi Atilius noster expresse dixisse
videatur sic in foro pueros a centumviralibus causis auspicari, ut ab Homero in scholis. Nam hic quoque, ut illic,
primum coepit esse quod maximum est. At hercule ante 10
memoriam meam (ita maiores natu solent dicere) ne nobi-
lissimis quidem adulescentibus locus erat nisi aliquo consulari
producente: tanta veneratione pulcherrimum opus colebatur.
Nunc refractis pudoris et reverentiae claustris omnia patent
omnibus, nec inducuntur, sed inrumpunt. Sequuntur audi- 15
tores actoribus similes, conducti et redempti: manceps convenitur: in media basilica tam palam sportulae quam in
triclinio dantur: ex iudicio in iudicium pari mercede trans-
itur. Inde iam non inurbane Σοφοκλεῖς vocantur [ἀπὸ τοῦ
σοφῶς καὶ καλεῖσθαι]: isdem latinum nomen inpositum est 20

Laudiceni. Et tamen crescit in dies foeditas utraque lingua
notata. Here duo nomenclatores mei (habent sane aetatem
eorum qui nuper togas sumpserint) ternis denariis ad laudan-
dum trahebantur. Tanti constat ut sis disertissimus. Hoc
25 pretio quamlibet numerosa subsellia inplentur, hoc ingens
corona colligitur, hoc infiniti clamores commoventur, cum
mesochorus dedit signum. Opus est enim signo apud non
intellegentes, ne audientes quidem : nam plerique non audiunt, nec ulli magis laudant. Siquando transibis per basili-
30 cam et voles scire quo modo quisque dicat, nihil est quod
tribunal ascendas, nihil quod praebeas aurem; facilis divinatio : scito eum pessime dicere, qui laudabitur maxime.
Primus hunc audiendi morem induxit Largius Licinius,
hactenus tamen ut auditores corrogaret : ita certe ex Quin-
35 tiliano, praeceptore meo, audisse memini. Narrabat ille
'adsectabar Domitium Afrum. Cum apud centumviros
diceret graviter et lente (hoc enim illi actionis genus erat),
audit ex proximo inmodicum insolitumque clamorem. Admiratus reticuit. Ubi silentium factum est, repetit quod
40 abruperat. Iterum clamor, iterum reticuit, et post silentium
coepit idem tertio. Novissime quis diceret quaesivit : re-
sponsum est "Licinus". Tum intermissa causa " centumviri "
inquit, "hoc artificium periit".' Quod alioqui perire incipiebat, cum perisse Afro videretur, nunc vero prope funditus
45 extinctum et eversum est. Pudet referre quae quam fracta
pronuntiatione dicantur, quibus quam tactris clamoribus
excipiantur. Plausus tantum ac potius sola cymbala et
tympana illis canticis desunt : ululatus quidem (neque enim
alio vocabulo potest exprimi theatris quoque indecora lauda-
50 tio) large supersunt. Nos tamen adhuc et utilitas amicorum
et ratio aetatis moratur ac retinet. Veremur enim ne forte
non has indignitates reliquisse, sed laborem fugisse videamur.
Sumus tamen solito rariores, quod initium est gradatim
desinendi. Vale.

A description of Pliny's Laurentine country house.

C. PLINIUS GALLO SUO S.

Miraris cur me Laurentinum vel, si ita mavis, Laurens
meum tanto opere delectet: desines mirari, cum cognoveris
gratiam villae, opportunitatem loci, litoris spatium. Decem
et septem milibus passuum ab urbe recessit, ut peractis quae
agenda fuerint salvo iam et composito die possis ibi manere. 5
Aditur non una via: nam et Laurentina et Ostiensis eodem
ferunt, sed Laurentina a quarto decimo lapide, Ostiensis ab
undecimo relinquenda est. Utrimque excipit iter aliqua ex
parte harenosum, iunctis paulo gravius et longius, equo breve
et molle. Varia hinc atque inde facies: nam modo occur- 10
rentibus silvis via coartatur, modo latissimis pratis diffunditur
et patescit; multi greges ovium, multa ibi equorum boum
armenta, quae montibus hieme depulsa herbis et tepore
verno nitescunt. Villa usibus capax, non sumptuosa tutela.
Cuius in prima parte atrium frugi nec tamen sordidum; 15
deinde porticus in D litterae similitudinem circumactae,
quibus parvula, sed festiva area includitur, egregium adversus
tempestates receptaculum: nam specularibus ac multo magis
imminentibus tectis muniuntur. Est contra medias cavaedium hilare, mox triclinium satis pulchrum, quod in litus ex- 20
currit, ac siquando africo mare inpulsum est, fractis iam et
novissimis fluctibus leviter adluitur. Undique valvas aut
fenestras non minores valvis habet, atque ita a lateribus, a
fronte quasi tria maria prospectat; a tergo cavaedium,
porticum, aream, porticum rursus, mox atrium, silvas et 25
longinquos respicit montes. Huius a laeva retractius paulo
cubiculum est amplum, deinde aliud minus, quod altera
fenestra admittit orientem, occidentem altera retinet, hac et
subiacens mare longius quidem, sed securius intuetur. Huius
cubiculi et triclinii illius obiectu includitur angulus, qui 30

purissimum solem continet et accendit. Hoc hibernaculum,
hoc etiam gymnasium meorum est : ibi omnes silent venti
exceptis qui nubilum inducunt et serenum ante quam usum
loci eripiunt. Adnectitur angulo cubiculum in hapsida
35 curvatum, quod ambitum solis fenestris omnibus sequitur.
Parieti eius in bibliothecae speciem armarium insertum est,
quod non legendos libros, sed lectitandos capit. Adhaeret
dormitorium membrum transitu interiacente, qui suspensus
et tubulatus conceptum vaporem salubri temperamento huc
40 illuc digerit et ministrat. Reliqua pars lateris huius servorum
libertorumque usibus detinetur, plerisque tam mundis, ut
accipere hospites possint. Ex alio latere cubiculum est
politissimum; deinde vel cubiculum grande vel modica
cenatio, quae plurimo sole, plurimo mari lucet; post hanc
45 cubiculum cum procoetone, altitudine aestivum, munimentis
hibernum : est enim subductum omnibus ventis. Huic
cubiculo aliud et procoeton communi pariete iunguntur.
Inde balinei cella frigidaria spatiosa et effusa, cuius in
contrariis parietibus duo baptisteria velut eiecta sinuantur,
50 abunde capacia, si mare in proximo cogites. Adiacet
unctorium, hypocauston, adiacet propnigeon balinei, mox
duae cellae magis elegantes quam sumptuosae : cohaeret
calida piscina mirifica, ex qua natantes mare aspiciunt; nec
procul sphaeristerium, quod calidissimo soli inclinato iam
55 die occurrit. Hic turris erigitur, sub qua diaetae duae,
totidem in ipsa, praeterea cenatio, quae latissimum mare,
longissimum litus, villas amoenissimas prospicit. Est et alia
turris : in hac cubiculum, in quo sol nascitur conditurque :
lata post apotheca et horreum : sub hoc triclinium, quod
60 turbati maris non nisi fragorem et sonum patitur, eumque
iam languidum ac desinentem ; hortum et gestationem videt,
qua hortus includitur. Gestatio buxo aut rore marino, ubi deficit buxus, ambitur : nam buxus, qua parte defenditur tectis,
abunde viret ; aperto caelo apertoque vento et quamquam

longinqua aspergine maris inarescit. Adiacet gestationi [65]
interiore circumitu vinea tenera et umbrosa nudisque etiam
pedibus mollis et cedens. Hortum morus et ficus frequens vestit, quarum arborum illa vel maxime ferax terra
est, malignior ceteris. Hac non deteriore quam maris facie
cenatio remota a mari fruitur: cingitur diaetis duabus a [70]
tergo, quarum fenestris subiacet vestibulum villae et hortus
alius pinguis et rusticus. Hinc cryptoporticus prope publici
operis extenditur. Utrimque fenestrae, a mari plures, ab
horto singulae, sed alternis pauciores. Hae, cum serenus
dies et inmotus, omnes, cum hinc vel inde ventis inquietus, [75]
qua venti quiescunt, sine iniuria patent. Ante cryptoporticum xystus violis odoratus: teporem solis infusi repercussu
cryptoporticus auget, quae ut tenet solem, sic aquilonem
inhibet summovetque, quantumque caloris ante tantum
retro frigoris. Similiter africum sistit atque ita diversissimos [80]
ventos alium alio latere frangit et finit. Haec iucunditas
eius hieme, maior aestate. Nam ante meridiem xystum,
post meridiem gestationis hortique proximam partem umbra
sua temperat, quae, ut dies crevit decrevitve, modo brevior
modo longior hac vel illa cadit. Ipsa vero cryptoporticus [85]
tum maxime caret sole, cum ardentissimus culmini eius
insistit. Ad hoc patentibus fenestris favonios accipit
transmittitque nec umquam aëre pigro et manente ingravescit. In capite xysti deinceps [cryptoporticus horti]
diaeta est, amores mei, re vera amores: ipse posui. In hac [90]
heliocaminus quidem alia xystum, alia mare, utraque solem,
cubiculum autem valvis cryptoporticum, fenestra prospicit
mare. Contra parietem medium zotheca perquam eleganter
recedit, quae specularibus et velis obductis reductisve modo
adicitur cubiculo, modo aufertur. Lectum et duas cathedras [95]
capit: a pedibus mare, a tergo villae, a capite silvae: tot
facies locorum totidem fenestris et distinguit et miscet.
Iunctum est cubiculum noctis et somni. Non illud voces

servulorum, non maris murmur, non tempestatum motus,
100 non fulgurum lumen ac ne diem quidem sentit, nisi fenestris
apertis.   Tam alti abditique secreti illa ratio, quod interia-
cens andron parietem cubiculi hortique distinguit atque ita
omnem sonum media inanitate consumit.   Adplicitum est
cubiculo hypocauston perexiguum, quod angusta fenestra
105 suppositum calorem, ut ratio exigit, aut effundit aut retinet.
Procoeton inde et cubiculum porrigitur in solem, quem
orientem statim exceptum ultra meridiem oblicum quidem,
sed tamen servat.   In hanc ego diaetam cum me recepi,
abesse mihi etiam a villa mea videor, magnamque eius volup-
110 tatem praecipue Saturnalibus capio, cum reliqua pars tecti
licentia dierum festisque clamoribus personat: nam nec ipse
meorum lusibus nec illi studiis meis obstrepunt.   Haec
utilitas, haec amoenitas deficitur aqua salienti, sed puteos ac
potius fontes habet: sunt enim in summo.   Et omnino
115 litoris illius mira natura: quocumque loco moveris humum,
obvius et paratus umor occurrit, isque sincerus ac ne leviter
quidem tanta maris vicinitate corruptus.   Suggerunt adfatim
ligna proximae silvae: ceteras copias Ostiensis colonia
ministrat.   Frugi quidem homini sufficit etiam vicus, quem
120 una villa discernit: in hoc balinea meritoria tria, magna
commoditas, si forte balineum domi vel subitus adventus vel
brevior mora calfacere dissuadeat.   Litus ornant varietate
gratissima nunc continua nunc intermissa tecta villarum, quae
praestant multarum urbium faciem, sive mari sive ipso litore
125 utare; quod non numquam longa tranquillitas mollit, saepius
frequens et contrarius fluctus indurat.   Mare non sane
pretiosis piscibus abundat, soleas tamen et squillas optimas
egerit.   Villa vero nostra etiam mediterraneas copias
praestat, lac in primis: nam illuc e pascuis pecora conve-
130 niunt, siquando aquam umbramve sectantur.   Iustisne de
causis iam tibi videor incolere, inhabitare, diligere secessum?
quem tu nimis urbanus es nisi concupiscis.   Atque utinam

concupiscas! ut tot tantisque dotibus villulae nostrae maxima
commendatio ex tuo contubernio accedat. Vale.

22. (BOOK 2. 18.)

Pliny gladly undertakes to find a school for the sons of Rusticus, and
will take real interest in the inquiry, though the choice will be invidious.

C. PLINIUS MAURICO SUOS.

Quid a te mihi iucundius potuit iniungi, quam ut praeceptorem fratris tui liberis quaererem? Nam beneficio tuo in
scholam redeo et illam dulcissimam aetatem quasi resumo :
sedeo inter iuvenes, ut solebam, atque etiam experior, quantum apud illos auctoritatis ex studiis habeam. Nam proxime 5
frequenti auditorio inter se coram multis ordinis nostri clare
loquebantur: intravi, conticuerunt; quod non referrem, nisi
ad illorum magis laudem quam ad meam pertineret, ac nisi
sperare te vellem posse fratris tui filios probe discere. Quod
superest, cum omnes qui profitentur audiero, quid de quoque 10
sentiam scribam efficiamque, quantum tamen epistula consequi
potero, ut ipse omnes audisse videaris. Debeo enim tibi, debeo
memoriae fratris tui hanc fidem, hoc studium, praesertim
super tanta re. Nam quid magis interest vestra, quam ut
liberi (dicerem tui, nisi nunc illos magis amares) digni illo 15
patre, te patruo reperiantur? quam curam mihi, etiam si non
mandasses, vindicassem. Nec ignoro suscipiendas offensas
in eligendo praeceptore ; sed oportet me non modo offensas
verum etiam simultates pro fratris tui filiis tam aequo animo
subire quam parentes pro suis. Vale.   20

23. (BOOK 2. 20.)

Pliny entertains Calvisius with three anecdotes about Regulus
and his shameless pursuit of legacies.

C. PLINIUS CALVISIO SUO S.

Assem para et accipe auream fabulam, fabulas immo:

nam me priorum nova admonuit, nec refert a qua potissimum incipiam. Verania Pisonis graviter iacebat, huius dico
Pisonis, quem Galba adoptavit. Ad hanc Regulus venit.
5 Primum inpudentiam hominis, qui venerit ad aegram, cuius
marito inimicissimus, ipsi invisissimus fuerat. Esto, si venit
tantum : at ille etiam proximus toro sedit, quo die, qua hora
nata esset interrogavit. Ubi audiit, componit vultum, intendit oculos, movet labra, agitat digitos, computat; nihil:
10 ut diu miseram expectatione suspendit, 'habes' inquit 'climactericum tempus, sed evades. Quod ut tibi magis liqueat,
haruspicem consulam, quem sum frequenter expertus.' Nec
mora: sacrificium facit, adfirmat exta cum siderum signi-
ficatione congruere. Illa, ut in periculo credula, poscit codi-
15 cillos, legatum Regulo scribit: mox ingravescit: clamat
moriens hominem nequam perfidum ac plus etiam quam
periurum, qui sibi per salutem filii perierasset. Facit hoc
Regulus non minus scelerate quam frequenter, quod iram
deorum, quos ipse cotidie fallit, in caput infelicis pueri
20 detestatur. Velleius Blaesus, ille locuples consularis, novissima valetudine conflictabatur : cupiebat mutare testamentum. Regulus, qui speraret aliquid ex novis tabulis,
quia nuper captare eum coeperat, medicos hortari, rogare
quoquo modo spiritum homini prorogarent. Postquam sig-
25 natum est testamentum, mutat personam, vertit adlocutionem,
isdemque medicis 'quousque miserum cruciatis? quid invi-
detis bona morte cui dare vitam non potestis?' Moritur
Blaesus, et tamquam omnia audisset, Regulo ne tantulum
quidem. Sufficiunt duae fabulae, an scholastica lege tertiam
30 poscis? Est unde fiat. Aurelia, ornata femina, signatura
testamentum sumpserat pulcherrimas tunicas. Regulus cum
venisset ad signandum, 'rogo' inquit 'has mihi leges.' Aurelia ludere hominem putabat, ille serio instabat : ne multa,
coegit mulierem aperire tabulas ac sibi tunicas quas erat
35 induta legare : observavit scribentem, inspexit an scripsisset.

Et Aurelia quidem vivit, ille tamen istud tamquam morituram coëgit, et hic hereditates, hic legata, quasi merc-
atur, accipit. Ἀλλὰ τί διατείνομαι in ea civitate, in qua iam
pridem non minora praemia, immo maiora, nequitia et im-
probitas quam pudor et virtus habent? Aspice Regulum, 40
qui ex paupere et tenui ad tantas opes per flagitia processit,
ut ipse mihi dixerit, cum consuleret, quam cito sestertium
sescenties inpleturus esset, invenisse se exta duplicia, quibus
portendi milies et ducenties habiturum. Et habebit, si modo,
ut coepit, aliena testamenta, quod est inprobissimum genus 45
falsi, ipsis quorum sunt illa dictaverit. Vale.

24. (BOOK 3. 1.)

Pliny describes with admiration the method and refinement with which
Spurinna disposes the leisure of his old age.

C. PLINIUS CALVISIO SUO S.

Nescio an ullum iucundius tempus exegerim, quam quo
nuper apud Spurinnam fui, adeo quidem, ut neminem magis
in senectute, si modo senescere datum est, aemulari velim:
nihil est enim illo vitae genere distinctius. Me autem ut
certus siderum cursus ita vita hominum disposita delectat, 5
senum praesertim. Nam iuvenes confusa adhuc quaedam
et quasi turbata non indecent; senibus placida omnia et
ordinata conveniunt, quibus industria sera, turpis ambitio
est. Hanc regulam Spurinna constantissime servat; quin
etiam parva haec, parva, si non cotidie fiant, ordine quodam 10
et velut orbe circumagit. Mane lectulo continetur, hora
secunda calceos poscit, ambulat milia passuum tria nec
minus animum quam corpus exercet. Si adsunt amici,
honestissimi sermones explicantur; si non, liber legitur,
interdum etiam praesentibus amicis, si tamen illi non gra- 15
vantur. Deinde considit, et liber rursus aut sermo libro
potior: mox vehiculum ascendit, adsumit uxorem singularis

exempli vel aliquem amicorum, ut me proxime. Quam
pulchrum illud, quam dulce secretum! quantum ibi antiqui-
20 tatis! quae facta, quos viros audias! quibus praeceptis
imbuare! quamvis ille hoc temperamentum modestiae suae
indixerit, ne praecipere videatur. Peractis septem milibus
passuum iterum ambulat mille, iterum residit vel se cubiculo
ac stilo reddit. Scribit enim, et quidem utraque lingua,
25 lyrica doctissime: mira illis dulcedo, mira suavitas, mira
hilaritas, cuius gratiam cumulat sanctitas scribentis. Ubi
hora balinei nuntiata est (est autem hieme nona, aestate
octava), in sole, si caret vento, ambulat nudus. Deinde
movetur pila vehementer et diu: nam hoc quoque exerci-
30 tationis genere pugnat cum senectute. Lotus accubat et
paulisper cibum differt: interim audit legentem remissius
aliquid et dulcius. Per hoc omne tempus liberum est amicis
vel eadem facere vel alia, si malint. Adponitur cena non
minus nitida quam frugi in argento puro et antiquo: sunt
35 in usu et Corinthia, quibus delectatur nec adficitur. Frequenter comoedis cena distinguitur, ut voluptates quoque
studiis condiantur. Sumit aliquid de nocte et aestate:
nemini hoc longum est; tanta comitate convivium trahitur.
Inde illi post septimum et septuagensimum annum aurium
40 oculorum vigor integer, inde agile et vividum corpus solaque
ex senectute prudentia. Hanc ego vitam voto et cogitatione
praesumo, ingressurus avidissime, ut primum ratio aetatis
receptui canere permiserit. Interim mille laboribus conteror,
quorum mihi et solacium et exemplum est idem Spurinna.
45 Nam ille quoque, quoad honestum fuit, obiit officia, gessit
magistratus, provincias rexit multoque labore hoc otium
meruit. Igitur eundem mihi cursum, eundem terminum
statuo, idque iam nunc apud te subsigno, ut, si me longius
evehi videris, in ius voces ad hanc epistulam meam et
50 quiescere iubeas, cum inertiae crimen effugero. Vale.

E

25.   (BOOK 3. 5.)

Pliny enumerates in order the books written by his uncle; and describes the habits of extraordinary industry which enabled him to complete so vast an amount of work.

C. PLINIUS BAEBIO MACRO SUO S.

Pergratum est mihi quod tam diligenter libros avunculi mei lectitas, ut habere omnes velis quaerasque qui sint omnes. Fungar indicis partibus atque etiam quo sint ordine scripti notum tibi faciam : est enim haec quoque studiosis non iniucunda cognitio. 'De iaculatione equestri unus :' 5 hunc, cum praefectus alae militaret, pari ingenio curaque conposuit.' 'De vita Pomponi Secundi duo,' a quo singulariter amatus hoc memoriae amici quasi debitum munus exsolvit. 'Bellorum Germaniae viginti,' quibus omnia quae cum Germanis gessimus bella collegit. Inchoavit, cum in 10 Germania militaret, somnio monitus : adstitit ei quiescenti Drusi Neronis effigies, qui Germaniae latissime victor ibi periit, commendabat memoriam suam orabatque ut se ab iniuria oblivionis adsereret. 'Studiosi tres,' in sex volumina propter amplitudinem divisi, quibus oratorem ab incunabulis 15 instituit et perficit. 'Dubii sermonis octo :' scripsit sub Nerone novissimis annis, cum omne studiorum genus paulo liberius et erectius periculosum servitus fecisset. 'A fine Aufidi Bassi triginta unus.' 'Naturae historiarum triginta septem,' opus diffusum, eruditum, nec minus varium quam 20 ipsa natura. Miraris quod tot volumina multaque in his tam scrupulosa homo occupatus absolverit : magis miraberis, si scieris illum aliquandiu causas actitasse, decessisse anno sexto et quinquagensimo, medium tempus distentum impeditumque qua officiis maximis qua amicitia principum 25 egisse. Sed erat acre ingenium, incredibile studium, summa vigilantia. Lucubrare Vulcanalibus incipiebat, non auspi-

candi causa, sed studendi, statim a nocte multa, hieme vero
ab hora septima, vel cum tardissime, octava, saepe sexta.
30 Erat sane somni paratissimi, non numquam etiam inter
ipsa studia instantis et deserentis. Ante lucem ibat ad
Vespasianum imperatorem (nam ille quoque noctibus uteba-
tur), inde ad delegatum sibi officium. Reversus domum,
quod reliquum temporis. studiis reddebat. Post cibum
35 saepe, quem interdiu levem et facilem veterum more
sumebat, aestate, siquid otii. iacebat in sole, liber legebatur,
adnotabat excerpebatque. Nihil enim legit quod non
excerperet: dicere etiam solebat nullum esse librum tam
malum, ut non aliqua parte prodesset. Post solem plerum-
40 que frigida lavabatur : deinde gustabat dormiebatque mini-
mum : mox quasi alio die studebat in cenae tempus. Super
hanc liber legebatur, adnotabatur, et quidem cursim. Memini quendam ex amicis, cum lector quaedam perperam
pronuntiasset, revocasse et repeti coëgisse, huic avunculum
45 meum dixisse 'intellexeras nempe?' cum ille adnuisset,
'cur ergo revocabas? decem amplius versus hac tua interpellatione perdidimus.' Tanta erat parsimonia temporis.
Surgebat aestate a cena luce, hieme intra primam noctis,
et tamquam aliqua lege cogente. Haec inter medios labores
50 urbisque fremitum. In secessu solum balinei tempus studiis
eximebatur : cum dico balinei, de interioribus loquor ; nam
dum destringitur tergiturque, audiebat aliquid aut dictabat.
In itinere quasi solutus ceteris curis huic uni vacabat: ad
latus notarius cum libro et pugillaribus, cuius manus hieme
55 manicis muniebantur, ut ne caeli quidem asperitas ullum
studiis tempus eriperet: qua ex causa Romae quoque sella
vehebatur. Repeto me correptum ab eo cur ambularem :
'poteras' inquit 'has horas non perdere;' nam perire omne
tempus arbitrabatur, quod studiis non impenderetur. Hac
60 intentione tot ista volumina peregit electorumque commentarios centum sexaginta mihi reliquit, opisthographos

quidem et minutissime scriptos; qua ratione multiplicatur
hic numerus. Referebat ipse potuisse se, cum procuraret
in Hispania, vendere hos commentarios Largio Licinio
quadringentis milibus nummum, et tunc aliquanto pauciores 65
erant. Nonne videtur tibi recordanti quantum legerit, quantum scripserit, nec in officiis ullis nec in amicitia principis
fuisse, rursus, cum audis quid studiis laboris inpenderit, nec
scripsisse satis nec legisse? Quid est enim quod non aut
illae occupationes inpedire aut haec instantia non possit 70
efficere? Itaque soleo ridere, cum me quidem studiosum
vocant, qui, si comparer illi, sum desidiosissimus. Ego
autem tantum, quem partim publica partim amicorum officia
distringunt? quis ex istis qui tota vita litteris adsident
collatus illi non quasi somno et inertiae deditus erubescat? 75
Extendi epistulam, cum hoc solum quod requirebas scribere
destinassem, quos libros reliquisset: confido tamen haec
quoque tibi non minus grata quam ipsos libros futura,
quae te non tantum ad legendos eos verum etiam ad
simile aliquid elaborandum possunt aemulationis stimulis 80
excitare. Vale.

26. (BOOK 3. 6.)

Pliny asks Severus to prepare a pedestal for a valuable and beautiful
bronze figure, which he has bought to present to the temple of Jupiter
at Comum.

C. PLINIUS ANNIO SEVERO SUO S.

Ex hereditate quae mihi obvenit emi proxime Corinthium
signum, modicum quidem, sed festivum et expressum,
quantum ego sapio, qui fortasse in omni re, in hac certe
perquam exiguum sapio: hoc tamen signum ego quoque
intellego. Est enim nudum nec aut vitia, siqua sunt, 5
celat aut laudes parum ostentat: effingit senem stantem;

ossa, musculi, nervi, venae, rugae etiam ut spirantis appar-
ent, rari et cedentes capilli, lata frons. contracta facies, exile
collum, pendent lacerti, papillae iacent, venter recessit. A
10 tergo quoque eadem aetas ut a tergo. Aes ipsum, quantum
verus color indicat, vetus et antiquum. Talia denique
omnia, ut possint artificum oculos tenere, delectare imperitorum. Quod me quamquam tirunculum sollicitavit ad
emendum. Emi autem, non ut haberem domi (neque enim
15 ullum adhuc Corinthium domi habeo), verum ut in patria
nostra celebri loco ponerem, ac potissimum in Iovis templo :
videtur enim dignum templo, dignum deo donum. Tu
ergo, ut soles omnia quae a me tibi iniunguntur, suscipe
hanc curam et iam nunc iube basim fieri ex quo voles
20 marmore, quae nomen meum honoresque capiat, si hos
quoque putabis addendos. Ego signum ipsum, ut primum
invenero aliquem qui non gravetur, mittam tibi vel ipse,
quod mavis, adferam mecum. Destino enim, si tamen
officii ratio permiserit, excurrere isto. Gaudes quod me
25 venturum esse polliceor, sed contrahes frontem, cum adiecero
ad paucos dies : neque enim diutius abesse me eadem haec
quae nondum exire patiuntur. Vale.

27. (BOOK 3. 7.)

Pliny gives a sketch of the life and abilities of Silius the poet ; and
takes occasion by his death both to reflect on the shortness of life, and
again to urge Caninius to literary effort.

C. PLINIUS CANINIO RUFO SUO S.

Modo nuntiatus est Silius Italicus in Neapolitano suo
inedia finisse vitam. Causa mortis valetudo. Erat illi natus
insanabilis clavus, cuius taedio ad mortem inrevocabili constantia decucurrit, usque ad supremum diem beatus et felix,
5 nisi quod minorem ex liberis duobus amisit ; sed maiorem

melioremque florentem atque etiam consularem reliquit. Laeserat famam suam sub Nerone, credebatur sponte accusasse; sed in Vitelli amicitia sapienter se et comiter gesserat, ex proconsulatu Asiae gloriam reportaverat, maculam veteris industriae laudabili otio abluerat. Fuit 10 inter principes civitatis sine potentia, sine invidia : salutabatur, colebatur multumque in lectulo iacens cubiculo semper non ex fortuna frequenti doctissimis sermonibus dies transigebat, cum a scribendo vacaret. Scribebat carmina maiore cura quam ingenio, non numquam iudicia hominum recita- 15 tionibus experiebatur. Novissime ita suadentibus annis ab urbe secessit seque in Campania tenuit, ac ne adventu quidem novi principis inde commotus est. Magna Caesaris laus, sub quo hoc liberum fuit, magna illius, qui hac libertate ausus est uti. Erat φιλόκαλος usque ad emacitatis reprehen- 20 sionem. Plures isdem in locis villas possidebat adamatisque novis priores neglegebat. Multum ubique librorum, multum statuarum, multum imaginum, quas non habebat modo verum etiam venerabatur, Vergili ante omnes, cuius natalem religiosius quam suum celebrabat, Neapoli maxime, ubi 25 monimentum eius adire ut templum solebat. In hac tranquillitate annum quintum et septuagensimum excessit, delicato magis corpore quam infirmo; utque novissimus a Nerone factus est consul, ita postremus ex omnibus quos Nero consules fecerat decessit. Illud etiam notabile, ultimus 30 ex Neronianis consularibus obiit quo consule Nero periit. Quod me recordantem fragilitatis humanae miseratio subit. Quid enim tam circumcisum, tam breve quam hominis vita longissima? an non videtur tibi Nero modo modo fuisse? cum interim ex iis qui sub illo gesserant consulatum 35 nemo iam superest. Quamquam quid hoc miror? nuper L. Piso, pater Pisonis illius qui a Valerio Festo per summum facinus in Africa occisus est, dicere solebat neminem se videre in senatu quem consul ipse sententiam rogavisset.

40 Tam angustis terminis tantae multitudinis vivacitas ipsa
concluditur, ut mihi non venia solum dignae verum etiam
laude videantur illae regiae lacrimae. Nam ferunt Xerxen,
cum inmensum exercitum oculis obisset, inlacrimasse, quod
tot milibus tam brevis immineret occasus. Sed tanto magis
45 hoc quidquid est temporis futilis et caduci, si non datur
factis (nam horum materia in aliena manu), certe studiis
proferamus, et quatenus nobis denegatur diu vivere, relin-
quamus aliquid quo nos vixisse testemur. Scio te stimulis
non egere; me tamen tui caritas evocat ut currentem
50 quoque instigem, sicut tu soles me. Ἀγαθὴ δ' ἔρις, cum
invicem se mutuis exhortationibus amici ad amorem inmor-
talitatis exacuunt. Vale.

28. (BOOK 3. 11.)

Pliny, while deprecating the excessive gratitude of Artemidorus,
relates with some satisfaction the dangerous services which he had
rendered to a man so worthy of his regard.

C. PLINIUS IULIO GENITORI SUO S.

Est omnino Artemidori nostri tam benigna natura, ut
officia amicorum in maius extollat: inde etiam meum
meritum ut vera ita supra meritum praedicatione circumfert.
Equidem, cum essent philosophi ab urbe summoti, fui apud
5 illum in suburbano, et quo notabilius, hoc est periculosius,
esset, fui praetor. Pecuniam etiam, qua tunc illi ampliore
opus erat, ut aes alienum exsolveret contractum ex pul-
cherrimis causis, mussantibus magnis quibusdam et locuple-
tibus amicis mutuatus ipse gratuitam dedi. Atque haec feci,
10 cum septem amicis meis aut occisis aut relegatis, occisis
Senecione Rustico Helvidio, relegatis Maurico Gratilla Arria
Fannia, tot circa me iactis fulminibus quasi ambustus mihi
quoque inpendere idem exitium certis quibusdam notis

augurarer. Non ideo tamen eximiam gloriam meruisse me, ut ille praedicat, credo, sed tantum effugisse flagitium. 15 Nam et C. Musonium, socerum eius, quantum licitum est per aetatem, cum admiratione dilexi et Artemidorum ipsum iam tum, cum in Syria tribunus militarem, arta familiaritate complexus sum, idque primum non nullius indolis dedi specimen, quod virum aut sapientem aut proximum similli- 20 mumque sapienti intellegere sum visus. Nam ex omnibus qui nunc se philosophos vocant vix unum aut alterum invenies tanta sinceritate, tanta veritate. Mitto qua patientia corporis hiemes iuxta et aestates ferat, ut nullis laboribus cedat, ut nihil in cibo, in potu voluptatibus tribuat, ut oculos 25 animumque contineat. Sunt haec magna, sed in alio; in hoc vero minima, si ceteris virtutibus comparentur, quibus meruit ut a C. Musonio ex omnibus omnium ordinum adsectatoribus gener adsumeretur. Quae mihi recordanti est quidem iucundum quod me cum apud alios tum apud 30 te tantis laudibus cumulat, vereor tamen ne modum excedat, quem benignitas eius (illuc enim unde coepi revertor) solet non tenere. Nam in hoc uno interdum vir alioqui pruden- tissimus honesto quidem sed tamen errore versatur, quod pluris amicos suos quam sunt arbitratur. Vale. 35

29. (BOOK 3. 12.)

Pliny accepts Catilius' invitation on condition that the fare shall be simple, and the party shall break up in time to avoid a repetition of Cato's misadventure.

C. PLINIUS CATILIO SEVERO SUO S.

Veniam ad cenam: sed iam nunc paciscor sit expedita, sit parca, Socraticis tantum sermonibus abundet, in his quo- que teneat modum. Erunt officia antelucana, in quae inci- dere inpune ne Catoni quidem licuit, quem tamen C.

5 Caesar ita reprehendit, ut laudet. Describit enim eos quibus
obvius fuerit, cum caput ebrii retexissent, erubuisse : deinde
adicit ' putares non ab illis Catonem, sed illos a Catone
deprehensos.' Potuitne plus auctoritatis tribui Catoni, quam
si ebrius quoque tam venerabilis erat ? Nostrae tamen cenae
10 ut apparatus et inpendii sic temporis modus constet. Neque
enim ii sumus quos vituperare ne inimici quidem possint,
nisi ut simul laudent. Vale.

30. (BOOK 3. 14.)

Pliny relates the murder of Largius Macedo by his slaves, and adds
an ominous circumstance from his previous life.

C. PLINIUS ACILIO SUO S.

Rem atrocem nec tantum epistula dignam Largius
Macedo, vir praetorius, a servis suis passus est, superbus
alioqui dominus et saevus et qui servisse patrem suum
parum, immo nimium meminisset. Lavabatur in villa For-
5 miana : repente eum servi circumsistunt : alius fauces in-
vadit, alius os verberat, alius pectus et ventrem atque etiam,
foedum dictu, verenda contundit ; et cum exanimem puta-
rent, abiciunt in fervens pavimentum, ut experirentur an
viveret. Ille, sive quia non sentiebat, sive quia se non
10 sentire simulabat, immobilis et extentus fidem peractae
mortis implevit. Tum demum quasi aestu solutus effertur :
excipiunt servi fideliores, concubinae cum ululatu et clamore concurrunt. Ita et vocibus excitatus et recreatus
loci frigore sublatis oculis agitatoque corpore vivere
15 se, et iam tutum erat, confitetur. Diffugiunt servi ;
quorum magna pars comprehensa est, ceteri requiruntur.
Ipse paucis diebus aegre focilatus non sine ultionis solacio
decessit, ita vivus vindicatus, ut occisi solent. Vides quot
periculis, quot contumeliis, quot ludibriis simus obnoxii

nec est quod quisquam possit esse securus, quia sit remissus 20
et mitis; non enim iudicio domini, sed scelere perimuntur.
Verum haec hactenus. Quid praeterea novi? quid? nihil;
alioqui subiungerem: nam et charta adhuc superest, et dies
feriatus patitur plura contexi. Addam quod opportune de
eodem Macedone succurrit. Cum in publico Romae 25
lavaretur, notabilis atque etiam, ut exitus docuit, ominosa
res accidit. Eques Romanus a servo eius ut transitum daret
manu leviter admonitus convertit se nec servum, a quo erat
tactus, sed ipsum Macedonem tam graviter palma percussit,
ut paene concideret. Ita balineum illi quasi per gradus 30
quosdam primum contumeliae locus, deinde exitii fuit.
Vale.

31. (BOOK 3. 16.)

To prove that the fame of noble acts is not determined by the proportion of their worth, Pliny relates instances of Arria's fortitude, affection, and stern resolution, all of which he considers grander than her
purpose in death.

C. PLINIUS NEPOTI SUO S.

Adnotasse videor facta dictaque virorum feminarumque
alia clariora esse alia maiora. Confirmata est opinio mea
hesterno Fanniae sermone. Neptis haec Arriae illius 'quae
marito et solacium mortis et exemplum fuit. Multa referebat aviae suae non minora hoc, sed obscuriora; quae tibi 5
existimo tam mirabilia legenti fore, quam mihi audienti
fuerunt. Aegrotabat Caecina Pactus, maritus eius, aegrotabat et filius, uterque mortifere, ut videbatur: filius decessit
eximia pulchritudine, pari verecundia, et parentibus non
minus ob alia carus, quam quod filius erat. Huic illa ita 10
funus paravit, ita duxit exequias, ut ignoraret maritus: quin
immo, quotiens cubiculum eius intraret, vivere filium atque
etiam commodiorem esse simulabat ac persaepe interroganti

quid ageret puer respondebat 'bene quievit, libenter cibum
15 sumpsit'. Deinde, cum diu cohibitae lacrimae vincerent
prorumperentque, egrediebatur: tunc se dolori dabat:
satiata siccis oculis composito vultu redibat, tamquam orbi-'
tatem foris reliquisset. Praeclarum quidem illud eiusdem,
ferrum stringere, perfodere pectus, extrahere pugionem,
20 porrigere marito, addere vocem immortalem ac paene
divinam 'Paete, non dolet.' Sed tamen ista facienti, ista
dicenti gloria et aeternitas ante oculos erant: quo maius
est sine praemio aeternitatis, sine praemio gloriae abdere
lacrimas, operire luctum, amissoque filio matrem adhuc
25 agere. Scribonianus arma in Illyrico contra Claudium mo-
verat: fuerat Paetus in partibus et occiso Scriboniano
Romam trahebatur. Erat ascensurus navem: Arria milites
orabat ut simul inponeretur. 'Nempe enim' inquit 'daturi
estis consulari viro servulos aliquos, quorum e manu cibum
30 capiat, a quibus vestiatur, a quibus calcietur: omnia sola
praestabo.' Non impetravit: conduxit piscatoriam nau-
culam ingensque navigium minimo secuta est. Eadem
apud Claudium uxori Scriboniani, cum illa profiteretur
indicium, 'ego' inquit 'te audiam, cuius in gremio Scribo-
35 nianus occisus est, et vivis?' ex quo manifestum est ei consilium pulcherrimae mortis non subitum fuisse. Quin etiam,
cum Thrasea, gener eius, deprecaretur ne mori pergeret
interque alia dixisset 'vis ergo filiam tuam, si mihi per-
eundum fuerit, mori mecum?' respondit 'si tam diu tantaque
40 concordia vixerit tecum, quam ego cum Paeto, volo.' Aux-
erat hoc responso curam suorum, attentius custodiebatur:
sensit et 'nihil agitis' inquit: 'potestis enim efficere ut male
moriar, ut non moriar non potestis.' Dum haec dicit,
exiluit cathedra adversoque parieti caput ingenti impetu
45 impegit et corruit. Focilata 'dixeram' inquit 'vobis inven-
turam me quamlibet duram ad mortem viam, si vos facilem
negassetis.' Videnturne haec tibi maiora illo 'Paete, non

dolet,' ad quod per haec perventum est? cum interim illud quidem ingens fama, haec nulla circumfert. Unde colligitur quod initio dixi, alia esse clariora alia maiora. Vale.   50

32. (BOOK 3. 18.)

Pliny is delighted with the favourable reception given to his public recitation of the Panegyric on Trajan, at first delivered by him in the senate, and since then enlarged and published.

C. PLINIUS CURIO SEVERO SUO S.

Officium consulatus iniunxit mihi ut rei publicae nomine principi gratias agerem. Quod ego in senatu cum ad rationem et loci et temporis ex more fecissem, bono civi convenientissimum credidi eadem illa spatiosius et uberius volumine amplecti, primum ut imperatori nostro virtutes 5 suae veris laudibus commendarentur; deinde ut futuri principes non quasi a magistro, sed tamen sub exemplo praemonerentur, qua potissimum via possent ad eandem gloriam niti. Nam praecipere qualis esse debeat princeps pulchrum quidem, sed onerosum ac prope superbum est; laudare vero 10 optimum principem ac per hoc posteris velut e specula lumen quod sequantur ostendere idem utilitatis habet, adrogantiae nihil. Cepi autem non mediocrem voluptatem, quod, hunc librum cum amicis recitare voluissem, non per codicillos, non per libellos, sed 'si commodum' et 'si valde 15 vacaret' admoniti (numquam porro aut valde vacat Romae aut commodum est audire recitantem), foedissimis insuper tempestatibus, per biduum convenerunt, cumque modestia mea finem recitationi facere voluisset, ut adicerem tertium diem exegerunt. Mihi hunc honorem habitum putem, an 20 studiis? Studiis malo, quae prope extincta refoventur. At cui materiae hanc sedulitatem praestiterunt? Nempe quam in senatu quoque, ubi perpeti necesse erat, gravari tamen

vel puncto temporis solebamus, eandem nunc et qui recitare
25 et qui audire triduo velint inveniuntur, non quia eloquentius
quam prius, sed quia liberius ideoque etiam libentius scri-
bitur. Accedet ergo hoc quoque laudibus principis nostri,
quod res antea tam invisa quam falsa nunc ut vera ita
amabilis facta est. Sed ego cum studium audientium tum
30 iudicium mire probavi: animadverti enim severissima quaeque vel maxime satisfacere. Memini quidem me non multis
recitasse quod omnibus scripsi, nihilo minus tamen, tamquam
sit eadem omnium futura sententia, hac severitate aurium
laetor, ac sicut olim theatra male musicos canere docuerunt,
35 ita nunc in spem adducor posse fieri ut eadem theatra bene
canere musicos doceant. Omnes enim qui placendi causa
scribunt qualia placere viderint scribent. Ac mihi quidem
confido in hoc genere materiae laetioris stili constare rationem, cum ea potius quae pressius et adstrictius quam illa
40 quae hilarius et quasi exultantius scripsi possint videri arcessita et inducta: non ideo tamen segnius precor ut quandoque veniat dies (utinamque iam venerit!), quo austeris illis
severisque dulcia haec blandaque vel iusta possessione
decedant. Habes acta mea tridui; quibus cognitis volui
45 tantum te voluptatis absentem et studiorum nomine et meo
capere, quantum praesens percipere potuisses. Vale.

33. (BOOK 3. 19.)

Pliny asks for advice in regard to the purchase of an estate which
runs into his property. He describes the advantages and disadvantages
of possessing it, among the latter the miserable condition of the culti-
vators.

C. PLINIUS CALVISIO RUFO SUO S.

Adsumo te in consilium rei familiaris, ut soleo. Praedia
agris meis vicina atque etiam inserta venalia sunt. In his
me multa sollicitant, aliqua nec minora deterrent. Sollicitat

primum ipsa pulchritudo iungendi, deinde quod non minus
utile quam voluptuosum posse utraque eadem opera, eodem 5
viatico invisere, sub eodem procuratore ac paene isdem
actoribus habere, unam villam colere et ornare, alteram
tantum tueri. Inest huic computationi sumptus supellectilis,
sumptus atriensium, topiariorum, fabrorum atque etiam
venatorii instrumenti; quae plurimum refert unum in locum 10
conferas, an in diversa dispergas. Contra vereor ne sit
incautum rem tam magnam isdem tempestatibus, isdem casi-
bus subdere: tutius videtur incerta fortunae possessionum
varietatibus experiri. Habet etiam multum iucunditatis soli
caelique mutatio ipsaque illa peregrinatio inter sua. Iam 15
quod deliberationis nostrae caput est, agri sunt fertiles
pingues aquosi, constant campis vineis silvis, quae materiam
et ex ea reditum sicut modicum ita statum praestant. Sed
haec felicitas terrae inbecillis cultoribus fatigatur. Nam
possessor prior saepius vendidit pignora, et dum reliqua 20
colonorum minuit ad tempus, vires in posterum exhausit,
quarum defectione rursus reliqua creverunt. Sunt ergo
instruendi eo pluris, quod frugi mancipiis: nam nec ipse
usquam vinctos habeo nec ibi quisquam. Superest ut scias
quanti videantur posse emi: sestertio tricies, non quia non 25
aliquando quinquagies fuerint, verum et hac paenuria colonorum et communi temporis iniquitate ut reditus agrorum
sic etiam pretium retro abiit. Quaeris an hoc ipsum tricies
facile colligere possimus? sum quidem prope totus in praediis, aliquid tamen fenero, nec molestum erit mutuari; acci- 30
piam a socru, cuius arca non secus ac mea utor. Proinde
hoc te non moveat, si cetera non refragantur, quae velim
quam diligentissime examines. Nam cum in omnibus
rebus tum in disponendis facultatibus plurimum tibi et usus
et providentiae superest. Vale. 35

34. (BOOK 3. 20.)

Pliny relates with some apprehension the sudden adoption of the
ballot by the senate in the election of magistrates, and expresses his
gratification at having found something of political interest to write
about, even under an imperial regime.

C. PLINIUS MESSIO MAXIMO SUO S.

Meministine te saepe legisse, quantas contentiones exci-
tarit lex tabellaria quantumque ipsi latori vel gloriae vel
reprehensionis attulerit? At nunc in senatu sine ulla dissen-
sione hoc idem ut optimum placuit: omnes comitiorum die
5 tabellas postulaverunt. Excesseramus sane manifestis illis
apertisque suffragiis licentiam contionum. Non tempus
loquendi, non tacendi modestia, non denique sedendi dignitas custodiebatur. Magni undique dissonique clamores,
procurrebant omnes cum suis candidatis, multa agmina in
10 medio multique circuli et indecora confusio: adeo desciver-
amus a consuetudine parentum, apud quos omnia disposita
moderata tranquilla maiestatem loci pudoremque retinebant.
Supersunt senes, ex quibus audire soleo hunc ordinem
comitiorum: citato nomine candidati silentium summum;
15 dicebat ipse pro se, explicabat vitam suam, testes et laudatores dabat vel eum sub quo militaverat vel eum cui quaestor fuerat vel utrumque, si poterat, addebat quosdam ex
suffragatoribus: illi graviter et paucis loquebantur. Plus
hoc quam preces proderat. Non numquam candidatus aut
20 natales competitoris aut annos aut etiam mores arguebat.
Audiebat senatus gravitate censoria. Ita saepius digni
quam gratiosi praevalebant. Quae nunc inmodico favore
corrupta ad tacita suffragia quasi ad remedium decucur-
rerunt; quod interim plane remedium fuit: erat enim
25 novum et subitum. Sed vereor ne procedente tempore ex
ipso remedio vitia nascantur. Est enim periculum ne
tacitis suffragiis inpudentia inrepat. Nam quoto cuique

eadem honestatis cura secreto quae palam? Multi famam, conscientiam pauci verentur. Sed nimis cito de futuris: interim beneficio tabellarum habebimus magistratus qui 30 maxime fieri debuerunt. Nam ut in reciperatoriis iudiciis sic nos in his comitiis quasi repente adprehensi sinceri iudices fuimus. Haec tibi scripsi, primum ut aliquid novi scriberem, deinde ut non numquam de re publica loquerer, cuius materiae nobis quanto rarior quam veteribus occasio 35 tanto minus omittenda est. Et hercule quousque illa vulgaria ' quid agis ? ecquid commode vales ?' Habeant nostrae quoque litterae aliquid non humile nec sordidum nec privatis rebus inclusum. Sunt quidem cuncta sub unius arbitrio, qui pro utilitate communi solus omnium curas laboresque 40 suscepit ; quidam tamen salubri temperamento ad nos quoque velut rivi ex illo benignissimo fonte decurrunt, quos et haurire ipsi et absentibus amicis quasi ministrare epistulis possumus. Vale.

35. (BOOK 3. 21.)

Pliny regrets the death of Martial the poet; and mentions that he had made Martial a present before he left Italy, in return for an epigram, which he subjoins.

C. PLINIUS CORNELIO PRISCO SUO S.

Audio Valerium Martialem decessisse et moleste fero. Erat homo ingeniosus acutus acer, et qui plurimum in scribendo et salis haberet et fellis nec candoris minus. Prosecutus eram viatico secedentem: dederam hoc amicitiae, dederam etiam versiculis quos de me composuit. 5 Fuit moris antiqui eos qui vel singulorum laudes vel urbium scripserant aut honoribus aut pecunia ornare ; nostris vero temporibus ut alia speciosa et egregia ita hoc in primis exolevit. Nam postquam desiimus facere laudanda, laudari quoque ineptum putamus. Quaeris qui 10

sint versiculi quibus gratiam rettuli. Remitterem te ad
ipsum volumen, nisi quosdam tenerem: tu, si placuerint hi,
ceteros in libro requires. Adloquitur Musam, mandat ut
domum meam Esquiliis quaerat, adeat reverenter:

15   Sed ne tempore non tuo disertam
       Pulses ebria ianuam videto:
       Totos dat tetricae dies Minervae,
       Dum centum studet auribus virorum
       Hoc quod saecula posterique possint
20   Arpinis quoque comparare chartis.
       Seras tutior ibis ad lucernas:
       Haec hora est tua, cum furit Lyaeus,
       Cum regnat rosa, cum madent capilli:
       Tunc me vel rigidi legant Catones.

25 Meritone eum qui haec de me scripsit et tunc dimisi
amicissime et nunc ut amicissimum defunctum esse doleo?
Dedit enim mihi quantum maximum potuit, daturus amplius,
si potuisset. Tametsi quid homini potest dari maius quam
gloria et laus et aeternitas? At non erunt aeterna quae
30 scripsit: non erunt fortasse, ille tamen scripsit tamquam
essent futura Vale.

36. (BOOK 4. 2.)

Regulus has lost his son, and Pliny describes the funeral, commenting
with great bitterness on the father's character and conduct.

C. PLINIUS ATTIO CLEMENTI SUO S.

Regulus filium amisit, hoc uno malo indignus, quod nescio
an malum putet. Erat puer acris ingenii, sed ambigui, qui
tamen posset recta sectari, si patrem non referret. Hunc
Regulus emancipavit, ut heres matris existeret; mancipatum
5 (ita vulgo ex moribus hominis loquebantur) foeda et insolita
parentibus indulgentiae simulatione captabat. Incredibile,

F

sed Regulum cogita. Amissum tamen luget insane. Habebat puer mannulos multos et iunctos et solutos, habebat canes maiores minoresque, habebat luscinias, psittacos, merulas: omnes Regulus circa rogum trucidavit. Nec 10 dolor erat ille, sed ostentatio doloris. Convenitur ad eum mira celebritate. Cuncti detestantur oderunt, et quasi probent, quasi diligant, cursant frequentant, utque breviter quod sentio enuntiem, in Regulo demerendo Regulum imitantur. Tenet se trans Tiberim in hortis, in quibus latissimum solum 15 porticibus inmensis, ripam statuis suis occupavit, ut est in summa avaritia sumptuosus, in summa infamia gloriosus. Vexat ergo civitatem insaluberrimo tempore, et quod vexat solacium putat. Dicit se velle ducere uxorem: hoc quoque, sicut alia, perverse: audies brevi nuptias lugentis, nuptias 20 senis: quorum alterum immaturum, alterum serum est. Unde hoc augurer quaeris: non quia adfirmat ipse, quo mendacius nihil est, sed quia certum est Regulum esse facturum quidquid fieri non oportet. Vale.

37.   (BOOK 4. 7.)

Pliny describes the perverse energy of Regulus now shown in his taste-less commemorations of his son's memory, as it had formerly been in his career as an advocate.

C. PLINIUS CATIO LEPIDO SUO S.

Saepe tibi dico inesse vim Regulo. Mirum est quam efficiat in quod incubuit. Placuit ei lugere filium; luget ut nemo: placuit statuas eius et imagines quam plurimas facere; hoc omnibus officinis agit, illum coloribus, illum cera, illum aere, illum argento, illum auro, ebore, marmore 5 effingit. Ipse vero nuper adhibito ingenti auditorio librum de vita eius recitavit, de vita pueri: recitavit tamen; eundem in exemplaria mille transscriptum per totam Italiam provinciasque dimisit: scripsit publice ut a decurionibus eligeretur

10 vocalissimus aliquis ex ipsis, qui legeret cum populo : factum est. Hanc ille vim, seu quo alio nomine vocanda est intentio quidquid velis obtinendi, si ad potiora vertisset, quantum boni efficere potuisset! Quamquam minor vis bonis quam malis inest, ac sicut ἀμαθία μὲν θράσος, λογισμὸς δὲ ὄκνον
15 φέρει, ita recta ingenia debilitat verecundia, perversa confirmat audacia. Exemplo est Regulus. Inbecillum latus, os confusum, haesitans lingua, tardissima inventio, memoria nulla, nihil denique praeter ingenium insanum ; et tamen eo impudentia ipsoque illo furore pervenit, ut orator habeatur.
20 Itaque Herennius Senecio mirifice Catonis illud de oratore in hunc e contrario vertit, 'orator est vir malus dicendi imperitus.' Non mehercule Cato ipse tam bene verum oratorem, quam hic Regulum expressit. Habesne quo tali epistulae parem gratiam referas? Habes, si scripseris, num
25 aliquis in municipio vestro ex sodalibus meis, num etiam ipse tu hunc luctuosum Reguli librum ut circulator in foro legeris, ἐπάρας scilicet, ut ait Demosthenes, τὴν φωνὴν καὶ γεγηθὼς καὶ λαρυγγίζων. Est enim tam ineptus, ut risum magis possit exprimere quam gemitum: credas non de
30 puero scriptum, sed a puero. Vale.

38. (BOOK 4. 10.)

As a man of honour Pliny cannot hesitate to give Modestus his liberty and his legacy, though Sabina's wish to that effect is not expressed in terms of legal force.

C. PLINIUS STATIO SABINO SUO S.

Scribis mihi Sabinam, quae nos reliquit heredes, Modestum servum suum nusquam liberum esse iussisse, eidem tamen sic adscripsisse legatum, 'Modesto, quem liberum esse iussi.' Quaeris quid sentiam. Contuli cum peritis
5 iuris : convenit inter omnes nec libertatem deberi, quia non sit data, nec legatum, quia servo suo dederit. Sed mihi

manifestus error videtur, ideoque puto nobis, quasi scripserit
Sabina, faciendum quod ipsa scripsisse se credidit.   Confido
accessurum te sententiae meae, cum religiosissime soleas
custodire defunctorum voluntatem, quam bonis heredibus 10
intellexisse pro iure est.   Neque enim minus apud nos
honestas quam apud alios necessitas valet.   Moretur ergo
in libertate sinentibus nobis, fruatur legato, quasi omnia
diligentissime caverit.   Cavit enim quae heredes bene elegit.
Vale.   15

30. (BOOK 4. 13.)

Pliny is promoting the establishment of a school at Comum; and
writes to ask Tacitus to look out for persons willing and able to under-
take the care of it, from among whom the parents of the children may
choose a master.

C. PLINIUS TACITO SUO S.

Salvum in urbem venisse gaudeo.   Venisti autem, siquando alias, nunc maxime mihi desideratus.   Ipse pauculis
adhuc diebus in Tusculano commorabor, ut opusculum
quod est in manibus absolvam.   Vereor enim ne, si hanc
intentionem iam in fine intermisero, aegre resumam.   In- 5
terim ne quid festinationi meae pereat, quod sum praesens
petiturus hac quasi praecursoria epistula rogo.   Sed prius
accipe causas rogandi.   Proxime cum in patria mea fui,
venit ad me salutandum municipis mei filius praetextatus.
Huic ego 'studes?' inquam.   Respondit 'etiam.' 'Ubi?' 10
'Mediolani.' 'Cur non hic?' et pater eius (erat enim una
atque etiam ipse adduxerat puerum), 'quia nullos hic praeceptores habemus.' 'Quare nullos? nam vehementer intererat vestra, qui patres estis,' et opportune conplures patres
audiebant, 'liberos vestros hic potissimum discere.   Ubi 15
enim aut iucundius morarentur, quam in patria, aut pudicius
continerentur, quam sub oculis parentum, aut minore
sumptu, quam domi?   Quantulum est ergo collata pecunia

conducere praeceptores, quodque nunc in habitationes, in
20 viatica, in ea quae peregre emuntur (omnia autem peregre
emuntur) inpenditis adicere mercedibus? Atque adeo ego,
qui nondum liberos habeo, paratus sum pro re publica
nostra, quasi pro filia vel parente, tertiam partem eius quod
conferre vobis placebit dare. Totum etiam pollicerer, nisi
25 timerem ne hoc munus meum quandoque ambitu corrumpe-
retur, ut accidere multis in locis video, in quibus praeceptores publice conducuntur. Huic vitio occurri uno remedio
potest, si parentibus solis ius conducendi relinquatur isdemque religio recte iudicandi necessitate collationis addatur.
30 Nam qui fortasse de alieno neglegentes, certe de suo diligentes erunt dabuntque operam ne a me pecuniam [non] nisi
dignus accipiat, si accepturus et ab ipsis erit. Proinde
consentite, conspirate maioremque animum ex meo sumite,
qui cupio esse quam plurimum quod debeam conferre.
35 Nihil honestius praestare liberis vestris, nihil gratius patriae
potestis. Educentur hic qui hic nascuntur statimque ab
infantia natale solum amare frequentare consuescant. Atque
utinam tam claros praeceptores inducatis, ut finitimis oppidis
studia hinc petantur, utque nunc liberi vestri aliena in loca,
40 ita mox alieni in hunc locum confluant!' Haec putavi altius
et quasi a fonte repetenda, quo magis scires, quam gratum
mihi foret, si susciperes quod iniungo. Iniungo autem et
pro rei magnitudine rogo ut ex copia studiosorum, quae ad
te ex admiratione ingenii tui convenit, circumspicias prae-
45 ceptores, quos sollicitare possimus, sub ea tamen condicione,
ne cui fidem meam obstringam. Omnia enim libera parentibus servo: illi iudicent, illi eligant; ego mihi curam tantum
et inpendium vindico. Proinde siquis fuerit repertus, qui
ingenio suo fidat, eat illuc ea lege, ut hinc nihil aliud certum
50 quam fiduciam suam ferat. Vale.

40. (BOOK 4. 17.)

Pliny willingly undertakes the case of Corellius' daughter, though in doing so he will have to act against another friend. That objection however vanishes when he remembers his relations with Corellius, and how the latter commended him to his daughter as her protector.

C. PLINIUS ASINIO GALLO SUO S.

Et admones et rogas ut suscipiam causam Corelliae absentis contra C. Caecilium, consulem designatum. Quod admones, gratias ago; quod rogas, queror. Admoneri enim debeo, ut sciam, rogari non debeo, ut faciam quod mihi non facere turpissimum est. An ego tueri Corelli filiam dubi- 5 tem? Est quidem mihi cum isto contra quem me advocas non plane familiaris, sed tamen amicitia. Accedit huc dignitas hominis atque hic ipse cui destinatus est honor; cuius nobis hoc maior agenda reverentia est, quod iam illo functi sumus. Naturale est enim ut ea quae quis adeptus 10 est ipse quam amplissima existimari velit. Sed mihi cogitanti adfuturum me Corelli filiae omnia ista frigida et inania videntur. Obversatur oculis ille vir, quo neminem aetas nostra graviorem sanctiorem subtiliorem tulit. Quem ego cum ex admiratione diligere coepissem, quod evenire contra 15 solet, magis admiratus sum, postquam penitus inspexi. Inspexi enim penitus: nihil a me ille secretum, non ioculare, non serium, non triste, non laetum. Adulescentulus eram, et iam mihi ab illo honor atque etiam, audebo dicere, reverentia ut aequali habebatur. Ille meus in petendis honoribus 20 suffragator et testis, ille in inchoandis deductor et comes, ille in gerendis consiliator et rector, ille denique in omnibus officiis nostris, quamquam et inbecillus et senior, quasi iuvenis et validus conspiciebatur. Quantum ille famae meae domi, in publico, quantum etiam apud principem 25 adstruxit! Nam cum forte de bonis iuvenibus apud Nervam imperatorem sermo incidisset et plerique me laudibus ferrent,

paulisper se intra silentium tenuit, quod illi plurimum auctoritatis addebat; deinde gravitate quam noras 'necesse est'
30 inquit 'parcius laudem Secundum, quia nihil nisi ex consilio
meo facit.' Qua voce tribuit mihi quantum petere voto
inmodicum erat, nihil me facere non sapientissime, cum
omnia ex consilio sapientissimi viri facerem. Quin etiam
moriens filiae suae (ipsa solet praedicare), 'multos quidem
35 amicos tibi ut longiore vita paravi, praecipuos tamen Secundum et Cornutum.' Quod cum recordor, 'intellego mihi
laborandum ne qua parte videar hanc de me fiduciam pro-
videntissimi viri destituisse.' Quare ego vero Corelliae adero
promptissime nec subire offensas recusabo: quamquam non
40 solum veniam me verum etiam laudem apud istum ipsum,
a quo, ut ais, nova lis fortasse ut feminae intenditur, arbitror
consecuturum, si haec eadem in actione, latius scilicet et
uberius, quam epistularum angustiae sinunt, vel in excusatio-
nem vel etiam commendationem meam dixero. Vale.

41. (BOOK 4. 19.)

Pliny describes to Hispulla, aunt of his wife Calpurnia, the interest
of the latter in all his pursuits, his consequent affection for her, and the
gratitude which he feels to Hispulla as the cause of their mutual
happiness.

C. PLINIUS CALPURNIAE HISPULLAE SUAE S.

Cum sis pietatis exemplum fratremque optimum et amantissimum tui pari caritate dilexeris filiamque eius ut tuam
diligas nec tantum amitae ei adfectum verum etiam patris
amissi repraesentes, non dubito maximo tibi gaudio fore,
5 cum cognoveris dignam patre, dignam te, dignam avo evadere. Summum est acumen, summa frugalitas: amat me,
quod castitatis indicium est. Accedit his studium litterarum,
quod ex mei caritate concepit: meos libellos habet, lectitat.
ediscit etiam. Qua illa sollicitudine, cum videor acturus,

quanto, cum egi, gaudio adficitur! Disponit qui nuntient 10
sibi, quem adsensum, quos clamores excitarim, quem even-
tum iudicii tulerim.   Eadem, siquando recito, in proximo
discreta velo sedet laudesque nostras avidissimis auribus
excipit.   Versus quidem meos cantat etiam formatque cithara,
non artifice aliquo docente, sed amore, qui magister est 15
optimus.   His ex causis in spem certissimam adducor perpetuam nobis maioremque in dies futuram esse concordiam.
Non enim aetatem meam aut corpus, quae paulatim occidunt
ac senescunt, sed gloriam diligit.   Nec aliud decet tuis
manibus educatam, tuis praeceptis institutam, quae nihil in 20
contubernio tuo viderit nisi sanctum honestumque, quae
denique amare me ex tua praedicatione consueverit.   Nam
cum matrem meam parentis loco verereris, me a pueritia
statim formare, laudare talemque, qualis nunc uxori meae
videor, ominari solebas.   Certatim ergo tibi gratias agimus, 25
ego quod illam mihi, illa quod me sibi dederis, quasi invicem
elegeris.   Vale.

42. (BOOK 4. 22.)

A bold remark by Junius Mauricus in Trajan's council on the subject
of the games at Vienne, leads Pliny to relate a bolder speech of the same
Mauricus at Nerva's table.

C. PLINIUS SEMPRONIO RUFO SUO S.

Interfui principis optimi cognitioni in consilium adsumptus.
Gymnicus agon apud Viennenses ex cuiusdam testamento
celebrabatur: hunc Trebonius Rufinus, vir egregius nobisque
amicus, in duumviratu tollendum abolendumque curavit:
negabatur ex auctoritate publica fecisse.   Egit ipse causam 5
non minus feliciter quam diserte.   Commendabat actionem
quod tamquam homo Romanus et bonus civis in negotio suo
mature et graviter loquebatur.   Cum sententiae perrogarentur,
dixit Iunius Mauricus, quo viro nihil firmius, nihil verius, non

10 esse restituendum Viennensibus agona: adiecit 'vellem
etiam Romae tolli posset.' Constanter, inquis, et fortiter.
Quidni? Sed hoc a Maurico novum non est. Idem apud
imperatorem Nervam non minus fortiter. Cenabat Nerva
cum paucis: Veiento proximus atque etiam in sinu recum-
15 bebat: dixi omnia, cum hominem nominavi. Incidit sermo
de Catullo Messalino, qui luminibus orbatus ingenio saevo
mala caecitatis addiderat: non verebatur, non erubescebat,
non miserebatur; quo saepius a Domitiano non secus ac
tela, quae et ipsa caeca et inprovida feruntur, in optimum
20 quemque contorquebatur. De huius nequitia sanguinariisque
sententiis in commune omnes super cenam loquebantur, cum
ipse imperator 'quid putamus passurum fuisse, si viveret?'
et Mauricus 'nobiscum cenaret.' Longius abii, libens tamen.
Placuit agona tolli, qui mores Viennensium infecerat, ut
25 noster hic omnium. Nam Viennensium vitia intra ipsos
resident, nostra late vagantur, utque in corporibus sic in
imperio gravissimus est morbus qui a capite diffunditur.
Vale.

43. (BOOK 4. 25.)

Pliny's fears about the use of the ballot in the Senate have been
justified by the vulgar folly with which it has been abused.

C. PLINIUS MESSIO MAXIMO SUO S.

Scripseram tibi verendum esse ne ex tacitis suffragiis vitium
aliquod existeret. Factum est. Proximis comitiis in quibusdam tabellis multa iocularia atque etiam foeda dictu, in
una vero pro candidatorum nominibus suffragatorum nomina
5 inventa sunt. Excanduit senatus magnoque clamore ei qui
scripsisset iratum principem est comprecatus. Ille tamen
fefellit et latuit, fortasse etiam inter indignantes fuit. Quid
hunc putamus domi facere, qui in tanta re tam serio
tempore tam scurriliter ludat, qui denique omnino in senatu

dicax et urbanus et bellus est? Tantum licentiae pravis 10
ingeniis adicit illa fiducia, 'quis enim sciet?' Poposcit
tabellam, stilum accepit, demisit caput, neminem veretur,
se contemnit. Inde ista ludibria scaena et pulpito digna.
Quo te vertas? Quae remedia conquiras? Ubique vitia
remediis fortiora. Ἀλλὰ ταῦτα τῷ ὑπὲρ ἡμᾶς μελήσει, cui 15
multum cotidie vigiliarum, multum laboris adicit haec
nostra iners et tamen effrenata petulantia. Vale.

44. (BOOK 5. 1.)

Pliny explains why the legacy just left him by Curianus had given him
so much pleasure; namely, because it was a recompense to him for
having formerly acted with equity and generosity towards Curianus, when
the latter had been disinherited by his mother Pomponia in favour of
Pliny, Severus and others.

C. PLINIUS ANNIO SEVERO SUO S.

Legatum mihi obvenit modicum, sed amplissimo gratius.
Cur amplissimo gratius? Pomponia Galla exheredato filio
Asudio Curiano heredem reliquerat me, dederat coheredes
Sertorium Severum, praetorium virum, aliosque splendidos
equites Romanos. Curianus orabat ut sibi donarem por- 5
tionem meam seque praeiudicio iuvarem; eandem tacita
conventione salvam mihi pollicebatur. Respondebam non
convenire moribus meis aliud palam, aliud agere secreto,
praeterea non esse satis honestum donare et locupleti et
orbo, in summa non profuturum ei, si donassem, profutu- 10
rum, si cessissem, esse autem me paratum cedere, si
inique exheredatum mihi liqueret. Ad hoc ille 'rogo
cognoscas.' Cunctatus paulum 'faciam' inquam : 'neque
enim video cur ipse me minorem putem, quam tibi videor.
Sed iam nunc memento non defuturam mihi constantiam, 15
si ita fides duxerit, secundum matrem tuam pronuntiandi.'
'Ut voles' ait : 'voles enim quod aequissimum.' Adhibui

in consilium duos quos tunc civitas nostra spectatissimos
habuit, Corellium et Frontinum.   His circumdatus in
20 cubiculo meo sedi: dixit Curianus quae pro se putabat:
respondi paucis ego (neque enim aderat alius qui defunctae
pudorem tueretur): deinde secessi et ex consilii sententia
'videtur' inquam, 'Curiane, mater tua iustas habuisse
causas irascendi tibi.'   Post hoc ille cum ceteris subscripsit
25 centumvirale iudicium, non subscripsit mecum.   Adpetebat
iudicii dies.   Coheredes mei conponere et transigere cupie-
bant, non diffidentia causae, sed metu temporum.   Vere-
bantur quod videbant multis accidisse, ne ex centumvirali
iudicio capitis rei exirent.   Et erant quidam in illis quibus
30 obici et Gratillae amicitia et Rustici posset.   Rogant me
ut cum Curiano loquar.   Convenimus in aedem Concordiae.
Ibi ego 'si mater' inquam 'te ex parte quarta scripsisset
heredem, num queri posses?   Quid si heredem quidem
instituisset ex asse, sed legatis ita exhausisset, ut non
35 amplius apud te quam quarta remaneret?   Igitur sufficere
tibi debet, si exheredatus a matre quartam partem ab
heredibus eius accipias, quam tamen ego augebo.   Scis
te non subscripsisse mecum et iam biennium transisse
omniaque me usu cepisse.   Sed ut te coheredes mei
40 tractabiliorem experiantur, utque tibi nihil abstulerit reverentia mei, offero pro mea parte tantundem.'   Tuli fructum
non conscientiae modo verum etiam famae.   Ille ergo
Curianus legatum mihi reliquit et factum meum, nisi forte
blandior mihi, antiquum notabili honore signavit.   Haec
45 tibi scripsi, quia de omnibus quae me vel delectant vel
angunt non aliter tecum quam mecum loqui soleo; deinde
quod durum existimabam te amantissimum mei fraudare
voluptate quam ipse capiebam.   Neque enim sum tam
sapiens, ut nihil mea intersit, an iis quae honeste fecisse
50 me credo testificatio quaedam et quasi praemium accedat.
Vale.

45. (BOOK 5. 2.)

Just now Pliny can send Calpurnius nothing but thanks in return for his present.

C. PLINIUS CALPURNIO FLACCO SUO S.

Accepi pulcherrimos turdos, cum quibus parem calculum ponere nec urbis copiis ex Laurentino nec maris tam turbidis tempestatibus possum. Recipies ergo epistulas steriles et simpliciter ingratas ac ne illam quidem sollertiam Diomedis in permutando munere imitantes. Sed quae facilitas tua, 5 hoc magis dabis veniam, quod se non mereri fatentur. Vale.

46. (BOOK 5. 5.)

Pliny is sorry to lose his friend Fannius,—sorry that he died before he could alter his will, but still more sorry that he has left unfinished his history of Nero's victims, a circumstance which had been intimated to Fannius himself by a strange vision.

C. PLINIUS NONIO MAXIMO SUO S.

Nuntiatum mihi est C. Fannium decessisse, qui nuntius me gravi dolore confudit, primum quod amavi hominem elegantem disertum, deinde quod iudicio eius uti solebam. Erat enim acutus natura, usu exercitatus, veritate prompt- issimus. Angit me super ista casus ipsius: decessit veteri 5 testamento, omisit quos maxime diligebat, prosecutus est quibus offensior erat. Sed hoc utcumque tolerabile, gravius illud, pulcherrimum opus inperfectum reliquit. Quamvis enim agendis causis distringeretur, scribebat tamen exitus occisorum aut relegatorum a Nerone et iam tres libros 10 absolverat, subtiles et diligentes et latinos atque inter ser- monem historiamque medios, ac tanto magis reliquos perficere cupiebat, quanto frequentius hi lectitabantur. Mihi autem videtur acerba semper et inmatura mors eorum qui immortale aliquid parant. Nam qui volupta- 15

tibus dediti quasi in diem vivunt vivendi causas cotidie
finiunt; qui vero posteros cogitant et memoriam sui
operibus extendunt, his nulla mors non repentina est, ut
quae semper inchoatum aliquid abrumpat.   Gaius quidem
20 Fannius quod accidit multo ante praesensit.   Visus est
sibi per nocturnam quietem iacere in lectulo suo compositus in habitum studentis, habere ante se scrinium (ita
solebat): mox imaginatus est venisse Neronem, in toro
resedisse, prompsisse primum librum quem de sceleribus
25 eius ediderat eumque ad extremum revolvisse, idem in
secundo ac tertio fecisse, tunc abisse.   Expavit et sic in-
terpretatus est, tamquam idem sibi futurus esset scribendi
finis, qui fuisset illi legendi, et fuit idem.   Quod me
recordantem miseratio subit, quantum vigiliarum, quantum
30 laboris exhauserit frustra.   Occursant animo mea mortalitas, mea scripta.   Nec dubito te quoque eadem cogitatione
terreri pro istis quae inter manus habes.   Proinde dum
suppetit vita, enitamur ut mors quam paucissima quae
abolere possit inveniat.   Vale.

47.   (BOOK 5. 10.)

Pliny begs Suetonius no longer to delay the publication of his work,
for which he says he has made himself responsible by some verses he
has written.

C. PLINIUS SUETONIO TRANQUILLO SUO S.

Libera tandem hendecasyllaborum meorum fidem, qui
scripta tua communibus amicis spoponderunt. Appellantur
cotidie et flagitantur, ac iam periculum est ne cogantur ad
exhibendum formulam accipere.   Sum et ipse in edendo
5 haesitator, tu tamen meam quoque cunctationem tardita-
temque vicisti.   Proinde aut rumpe iam moras aut cave
ne eosdem istos libellos, quos tibi hendecasyllabi nostri blan-
ditiis elicere non possunt, convicio scazontes extorqueant.

Perfectum opus absolutumque est nec iam splendescit lima, sed atteritur. Patere me videre titulum tuum, patere audire 10 describi legi venire volumina Tranquilli mei. Aequum est nos in amore tam mutuo eandem percipere ex te voluptatem, qua tu perfrueris ex nobis. Vale.

48. (BOOK 5. 14.)

While Pliny was enjoying country retirement with his wife's family, the news has reached him of Cornutus' appointment as guardian of the Aemilian way, an event which gives him sincere satisfaction.

C. PLINIUS PONTIO SUO S.

Secesseram in municipium, cum mihi nuntiatum est Cornutum Tertullum accepisse Aemiliae viae curam. Exprimere non possum, quanto sim gaudio adfectus et ipsius et meo nomine; ipsius, quod, sit licet, sicut est, ab omni ambitione longe remotus, debet tamen ei iucundus honor 5 esse ultro datus; meo, quod aliquanto magis me delectat mandatum mihi officium, postquam par Cornuto datum video. Neque enim augeri dignitate quam aequari bonis gratius. Cornuto autem quid melius? quid sanctius? quid in omni genere laudis ad exemplar antiquitatis expressius? 10 Quod mihi cognitum est non fama, qua alioqui optima et meritissima fruitur, sed longis magnisque experimentis. Una diligimus, una dileximus omnes fere quos aetas nostra in utroque sexu aemulandos tulit; quae societas amicitiarum artissima nos familiaritate coniunxit. Accessit vinculum 15 necessitudinis publicae. Idem enim mihi, ut scis, collega quasi voto petitus in praefectura aerarii fuit, fuit et in consulatu. Tum ego qui vir et quantus esset altissime inspexi, cum sequerer ut magistrum, ut parentem vererer; quod non tam aetatis maturitate quam vitae merebatur. 20 His ex causis ut illi sic mihi gratulor, nec privatim magis quam publice, quod tandem homines non ad pericula, ut

prius, verum ad honores virtute perveniunt. In infinitum
epistulam extendam, si gaudio meo indulgeam. Praevertor
25 ad ea quae me agentem hic nuntius deprehendit. Eram
cum prosocero meo, eram cum amita uxoris, eram cum
amicis diu desideratis, circumibam agellos, audiebam
multum rusticarum querellarum, rationes legebam invitus
et cursim (aliis enim chartis, aliis sum litteris initiatus),
30 coeperam etiam itineri me praeparare. Nam includor
angustiis commeatus eoque ipso, quod delegatum Cornuto
audio officium, mei admoneor. Cupio te quoque sub
idem tempus Campania tua remittat, ne quis, cum in
urbem rediero, contubernio nostro dies pereat. Vale.

49. (BOOK 5. 16.)

Pliny expresses with real feeling his grief for the death on the eve of
marriage of Fundanus' charming daughter.

C. PLINIUS MARCELLINO SUO S.

Tristissimus haec tibi scribo Fundani nostri filia minore
defuncta. Qua puella nihil umquam festivius, amabilius
nec modo longiore vita, sed prope immortalitate dignius
vidi. Nondum annos quattuordecim impleverat, et iam illi
5 anilis prudentia, matronalis gravitas erat, et tamen suavitas
puellaris cum virginali verecundia. Ut illa patris cervicibus
inhaerebat! Ut nos amicos paternos et amanter et modeste
complectebatur! Ut nutrices, ut paedagogos, ut praeceptores
pro suo quemque officio diligebat! Quam studiose, quam
10 intellegenter lectitabat! Ut parce custoditeque ludebat! Qua
illa temperantia, qua patientia, qua etiam constantia novissimam valetudinem tulit! Medicis obsequebatur, sororem,
patrem adhortabatur ipsamque se destitutam corporis viribus
vigore animi sustinebat. Duravit hic illi usque ad extremum
15 nec aut spatio valetudinis aut metu mortis infractus est, quo
plures gravioresque nobis causas relinqueret et desiderii et

doloris. O triste plane acerbumque funus! O morte ipsa mortis tempus indignius! Iam destinata erat egregio iuveni, iam electus nuptiarum dies, iam nos vocati. Quod gaudium quo maerore mutatum est! Non possum ex- 20 primere verbis, quantum animo vulnus acceperim, cum audivi Fundanum ipsum, ut multa luctuosa dolor invenit, praecipientem, quod in vestes margarita gemmas fuerat erogaturus, hoc in tus et unguenta et odores inpenderetur. Est quidem ille eruditus et sapiens, ut qui se ab incunte 25 aetate altioribus studiis artibusque dediderit: sed nunc omnia quae audiit saepe, quae dixit aspernatur expulsisque virtutibus aliis pietatis est totus. Ignosces, laudabis etiam, si cogitaveris quid amiserit. Amisit enim filiam quae non minus mores eius quam os voltumque referebat totumque patrem 30 mira similitudine exscripserat. Proinde siquas ad eum de dolore tam iusto litteras mittes, memento adhibere solacium, non quasi castigatorium et nimis forte, sed molle et humanum. Quod ut facilius admittat multum faciet medii temporis spatium. Ut enim crudum adhuc vulnus medentium manus 35 reformidat, deinde patitur atque ultro requirit, sic recens animi dolor consolationes reicit ac refugit, mox desiderat et clementer admotis adquiescit. Vale.

50. (BOOK 5. 19.)

Pliny asks Paulinus to allow the use of his villa at Forum Julii to his freedman Zosimus, who is going there for his health.

C. PLINIUS PAULINO SUO S.

Video quam molliter tuos habeas, quo simplicius tibi confitebor qua indulgentia meos tractem. Est mihi semper in animo et Homericum illud πατὴρ δ' ὡς ἤπιος ἦεν et hoc nostrum 'pater familiae.' Quod si essem natura asperior et durior, frangeret me tamen infirmitas liberti mei Zosimi, cui 5 tanto maior humanitas exhibenda est, quanto nunc illa magis eget. Homo probus officiosus litteratus; et ars quidem eius

et quasi inscriptio comoedus, in qua plurimum facit. Nam
pronuntiat acriter, sapienter, apte, decenter etiam ; utitur et
10 cithara perite, ultra quam comoedo necesse est. Idem tam
commode orationes et historias et carmina legit, ut hoc
solum didicisse videatur. Haec tibi sedulo exposui, quo
magis scires quam multa unus mihi et quam iucunda ministeria praestaret. Accedit longa iam caritas hominis, quam
15 ipsa pericula auxerunt. Est enim ita natura comparatum, ut
nihil aeque amorem incitet et accendat quam carendi metus,
quem ego pro hoc non semel patior. Nam ante aliquot
annos, dum intente instanterque pronuntiat, sanguinem
reiecit atque ob hoc in Aegyptum missus a me post longam
20 peregrinationem confirmatus rediit nuper ; deinde dum per
continuos dies nimis imperat voci, veteris infirmitatis tus-
sicula admonitus rursus sanguinem reddidit. Qua ex causa
destinavi eum mittere in praedia tua, quae Foro Iuli
possides. Audivi enim te saepe referentem esse ibi et aëra
25 salubrem et lac eius modi curationibus accommodatissimum.
Rogo ergo scribas tuis ut illi villa, ut domus pateat, offerant
etiam sumptibus eius, siquid opus erit ; erit autem opus
modico. Est enim tam parcus et continens, ut non solum
delicias verum etiam necessitates valetudinis frugalitate res-
30 tringat. Ego proficiscenti tantum viatici dabo, quantum
sufficiat eunti in 'ua. Vale.

51. (BOOK 5. 21.)

Pliny is glad to hear that Saturninus is waiting for his arrival to give
a recitation, but is distressed by his report of the dangerous illness of one
friend, and the premature death of another.

C. PLINIUS SATURNINO SUO S.

Varie me adfecerunt litterae tuae. Nam partim laeta
partim tristia continebant : laeta, quod te in urbe teneri
nuntiabant ; 'nollem' inquis, sed ego volo : praeterea quod

recitaturum statim ut venissem pollicebantur; ago gratias, quod expector. Triste illud, quod Iulius Valens graviter iacet: 5 quamquam ne hoc quidem triste, si illius utilitatibus aestimetur, cuius interest quam maturissime inexplicabili morbo liberari. Illud plane non triste solum verum etiam luctuosum, quod Iulius Avitus decessit, dum ex quaestura redit, decessit in nave, procul a fratre amantissimo, procul a matre, 10 a sororibus. Nihil ista ad mortuum pertinent, sed pertinuerunt, cum moreretur, pertinent ad hos qui supersunt. Iam quod in flore primo tantae indolis iuvenis extinctus est summa consecuturus, si virtutes eius maturuissent! Quo ille studiorum amore flagrabat! Quantum legit, quantum etiam 15 scripsit! Quae nunc omnia cum ipso sine fructu posteritatis abierunt. Sed quid ego indulgeo dolori? Cui si frenos remittas, nulla materia non maxima est. Finem epistulae faciam: ut facere possim etiam lacrimis, quas epistula expressit! Vale.   20

52. (BOOK 6. 2.)

Even the loss of Regulus must be regretted as that of a painstaking advocate, and a steady opponent of the modern fashion of hurrying cases through the courts.

C. PLINIUS ARRIANO SUO S.

Soleo non numquam in iudiciis quaerere M. Regulum: nolo enim dicere desiderare. Cur ergo quaero? Habebat studiis honorem, timebat, pallebat, scribebat, quamvis non posset ediscere. Illud ipsum, quod oculum modo dextrum modo sinistrum circumlinebat, dextrum, si a petitore, alte- 5 rum, si a possessore esset acturus, quod candidum splenium in hoc aut in illud supercilium transferebat, quod semper haruspices consulebat de actionis eventu, a nimia superstitione, sed tamen et a magno studiorum honore veniebat. Iam illa perquam iucunda una dicentibus, quod libera tem- 10

pora petebat, quod audituros corrogabat. Quid enim iucundius, quam sub alterius invidia quam diu velis et in alieno
auditorio quasi deprehensum commode dicere? Sed utcumque se habent ista, bene fecit Regulus quod est mortuus;
15 melius, si ante. Nunc enim sane poterat sine malo publico
vivere sub eo principe, sub quo nocere non poterat. Ideo fas
est non numquam eum quaerere. Nam postquam obiit ille,
increbruit passim et invaluit consuetudo binas vel singulas
clepsydras, interdum etiam dimidias, et dandi et petendi.
20 Nam et qui dicunt egisse malunt quam agere et qui audiunt
finire quam iudicare. Tanta neglegentia, tanta desidia, tanta
denique inreverentia studiorum periculorumque est. An nos
sapientiores maioribus nostris, nos legibus ipsis iustiores,
quae tot horas, tot dies, tot comperendinationes largiuntur?
25 Hebetes illi et supra modum tardi, nos apertius dicimus,
celerius intellegimus, religiosius iudicamus, quia paucioribus
clepsydris praecipitamus causas, quam diebus explicari solebant? O Regule, qui ambitione ab omnibus obtinebas quod
fidei paucissimi praestant? Equidem quotiens iudico, quod
30 vel saepius facio, quam dico, quantum quis plurimum postulat
aquae do. Etenim temerarium existimo divinare, quam spatiosa sit causa inaudita, tempusque negotio finire, cuius
modum ignores, praesertim cum primam religioni suae iudex
patientiam debeat, quae pars magna iustitiae est. At quae-
35 dam supervacua dicuntur. Etiam: sed satius est et haec dici,
quam non dici necessaria. Praeterea an sint supervacua,
nisi cum audieris, scire non possis. Sed de his melius
coram, ut de pluribus vitiis civitatis. Nam tu quoque amore
communium soles emendari cupere quae iam corrigere
40 difficile est. Nunc respiciamus domos nostras. Ecquid
omnia in tua recte? In mea novi nihil. Mihi autem et
gratiora sunt bona, quod perseverant, et leviora incommoda,
quod adsuevi. Vale.

53. (BOOK 6. 3.)

Pliny is glad that the farm which he had given to his nurse is now in the hands of a good tenant.

C. PLINIUS VERO SUO S.

Gratias ago, quod agellum quem nutrici meae donaveram colendum suscepisti. Erat, cum donarem, centum milium nummum; postea decrescente reditu etiam pretium minuit, quod nunc te curante reparabit. Tu modo memineris com-mendari tibi a me non arbores et terram, quamquam haec 5 quoque, sed munusculum meum; quod esse quam fructuo-sissimum non illius magis interest, quae accepit, quam mea, qui dedi. Vale.

54. (BOOK 6. 4.)

Pliny expresses his affectionate anxiety for his wife, and begs her to relieve it by frequent letters.

C. PLINIUS CALPURNIAE SUAE S.

Numquam sum magis de occupationibus meis questus, quae me non sunt passae aut proficiscentem te valetudinis causa in Campaniam prosequi aut profectam e vestigio sub-sequi. Nunc enim praecipue simul esse cupiebam, ut oculis meis crederem, quid viribus, quid corpusculo adparares, 5 ecquid denique secessus voluptates regionisque abundantiam inoffensa transmitteres. Equidem etiam fortem te non sine cura desiderarem: est enim suspensum et anxium de eo quem ardentissime diligas interdum nihil scire: nunc vero me cum absentiae tum infirmitatis tuae ratio incerta et varia 10 sollicitudine exterret. Vereor omnia, imaginor omnia, quae-que natura metuentium est, ea maxime mihi quae maxime abominor fingo. Quo inpensius rogo ut timori meo cotidie singulis vel etiam binis epistulis consulas. Ero enim secu-rior, dum lego, statimque timebo, cum legero. Vale. 15

55. (BOOK 6. 6.)

Pliny begs Fundanus to come to Rome and help him in his support
of Julius Naso in his candidature for the quaestorship, a young man
whom Pliny values both for his own sake, and his father's.

C. PLINIUS FUNDANO SUO S.

Siquando, nunc praecipue cuperem esse te Romae, et sis
rogo. Opus est mihi voti laboris sollicitudinis socio. Petit
honores Iulius Naso, petit cum multis, cum bonis, quos ut
gloriosum sic est difficile superare. Pendeo ergo et exer-
5 ceor spe, adficior metu et me consularem esse non sentio :
nam rursus mihi videor omnium quae decucurri candidatus.
Meretur hanc curam longa mei caritate. Est mihi cum illo
non sane paterna amicitia (neque enim esse potuit per
meam aetatem) ; solebat tamen vixdum adulescentulo mihi
10 pater eius cum magna laude monstrari. Erat non studiorum
tantum verum etiam studiosorum amantissimus ac prope
cotidie ad audiendos, quos tunc ego frequentabam, Quintilianum, Niceten Sacerdotem ventitabat, vir alioqui clarus et
gravis et qui prodesse filio memoria sui debeat. Sed multi
15 nunc in senatu quibus ignotus ille, multi quibus notus, sed
non nisi viventes reverentur. Quo magis huic omissa gloria
patris, in qua magnum ornamentum, gratia infirma, ipsi
enitendum, ipsi elaborandum est. Quod quidem semper,
quasi provideret hoc tempus, sedulo fecit : paravit amicos,
20 quos paraverat coluit, me certe, ut primum sibi iudicare
permisit, ad amorem imitationemque delegit. Dicenti mihi
sollicitus adsistit, adsidet recitanti : primis etiam et cum
maxime nascentibus opusculis meis interest, nunc solus,
ante cum fratre, cuius nuper amissi ego suscipere partes,
25 ego vicem debeo inplere. Doleo enim et illum inmatura
morte indignissime raptum et hunc optimi fratris adiumento
destitutum solisque amicis relictum. Quibus ex causis exigo
ut venias et suffragio meo tuum iungas. Permultum interest

mea te ostentare, tecum circumire. Ea est auctoritas tua,
ut putem me efficacius tecum etiam meos amicos rogaturum. 30
Abrumpe, siqua te retinent: hoc tempus meum, hoc fides,
hoc etiam dignitas postulat. Suscepi candidatum, et sus-
cepisse me notum est: ego ambio, ego periclitor: in summa, si datur Nasoni quod petit, illius honor; si negatur, mea
repulsa est. Vale.   35

56. (BOOK 6. 7.)

Pliny is glad that his wife finds the same pleasure and comfort in his
letters, as he does in hers.

C. PLINIUS CALPURNIAE SUAE S.

Scribis te absentia mea non mediocriter adfici unumque
habere solacium, quod pro me libellos meos teneas, saepe
etiam in vestigio meo conloces. Gratum est quod nos
requiris, gratum quod his fomentis adquiescis: invicem ego
epistulas tuas lectito atque identidem in manus quasi novas 5
sumo; sed eo magis ad desiderium tui accendor. Nam
cuius litterae tantum habent suavitatis, huius sermonibus
quantum dulcedinis inest! Tu tamen quam frequentissime
scribe, licet hoc ita me delectet, ut torqueat. Vale.

57. (BOOK 6. 10.)

Pliny visiting the former residence of Verginius is distressed to find
that the monument of that illustrious man is still unfinished.

C. PLINIUS ALBINO SUO S.

Cum venissem in socrus meae villam Alsiensem, quae
aliquando Rufi Vergini fuit, ipse mihi locus optimi illius et
maximi viri desiderium non sine dolore renovavit. Hunc
enim incolere secessum atque etiam senectutis suae nidulum
vocare consueverat. Quocumque me contulissem, illum 5
animus, illum oculi requirebant. Libuit etiam monimentum

eius videre, et vidisse paenituit. Est enim adhuc inperfectum, nec difficultas operis in causa modici ac potius exigui,
sed inertia eius cui cura mandata est. Subit indignatio cum
10 miseratione, post decimum mortis annum reliquias neglec-
tumque cinerem sine titulo, sine nomine iacere, cuius memoria orbem terrarum gloria pervagetur. At ille mandaverat
caveratque ut divinum illud et inmortale factum versibus
inscriberetur,

15   Hic situs est Rufus, pulso qui Vindice quondam
        Imperium adseruit non sibi sed patriae.

Tam rara in amicitiis fides, tam parata oblivio mortuorum, ut
ipsi nobis debeamus etiam conditoria extruere omniaque
heredum officia praesumere. Nam cui non est verendum
20 quod videmus accidisse Verginio? Cuius iniuriam ut indigni-
orem sic etiam notiorem ipsius claritas facit. Vale.

58. (BOOK 6. 15.)

Pliny relates the unfortunate interruption of Paulus' recitation by an
audacious jest.

C. PLINIUS ROMANO SUO S.

Mirificae rei non interfuisti: ne ego quidem; sed me
recens fabula excepit. Passennus Paulus, splendidus eques
Romanus et in primis eruditus, scribit elegos. Gentilicium
hoc illi: est enim municeps Properti atque etiam inter
5 maiores suos Propertium numerat. Is cum recitaret, ita
coepit dicere, 'Prisce, iubes.' Ad hoc Iavolenus Priscus
(aderat enim, ut Paulo amicissimus) 'ego vero non iubeo.'
Cogita qui risus hominum, qui ioci. Est omnino Priscus
dubiae sanitatis, interest tamen officiis, adhibetur consiliis
10 atque etiam ius civile publice respondet: quo magis quod
tunc fecit et ridiculum et notabile fuit. Interim Paulo aliena
deliratio aliquantum frigoris attulit. Tam sollicite recitaturis
providendum est non solum ut sint ipsi sani, verum etiam
ut sanos adhibeant. Vale.

59. (BOOK 6. 16.)

Pliny, at the request of Tacitus, relates how his uncle being in command at Misenum crossed the bay of Naples to assist the sufferers from the eruption of Vesuvius, and expired during the eruption, apparently from the effect of the sulphurous vapours accompanying it.

C. PLINIUS TACITO SUO S.

Petis ut tibi avunculi mei exitum scribam, quo verius tradere posteris possis. Gratias ago : nam video morti eius, si celebretur a te, inmortalem gloriam esse propositam. Quamvis enim pulcherrimarum clade terrarum, ut populi, ut urbes, memorabili casu quasi semper victurus occiderit, 5 quamvis ipse plurima opera et mansura condiderit, multum tamen perpetuitati eius scriptorum tuorum aeternitas addet. Equidem beatos puto quibus deorum munere datum est aut facere scribenda aut scribere legenda, beatissimos vero quibus utrumque. Horum in numero avunculus meus et suis 10 libris et tuis erit. Quo libentius suscipio, deposco etiam quod iniungis. Erat Miseni classemque imperio praesens regebat. Nonum Kal. Septembres hora fere septima mater mea indicat ei apparere nubem inusitata et magnitudine et specie. Usus ille sole, mox frigida, gustaverat iacens stu- 15 debatque : poscit soleas, ascendit locum ex quo maxime miraculum illud conspici poterat. Nubes, incertum procul intuentibus ex quo monte (Vesuvium fuisse postea cognitum est), oriebatur, cuius similitudinem et formam non alia magis arbor quam pinus expresserit. Nam longissimo velut trunco 20 elata in altum quibusdam ramis diffundebatur, credo, quia recenti spiritu evecta, dein senescente eo destituta aut etiam pondere suo victa in latitudinem vanescebat : candida interdum, interdum sordida et maculosa, prout terram cineremve sustulerat. Magnum propiusque noscendum, ut eruditis- 25 simo viro, visum. Iubet liburnicam aptari : mihi, si venire

una vellem, facit copiam: respondi studere me malle, et
forte ipse quod scriberem dederat. Egrediebatur domo:
accipit codicillos Rectinae Tasci inminenti periculo exter-
30 ritae (nam villa eius subiacebat, nec ulla nisi navibus fuga):
ut se tanto discrimini eriperet orabat. Vertit ille consilium
et quod studioso animo inchoaverat obit maximo. Deducit
quadriremes, ascendit ipse non Rectinae modo sed multis
(erat enim frequens amoenitas orae) laturus auxilium. Pro-
35 perat illuc unde alii fugiunt rectumque cursum, recta gubernacula in periculum tenet, adeo solutus metu, ut omnes illius
mali motus, omnes figuras, ut deprenderat oculis, dictaret
enotaretque. Iam navibus cinis incidebat, quo propius
accederent, calidior et densior, iam pumices etiam nigrique
40 et ambusti et fracti igne lapides, iam vadum subitum ruinaque montis litora obstantia. Cunctatus paulum, an retro
flecteret, mox gubernatori ut ita faceret monenti ‘fortes’
inquit ‘fortuna iuvat, Pomponianum pete.’ Stabiis erat,
diremptus sinu medio (nam sensim circumactis curvatisque
45 litoribus mare infunditur): ibi, quamquam nondum periculo
adpropinquante, conspicuo tamen et cum cresceret proximo,
sarcinas contulerat in naves certus fugae, si contrarius ventus
resedisset. Quo tunc avunculus meus secundissimo invec-
tus complectitur trepidantem, consolatur, hortatur, utque
50 timorem eius sua securitate leniret, deferri in balineum
iubet: lotus accubat, cenat aut hilaris aut, quod aeque
magnum, similis hilari. Interim e Vesuvio monte pluribus
in locis latissimae flammae altaque incendia relucebant,
quorum fulgor et claritas tenebris noctis excitabatur. Ille
55 agrestium trepidatione ignes relictos desertasque villas per
solitudinem ardere in remedium formidinis dictitabat. Tum
se quieti dedit et quievit verissimo quidem somno. Nam
meatus animae, qui illi propter amplitudinem corporis
gravior et sonantior erat, ab iis qui limini obversabantur
60 audiebatur. Sed area ex qua diaeta adibatur ita iam cinere

mixtisque pumicibus oppleta surrexerat, ut, si longior in
cubiculo mora, exitus negaretur. Excitatus procedit seque
Pomponiano ceterisque qui pervigilaverant reddit. In commune consultant, intra tecta subsistant an in aperto vagentur.
Nam crebris vastisque tremoribus tecta nutabant et quasi 65
emota sedibus suis nunc huc, nunc illuc abire aut referri
videbantur. Sub dio rursus quamquam levium exesorumque
pumicum casus metuebatur; quod tamen periculorum colla-
tio elegit. Et apud illum quidem ratio rationem, apud alios
timorem timor vicit. Cervicalia capitibus inposita linteis 70
constringunt : id munimentum adversus incidentia fuit.
Iam dies alibi, illic nox omnibus noctibus nigrior densiorque, quam tamen faces multae variaque lumina solabantur.
Placuit egredi in litus et ex proximo aspicere, ecquid iam
mare admitteret, quod adhuc vastum et adversum permane- 75
bat. Ibi super abiectum linteum recubans semel atque
iterum frigidam poposcit hausitque. Deinde flammae flam-
marumque praenuntius odor sulpuris alios in fugam vertunt,
excitant illum. Innitens servulis duobus adsurrexit et statim
concidit, ut ego colligo, crassiore caligine spiritu obstructo 80
clausoque stomacho, qui illi natura invalidus et angustus et
frequenter aestuans erat. Ubi dies redditus (is ab eo quem
novissime viderat *erat* tertius), corpus inventum integrum,
inlaesum opertumque, ut fuerat indutus : habitus corporis
quiescenti quam defuncto similior. Interim Miseni ego et 85
mater—sed nihil ad historiam, nec tu aliud quam de exitu
eius scire voluisti. Finem ergo faciam. Unum adiciam,
omnia me quibus interfueram quaeque statim, cum maxime
vera memorantur, audieram persecutum. Tu potissima ex-
cerpes. Aliud est enim epistulam aliud historiam, aliud 90
amico, aliud omnibus scribere. Vale.

60. (BOOK 6. 19.)

The senate endeavouring to purify its elections to the magistracies, has been seconded by the Emperor, who has promulgated a law limiting the expenditure of candidates, and requires them to be qualified by the possession of property in Italy. This enactment has raised the value of landed property near the city.

C. PLINIUS NEPOTI SUO S.

Scis tu accessise pretium agris, praecipue suburbanis? Causa subitae caritatis res multis agitata sermonibus: proximis comitiis honestissimas voces senatus expressit, 'candidati ne conviventur, ne mittant munera, ne pecunias 5 deponant.' Ex quibus duo priora tam aperte quam immodice fiebant, hoc tertium, quamquam occultaretur, pro comperto habebatur. Homullus deinde noster, vigilanter usus hoc consensu senatus, sententiae loco postulavit ut consules desiderium universorum notum principi facerent 10 peterentque, sicut aliis vitiis huic quoque providentia sua occurreret. Occurrit: nam sumptus candidatorum, foedos illos et infames, ambitus lege restrinxit: eosdem patrimonii tertiam partem conferre iussit in ea quae solo continerentur, deforme arbitratus, et erat, honorem petituros urbem 15 Italiamque non pro patria, sed pro hospitio aut stabulo quasi peregrinantes habere. Concursant ergo candidati: certatim quidquid venale audiunt emptitant quoque sint plura venalia efficiunt. Proinde si paenitet te Italicorum praediorum, hoc vendendi tempus tam hercule quam in 20 provinciis comparandi, dum iidem candidati illic vendunt, ut hic emant. Vale.

61. (BOOK 6. 20.)

Pliny gives Tacitus a narrative of his own observations and adventures during the eruption, after his uncle left him at Misenum.

C. PLINIUS TACITO SUO S.

Ais te adductum litteris quas exigenti tibi de morte

avunculi mei scripsi cupere cognoscere, quos ego Miseni
relictus (id enim ingressus abruperam) non solum metus
verum etiam casus pertulerim. 'Quamquam animus meminisse horret, incipiam.' Profecto avunculo ipse reliquum 5
tempus studiis (ideo enim remanseram) inpendi : mox
balineum, cena, somnus inquietus et brevis. Praecesserat
per multos dies tremor terrae minus formidolosus, quia
Campaniae solitus. Illa vero nocte ita invaluit, ut non
moveri omnia sed verti crederentur. Inrumpit cubiculum 10
meum mater : surgebam invicem, si quiesceret, excitaturus.
Residimus in area domus, quae mare a tectis modico
spatio dividebat. Dubito constantiam vocare an inpru-
dentiam debeam (agebam enim duodevicensimum annum) :
posco librum Titi Livi et quasi per otium lego atque 15
etiam, ut coeperam, excerpo. Ecce amicus avunculi, qui
nuper ad eum ex Hispania venerat, ut me et matrem
sedentes, me vero etiam legentem videt, illius patientiam,
securitatem meam corripit. Nihilo segnius ego intentus
in librum. Iam hora diei prima, et adhuc dubius et quasi 20
languidus dies : iam quassatis circumiacentibus tectis, quamquam in aperto loco, angusto tamen, magnus et certus
ruinae metus. Tum demum excedere oppido visum : sequitur vulgus attonitum, quodque in pavore simile pru-
dentiae, alienum consilium suo praefert ingentique agmine 25
abeuntes premit et inpellit. Egressi tecta consistimus.
Multa ibi miranda, multas formidines patimur. Nam vehi-
cula quae produci iusseramus, quamquam in planissimo
campo, in contrarias partes agebantur ac ne lapidibus quidem fulta in eodem vestigio quiescebant. Praeterea mare 30
in se resorberi et tremore terrae quasi repelli videbamus.
Certe processerat litus multaque animalia maris siccis ha-
renis detinebat. Ab altero latere nubes atra et horrenda
ignei spiritus tortis vibratisque discursibus rupta in longas
flammarum figuras dehiscebat : fulguribus illae et similes 35

et maiores erant. Tum vero idem ille ex Hispania amicus acrius et instantius 'si frater' inquit 'tuus, tuus avunculus vivit, vult esse vos salvos; si periit, superstites voluit. Proinde quid cessatis evadere?' Respondimus non
40 commissuros nos ut de salute illius incerti nostrae consuleremus. Non moratus ultra proripit se effusoque cursu
periculo aufertur. Nec multo post illa nubes descendere
in terras, operire maria: cinxerat Capreas et absconderat,
Miseni quod procurrit abstulerat. Tum mater orare, hor-
45 tari, iubere quoquo modo fugerem; posse enim iuvenem,
se et annis et corpore gravem bene morituram, si mihi
causa mortis non fuisset. Ego contra, salvum me nisi
una non futurum: dein manum eius amplexus addere
gradum cogo. Paret aegre incusatque se, quod me more-
50 tur. Iam cinis, adhuc tamen rarus: respicio; densa caligo
tergis imminebat, quae nos torrentis modo infusa terrae
sequebatur. 'Deflectamus' inquam, 'dum videmus ne in
via strati comitantium turba in tenebris obteramur.' Vix
consideramus, et nox, non qualis inlunis aut nubila, sed
55 qualis in locis clausis lumine extincto. Audires ululatus
feminarum, infantum quiritatus, clamores virorum: alii parentes, alii liberos, alii coniuges vocibus requirebant, vocibus noscitabant: hi suum casum, illi suorum miseraban-
tur: erant qui metu mortis mortem precarentur: multi ad
60 deos manus tollere, plures nusquam iam deos ullos aeter-
namque illam et novissimam noctem mundo interpreta-
bantur. Nec defuerunt qui fictis mentitisque terroribus
vera pericula augerent. Aderant qui Miseni illud ruisse,
illud ardere falso, sed credentibus nuntiabant. Paulum re-
65 luxit, quod non dies nobis, sed adventantis ignis indicium
videbatur. Et ignis quidem longius substitit, tenebrae
rursus, cinis rursus multus et gravis. Hunc identidem ad-
surgentes excutiebamus; operti alioqui atque etiam oblisi
pondere essemus. Possem gloriari non gemitum mihi, non

vocem parum fortem in tantis periculis excidisse, nisi me 70
cum omnibus, omnia mecum perire misero, magno tamen
mortalitatis solacio credidissem.　Tandem illa caligo tenu-
ata quasi in fumum nebulamve discessit: mox dies verus,
sol etiam effulsit, luridus tamen, qualis esse, cum deficit,
solet.　Occursabant trepidantibus adhuc oculis mutata omnia 75
altoque cinere tamquam nive obducta.　Regressi Misenum
curatis utcumque corporibus suspensam dubiamque noctem
spe ac metu exegimus.　Metus praevalebat: nam et tremor terrae perseverabat, et plerique lymphati terrificis vati-
cinationibus et sua et aliena mala ludificabantur.　Nobis 80
tamen ne tunc quidem, quamquam et expertis periculum
et expectantibus, abeundi consilium, donec de avunculo
nuntius.　Haec nequaquam historia digna non scripturus
leges et tibi, scilicet qui requisisti, imputabis, si digna ne
epistula quidem videbuntur.　Vale.　　　　　　　　　　85

62.　(BOOK 6. 33.)

Pliny sends Romanus his masterpiece of oratory, his speech on behalf of Attia Viriola, unjustly disinherited by the influence of her
stepmother.

C. PLINIUS ROMANO SUO S.

'Tollite cuncta' inquit 'coeptosque auferte labores.'
Seu scribis aliquid seu legis, tolli auferri iube et accipe
orationem meam, ut illa arma, divinam (num superbius
potui?), re vera ut inter meas pulchram: nam mihi satis
est certare mecum.　Est haec pro Attia Viriola, et dig- 5
nitate personae et exempli raritate et iudicii magnitudine
insignis.　Nam femina splendide nata, nupta praetorio viro,
exheredata ab octogenario patre intra undecim dies, quam
illi novercam amore captus induxerat, quadruplici iudicio
bona paterna repetebat.　Sedebant centum et octoginta 10
iudices (tot enim quattuor consiliis colliguntur): ingens

utrimque advocatio et numerosa subsellia, praeterea densa
circumstantium corona latissimum iudicium multiplici cir-
culo ambibat. Ad hoc stipatum tribunal, atque etiam ex
15 superiore basilicae parte qua feminae qua viri et audiendi,
quod difficile, et, quod facile, visendi studio imminebant.
Magna expectatio patrum, magna filiarum, magna etiam
novercarum. Secutus est varius eventus. Nam duobus
consiliis vicimus, totidem victi sumus. Notabilis prorsus
20 et mira eadem in causa, isdem iudicibus, isdem advocatis,
eodem tempore tanta diversitas accidit casu, non quod
casus videretur. Victa est noverca, ipsa heres ex parte
sexta, victus Suberinus, qui exheredatus a patre singulari
inpudentia alieni patris bona vindicabat, non ausus sui
25 petere. Haec tibi exposui, primum ut ex epistula scires
quae ex oratione non poteras; deinde (nam detegam
artes) ut orationem libentius legeres, si non legere tibi,
sed interesse iudicio videreris: quam, sit licet magna, non
despero gratiam brevissimae impetraturam. Nam et copia
30 rerum et arguta divisione et narratiunculis pluribus et
eloquendi varietate renovatur. Sunt multa (non auderem
nisi tibi dicere) elata, multa pugnacia, multa subtilia.
Intervenit enim acribus illis et erectis frequens necessitas
conputandi ac paene calculos tabulamque poscendi, ut
35 repente in privati iudicii formam centumvirale vertatur.
Dedimus vela indignationi, dedimus irae, dedimus dolori
et in amplissima causa, quasi magno mari, pluribus ventis
sumus vecti. In summa solent quidam ex contubernalibus
nostris existimare hanc orationem, iterum dicam, ut inter
40 meas ὑπὲρ Κτησιφῶντος esse: an vere, tu facillime iudicabis,
qui tam memoriter tenes omnes, ut conferre cum hac,
dum hanc solam legis, possis. Vale.

63. (BOOK 6. 34.)

Pliny approves of Maximus' conduct in acceding to the request of Verona that he would celebrate his wife's memory by a gladiatorial exhibition.

C. PLINIUS MAXIMO SUO S.

Recte fecisti quod gladiatorum munus Veronensibus nostris promisisti, a quibus olim amaris, suspiceris, ornaris. Inde etiam uxorem carissimam tibi et probatissimam habuisti, cuius memoriae aut opus aliquod aut spectaculum atque 5 hoc potissimum quod maxime funeri debebatur. Praeterea tanto consensu rogabaris, ut negare non constans, sed durum videretur. Illud quoque egregie, quod tam facilis, tam liberalis in edendo fuisti. Nam per haec etiam magnus animus ostenditur. Vellem Africanae, quas coemeras 10 plurimas, ad praefinitum diem occurrissent : sed licet cessaverint illae tempestate detentae, tu tamen meruisti ut acceptum tibi fieret, quod quo minus exhiberes non per te stetit. Vale.

64. (BOOK 7. 11.)

Pliny explains to Fabatus the obligations of friendship which induce him to sell to Corellia, at an inadequate price, the share which has lately been left to him in a property near the Lago di Como.

C. PLINIUS FABATO PROSOCERO SUO S.

Miraris quod Hermes, libertus meus, hereditarios agros, quos ego iusseram proscribi, non expectata auctione pro meo quincunce ex septingentis milibus Corelliae addixerit. Adicis hos nongentis milibus posse venire ac tanto magis quaeris, an quod gessit ratum servem. Ego vero servo : 5 quibus ex causis, accipe. Cupio enim et tibi probatum et coheredibus meis excusatum esse, quod me ab illis maiore officio iubente secerno. Corelliam cum summa reverentia

diligo, primum ut sororem Corelli Rufi, cuius mihi memoria
10 sacrosancta est, deinde ut matri meae familiarissimam.
Sunt mihi et cum marito eius, Minicio Iusto, optimo viro,
vetera iura; fuerunt et cum filio maxima, adeo quidem, ut
praetore me ludis meis praesederit. Haec, cum proxime
istic fui, indicavit mihi cupere se aliquid circa Larium nostrum
15 possidere. Ego illi ex praediis meis quod vellet et quanti
vellet obtuli exceptis maternis paternisque: his enim cedere
ne Corelliae quidem possum. Igitur cum obvenisset mihi
hereditas, in qua praedia ista, scripsi ei venalia futura. Has
epistulas Hermes tulit exigentique ut statim portionem meam
20 sibi addiceret paruit. Vides, quam ratum debeam habere
quod libertus meus meis moribus gessit. Superest ut coheredes aequo animo ferant separatim me vendidisse quod mihi
licuit omnino non vendere. Nec vero coguntur imitari meum
exemplum: non enim illis eadem cum Corellia iura. Possunt
25 ergo intueri utilitatem suam, pro qua mihi fuit amicitia. Vale.

65. (BOOK 7. 14.)

Corellia has found out the advantage she has been allowed in her
purchase, and wishes to pay the full price, which however Pliny gently
but firmly refuses.

C. PLINIUS CORELLIAE SUAE S.

Tu quidem honestissime, quod tam inpense et rogas et
exigis ut accipi iubeam a te pretium agrorum non ex septingentis milibus, quanti illos a liberto meo, sed ex nongentis,
quanti a publicanis partem vicesimam emisti. Invicem ego
5 et rogo et exigo ut non solum quid te, verum etiam quid me
deceat aspicias patiarisque me in hoc uno tibi eodem animo
repugnare, quo in omnibus obsequi soleo. Vale.

66.   (BOOK 7. 18.)

Caninius, anxious about an endowment he is establishing at Comum, is advised by Pliny to adopt his method, namely, to establish a permanent rent charge on a portion of his property, which shall be payable to the authorities of the borough.

C. PLINIUS CANINIO SUO S.

Deliberas mecum, quem ad modum pecunia, quam municipibus nostris in epulum obtulisti, post te quoque salva sit. Honesta consultatio, non expedita sententia. Numeres rei publicae summam? verendum est ne dilabatur. Des agros? ut publici neglegentur. Equidem nihil commodius invenio, 5 quam quod ipse feci. Nam pro quingentis milibus nummum, quae in alimenta ingenuorum ingenuarumque promiseram, agrum ex meis longe pluris actori publico mancipavi: eundem vectigali inposito recepi, tricena milia annua daturus. Per hoc enim et rei publicae sors in tuto nec reditus incertus, et 10 ager ipse propter id, quod vectigal large supercurrit, semper dominum, a quo exerceatur, inveniet. Nec ignoro me plus aliquanto quam donasse videor erogavisse, cum pulcherrimi agri pretium necessitas vectigalis infregerit. Sed oportet privatis utilitatibus publicas, mortalibus aeternas anteferre, 15 multoque diligentius muneri suo consulere quam facultatibus. Vale.

67.   (BOOK 7. 19.)

The illness of Fannia gives occasion for a sketch of her virtues, and a eulogy of her family.

C. PLINIUS PRISCO SUO S.

Angit me Fanniae valetudo. Contraxit hanc, dum adsidet Iuniae virgini, sponte primum (est enim adfinis), deinde etiam ex auctoritate pontificum. Nam virgines, cum vi morbi atrio Vestae coguntur excedere, matronarum curae

5 custodiaeque mandantur. Quo munere Fannia dum sedulo
fungitur, hoc discrimine inplicita est. Insident febres, tussis
increscit, summa macies, summa defectio: animus tantum et
spiritus viget Helvidio marito, Thrasea patre dignissimus;
reliqua labuntur meque non metu tantum verum etiam dolore
10 conficiunt. Doleo enim feminam maximam eripi oculis
civitatis nescio an aliquid simile visuris. Quae castitas illi!
quae sanctitas! quanta gravitas! quanta constantia! bis
maritum secuta in exilium est, tertio ipsa propter maritum
relegata. Nam cum Senecio reus esset, quod de vita
15 Helvidi libros composuisset, rogatumque se a Fannia in
defensione dixisset, quaerente minaciter Mettio Caro, an
rogasset, respondit 'rogavi,' an commentarios scripturo
dedisset, 'dedi,' an sciente matre, 'nesciente'; postremo
nullam vocem cedentem periculo emisit. Quin etiam illos
20 ipsos libros, quamquam ex necessitate et metu temporum
abolitos senatus consulto, publicatis bonis servavit, habuit
tulitque in exilium exilii causam. Eadem quam iucunda,
quam comis, quam denique, quod paucis datum est, non
minus amabilis quam veneranda! Eritne quam postea uxo-
25 ribus nostris ostentare possimus? Erit a qua viri quoque
fortitudinis exempla sumamus, quam sic cernentes audien-
tesque miremur, ut illas quae leguntur? Ac mihi domus
ipsa nutare convulsaque sedibus suis ruitura supra videtur,
licet adhuc posteros habeat. Quantis enim virtutibus
30 quantisque factis adsequentur ut haec non novissima
occiderit? Me quidem illud etiam adfligit et torquet, quod
matrem eius, illam (nihil possum inlustrius dicere) tantae
feminae matrem, rursus videor amittere, quam haec, ut
reddit ac refert nobis, sic auferet secum meque et novo
35 pariter et rescisso vulnere adficiet. Utramque dilexi; utram
magis, nescio, nec discerni volebant. Habuerunt officia mea
in secundis, habuerunt in adversis. Ego solacium relega-
tarum, ergo ultor reversarum; non feci tamen paria atque

co magis hanc cupio servari, ut mihi solvendi tempora
supersint.   In his eram curis, cum scriberem ad te; quas 40
si deus aliquis in gaudium verterit, de metu non querar.
Vale.

68.   (BOOK 7. 27.)

Pliny, under cover of inquiring Sura's opinion about ghosts, relates
appearances seen by Curtius Rufus, Athenodorus, and one of Pliny's
own slaves.

C. PLINIUS SURAE SUO S.

Et mihi discendi et tibi docendi facultatem otium praebet.
Igitur perquam velim scire, esse phantasmata et habere
propriam figuram numenque aliquod putes, an inania et
vana ex metu nostro imaginem accipere.   Ego ut esse
credam in primis eo ducor, quod audio accidisse Curtio 5
Rufo.   Tenuis adhuc et obscurus obtinenti Africam comes
haeserat: inclinato die spatiabatur in porticu: offertur ei
mulieris figura humana grandior pulchriorque: perterrito
Africam se, futurorum praenuntiam, dixit; iturum enim
Romam honoresque gesturum atque etiam cum summo 10
imperio in eandem provinciam reversurum ibique mori-
turum.   Facta sunt omnia.   Praeterea accedenti Carthaginem
egredientique nave eadem figura in litore occurrisse narratur.
Ipse certe inplicitus morbo, futura praeteritis, adversa
secundis auguratus, spem salutis nullo suorum desperante 15
proiecit.   Iam illud nonne et magis terribile et non minus
mirum est, quod exponam ut accepi?   Erat Athenis spatiosa
et capax domus, sed infamis et pestilens.   Per silentium
noctis sonus ferri et, si attenderes acrius, strepitus vinculorum
longius primo, deinde e proximo reddebatur: mox apparebat 20
idolon, senex macie et squalore confectus, promissa barba,
horrenti capillo: cruribus compedes, manibus catenas ge-
rebat quatiebatque.   Inde inhabitantibus tristes diraeque

noctes per metum vigilabantur: vigiliam morbus et crescente
25 formidine mors sequebatur. Nam interdiu quoque, quamquam abscesserat imago, memoria imaginis oculis inerrabat,
longiorque causis timoris timor erat. Deserta inde et dam-
nata solitudine domus totaque illi monstro relicta; proscribebatur tamen, seu quis emere, seu quis conducere ignarus
30 tanti mali vellet. Venit Athenas philosophus Athenodorus,
legit titulum auditoque pretio, quia suspecta vilitas, percunc-
tatus omnia docetur ac nihilo minus, immo tanto magis
conducit. Ubi coepit advesperascere, iubet sterni sibi in
prima domus parte, poscit pugillares stilum lumen; suos
35 omnes in interiora dimittit, ipse ad scribendum animum
oculos manum intendit, ne vacua mens audita simulacra et
inanes sibi metus fingeret. Initio, quale ubique, silentium
noctis, dein concuti ferrum, vincula moveri: ille non tollere
oculos, non remittere stilum, sed offirmare animum auribus-
40 que praetendere: tum crebrescere fragor, adventare et iam
ut in limine, iam ut intra limen audiri: respicit, videt ag-
noscitque narratam sibi effigiem. Stabat innuebatque digito
similis vocanti: hic contra ut paulum expectaret manu
significat rursusque ceris et stilo incumbit: illa scribentis
45 capiti catenis insonabat: respicit rursus idem quod prius
innuentem nec moratus tollit lumen et sequitur. Ibat illa
lento gradu, quasi gravis vinculis: postquam deflexit in
aream domus, repente dilapsa deserit comitem: desertus
herbas et folia concerpta signum loco ponit. Postero die
50 adit magistratus, monet ut illum locum effodi iubeant. Inveniuntur ossa inserta catenis et inplicita, quae corpus aevo
terraque putrefactum nuda et exesa reliquerat vinculis:
collecta publice sepeliuntur. Domus postea rite conditis
manibus caruit. Et haec quidem adfirmantibus credo;
55 illud adfirmare aliis possum. Est libertus mihi non inlitter-
atus: cum hoc minor frater eodem lecto quiescebat: is visus
est sibi cernere quendam in toro residentem admoventemque

capiti suo cultros atque etiam ex ipso vertice amputantem capillos. Ubi inluxit, ipse circa verticem tonsus, capilli iacentes reperiuntur. Exiguum temporis medium, et rursus 60 simile aliud priori· fidem fecit. Puer in paedagogio mixtus pluribus dormiebat: venerunt per fenestras (ita narrat) in tunicis albis duo cubantemque detonderunt et qua venerant recesserunt. Hunc quoque tonsum sparsosque circa capillos dies ostendit. Nihil notabile secutum, nisi forte quod 65 non fui reus, futurus, si Domitianus, sub quo haec acciderunt, diutius vixisset. Nam in scrinio eius datus a Caro de me libellus inventus est; ex quo coniectari potest, quia reis moris est summittere capillum, recisos meorum capillos depulsi quod imminebat periculi signum fuisse. Proinde 70 rogo eruditionem tuam intendas. Digna res est quam diu multumque consideres, ne ego quidem indignus cui copiam scientiae tuae facias. Licet etiam utramque in partem, ut soles, disputes, ex altera tamen fortius, ne me suspensum incertumque dimittas, cum mihi consulendi causa fuerit ut 75 dubitare desinerem. Vale.

69. (BOOK 7. 33.)

Pliny begs Tacitus to insert in his Histories some mention of the fearless zeal with which he, together with Senecio, followed up their joint attack on Baebius Massa.

C. PLINIUS TACITO SUO S.

Auguror, nec me fallit augurium, historias tuas immortales futuras; quo magis illis, ingenue fatebor, inseri cupio. Nam si esse nobis curae solet ut facies nostra ab optimo quoque artifice exprimatur, nonne debemus optare ut operibus nostris similis tui scriptor praedicatorque contingat? De- 5 monstro ergo, quamquam diligentiam tuam fugere non possit, cum sit in publicis actis, demonstro tamen, quo magis credas iucundum mihi futurum, si factum meum,

cuius gratia periculo crevit, tuo ingenio, tuo testimonio
10 ornaveris. Dederat me senatus cum Herennio Senecione advocatum provinciae Baeticae contra Baebium
Massam damnatoque Massa censuerat ut bona eius publice
custodirentur. Senecio, cum explorasset consules postu-
lationibus vacaturos, convenit me et 'qua concordia' inquit
15 'iniunctam nobis accusationem exsecuti sumus, hac adeamus
consules petamusque ne bona dissipari sinant quorum esse
in custodia debent.' Respondi 'cum simus advocati a
senatu dati, dispice num peractas putes partes nostras
senatus cognitione finita.' Et ille 'tu quem voles tibi
20 terminum statues, cui nulla cum provincia necessitudo nisi
ex beneficio tuo, et hoc recenti; ipse et natus ibi et quaestor
in ea fui.' Tum ego 'si fixum tibi istud ac deliberatum,
sequar te, ut, siqua ex hoc invidia, non tantum tua.' Ve-
nimus ad consules, dicit Senecio quae res ferebat, aliqua
25 subiungo. Vixdum conticueramus, et Massa questus Sene-
cionem non advocati fidem, sed inimici amaritudinem
inplesse, impietatis reum postulat. Horror omnium : ego
autem 'vereor' inquam, 'clarissimi consules, ne mihi Massa
silentio suo praevaricationem obiecerit, quod non et me reum
30 postulavit.' Quae vox et statim excepta et postea multo
sermone celebrata est. Divus quidem Nerva (nam privatus
quoque attendebat his quae recte in publico fierent) missis
ad me gravissimis litteris non mihi solum verum etiam
saeculo est gratulatus, cui exemplum (sic enim scripsit)
35 simile antiquis contigisset. Haec, utcumque se habent,
notiora clariora maiora tu facies : quamquam non exigo ut
excedas actae rei modum. Nam nec historia debet egredi
veritatem, et honeste factis veritas sufficit. Vale.

70.   (BOOK 8. 2.)

Pliny has felt obliged, by the failure of the crop, to throw back to the
purchasers of his vintages part of the price agreed on ; and points out
that he has made his remissions on a scale proportionate to the size of the
various bargains, and at the same time has encouraged prompt payers.

C. PLINIUS CALVISIO SUO S.

Alii in praedia sua proficiscuntur, ut locupletiores rever-
tantur, ego, ut pauperior.   Vendideram vindemias certatim
negotiatoribus ementibus.   Invitabat pretium, et quod tunc
et quod fore videbatur.   Spes fefellit.   Erat expeditum
omnibus remittere aequaliter, sed non satis aequum.   Mihi 5
autem egregium in primis videtur ut foris ita domi, ut in
magnis ita in parvis, ut in alienis ita in suis agitare iustitiam.
Nam si paria peccata, pares etiam laudes.   Itaque omnibus
quidem, ne quis mihi non donatus abiret, partem octavam
pretii quo quis emerat concessi ; deinde iis qui amplissimas 10
summas emptionibus occupaverant separatim consului.   Nam
et me magis iuverant et maius ipsi fecerant damnum.   Igitur
iis qui pluris quam decem milibus emerant ad illam communem et quasi publicam octavam addidi decumam eius sum-
mae, qua decem milia excesserant.   Vereor ne parum 15
expresserim ;   apertius calculos ostendam.   Siqui forte
quindecim milibus emerant, hi et quindecim milium octavam
et quinque milium decimam tulerunt.   Praeterea, cum ·
reputarem quosdam ex debito aliquantum, quosdam aliquid,
quosdam nihil reposuisse, nequaquam verum arbitrabar, 20
quos non aequasset fides solutionis, hos benignitate remissionis aequari.   Rursus ergo iis qui solverant eius quod
solverant decimam remisi.   Per hoc enim aptissime et in
praeteritum singulis pro cuiusque merito gratia referri, et in
futurum omnes cum ad emendum tum etiam ad solvendum 25
allici videbantur.   Magno mihi seu ratio haec seu facilitas
stetit, sed fuit tanti.   Nam regione tota et novitas remissionis

et forma laudatur. Ex ipsis etiam, quos non una, ut dicitur,
pertica, sed distincte gradatimque tractavi, quanto quis melior
30 et probior, tanto mihi obligatior abiit, expertus non esse apud
me ἐν δὲ ἰῇ τιμῇ ἠμὲν κακὸν ἠδέ καὶ ἐσθλόν. Vale.

71. (BOOK 8. 4.)

Pliny congratulates Caninius on having chosen Trajan's Dacian
campaigns for the subject of an epic ; hints at the difficulty of adapt-
ing the barbaric names to verse ; and begs that the author will let
him see something of his work while it is still in the rough.

C. PLINIUS CANINIO SUO S.

Optime facis quod bellum Dacicum scribere paras. Nam
quae tam recens, tam copiosa, tam lata, quae denique tam
poetica et quamquam in verissimis rebus tam fabulosa
materia ? Dices inmissa terris nova flumina, novos pontes
5 fluminibus iniectos, insessa castris montium abrupta, pulsum regia, pulsum etiam vita regem nihil desperantem;
super haec actos bis triumphos, quorum alter ex invicta
gente primus, alter novissimus fuit. Una, sed maxima
difficultas, quod haec aequare dicendo arduum inmensum,
10 etiam tuo ingenio, quamquam altissime adsurgat et am-
plissimis operibus increscat. Non nullus et in illo labor,
ut barbara et fera nomina, in primis regis ipsius, graecis
versibus non resultent. Sed nihil est quod non arte curaque, si non potest vinci, mitigetur. Praeterea, si datur
15 Homero et mollia vocabula et graeca ad levitatem versus
contrahere, extendere, inflectere, cur tibi similis audentia,
praesertim non delicata sed necessaria, non detur ? Proinde
iure vatum invocatis dis et inter deos ipso, cuius res
opera consilia dicturus es, immitte rudentes, pande vela,
20 ac siquando alias, toto ingenio vehere. Cur enim non
ego quoque poetice cum poeta ? Illud iam nunc paciscor: prima quaeque ut absolveris, mittito, immo etiam
ante quam absolvas, sicut erunt recentia et rudia et adhuc

similia nascentibus. Respondebis non posse perinde carp-
tim ut contexta, perinde inchoata placere ut effecta. Scio: 25
itaque et a me aestimabuntur ut coepta, spectabuntur ut
membra extremamque limam tuam opperientur in scrinio
nostro. Patere hoc me super cetera habere amoris tui
pignus, ut ea quoque norim, quae nosse neminem velles.
In summa potero fortasse scripta tua magis probare lau- 30
dare, quanto illa tardius cautiusque, sed ipsum te magis
amabo magisque laudabo, quanto celerius et incautius
miseris. Vale.

72. (BOOK 8. 8.)

Pliny describes the source of the Clitumnus, its sudden expansion
into a river, and the various attractions of the spot.

C. PLINIUS ROMANO SUO S.

Vidistine aliquando Clitumni fontem? Si nondum (et
puto nondum; alioqui narrasses mihi), vide, quem ego
(paenitet tarditatis) proxime vidi. Modicus collis adsurgit
antiqua cupresso nemorosus et opacus: hunc subter exit
fons et exprimitur pluribus venis, sed inparibus, eluctatus- 5
que quem facit gurgitem lato gremio patescit purus et
vitreus, ut numerare iactas stipes et relucentes calculos
possis. Inde non loci devexitate, sed ipsa sui copia et
quasi pondere inpellitur. Fons adhuc et iam amplissimum flumen atque etiam navium patiens, quas obvias 10
quoque et contrario nisu in diversa tendentes transmittit
et perfert, adeo validus, ut illa qua properat ipse, quamquam per solum planum, remis non adiuvetur, idem aeger-
rime remis contisque superetur adversus. Iucundum utrumque per iocum ludumque fluitantibus, ut flexerint cursum, 15
laborem otio, otium labore variare. Ripae fraxino multa,
multa populo vestiuntur, quas perspicuus amnis velut
mersas viridi imagine adnumerat. Rigor aquae certaverit
nivibus, nec color cedit. Adiacet templum priscum et

20 religiosum : stat Clitumnus ipse amictus ornatusque prae-
texta : praesens numen atque etiam fatidicum indicant
sortes. Sparsa sunt circa sacella complura totidemque
di, Sui cuique veneratio, suum nomen, quibusdam vero
etiam fontes. Nam praeter illum quasi parentem cetero-
25 rum sunt minores capite discreti; sed flumini miscentur,
quod ponte transmittitur. Is terminus sacri profanique.
In superiore parte navigare tantum, infra etiam natare
concessum. Balineum Hispellates, quibus illum locum
divus Augustus dono dedit, publice praebent, praebent et
30 hospitium. Nec desunt villae, quae secutae fluminis amoen-
itatem margini insistunt. In summa nihil erit ex quo non
capias voluptatem. Nam studebis quoque; leges multa
multorum omnibus columnis, omnibus parietibus inscripta,
quibus fons ille deusque celebratur. Plura laudabis, non
35 nulla ridebis; quamquam tu vero, quae tua humanitas,
nulla ridebis. Vale.

73. (BOOK 8. 16.)

Although Pliny comforts himself for the loss of his slaves by manu-
mitting them before death, and permitting them to dispose of their
property by will, yet the humanity which prompts this concession is
deeply affected by their decease.

C. PLINIUS PATERNO SUO S.

Confecerunt me infirmitates meorum, mortes etiam, et
quidem iuvenum. Solacia duo nequaquam paria tanto
dolori, solacia tamen : unum facilitas manumittendi; videor
enim non omnino inmaturos perdidisse quos iam liberos
5 perdidi : alterum, quod permitto servis quoque quasi testamenta facere eaque ut legitima custodio. Mandant rogant-
que quod visum; pareo ut iussus: dividunt, donant,
relinquunt, dumtaxat intra domum: nam servis res publica
quaedam et quasi civitas domus est. Sed quamquam
10 his solaciis adquiescam, debilitor et frangor eadem illa

humanitate, quae me ut hoc ipsum permitterem induxit.
Non ideo tamen velim durior fieri.   Nec ignoro alios
eius modi casus nihil amplius vocare quam damnum eoque
sibi magnos homines et sapientes videri.   Qui an magni
sapientesque sint nescio, homines non sunt.   Hominis est 15
enim adfici dolore, sentire, resistere tamen et solacia ad-
mittere, non solaciis non egere.   Verum de his plura
fortasse quam debui, sed pauciora quam volui.   Est enim
quaedam etiam dolendi voluptas, praesertim si in amici
sinu defleas, apud quem lacrimis tuis vel laus sit parata 20
vel venia.   Vale.

74.   (BOOK 9. 3.)

Men should either consider the immortality of fame, and work for
it, or the shortness of life, and enjoy it; and Pliny knows that Paulinus
agrees with him in preferring the former course.

C. PLINIUS PAULINO SUO S.

Alius aliud, ego beatissimum existimo qui bonae man-
suraeque famae praesumptione perfruitur certusque posteritatis cum futura gloria vivit.   Ac mihi nisi praemium
aeternitatis ante oculos, pingue illud altumque otium
placeat.   Etenim omnes homines arbitror oportere aut 5
inmortalitatem suam aut mortalitatem cogitare, et illos
quidem contendere eniti, hos quiescere remitti nec brevem
vitam caducis laboribus fatigare, ut video multos misera
simul et ingrata imagine industriae ad vilitatem sui per-
venire.   Haec ego tecum, quae cotidie mecum, ut desinam 10
mecum, si dissenties tu; quamquam non dissenties, ut qui
semper clarum aliquid et inmortale meditere.   Vale.

75. (BOOK 9. 6.)

The occupation of the Romans in the games of the Circus, in which Pliny can see no element of rational interest, has given Pliny a few days' leisure for literary pursuits.

C. PLINIUS CALVISIO SUO S.

Omne hoc tempus inter pugillares ac libellos iucundissima quiete transmisi. 'Quem ad modum' inquis 'in urbe potuisti?' Circenses erant, quo genere spectaculi ne levissime quidem teneor. Nihil novum, nihil varium, nihil 5 quod non semel spectasse sufficiat. Quo magis miror tot milia virorum tam pueriliter identidem cupere currentes equos, insistentes curribus homines videre. Si tamen aut velocitate equorum aut hominum arte traherentur, esset ratio non nulla: nunc favent panno, pannum amant, et 10 si in ipso cursu medioque certamine hic color illuc, ille huc transferatur, studium favorque transibit, et repente agitatores illos, equos illos, quos procul noscitant, quorum clamitant nomina, relinquent. Tanta gratia, tanta auctoritas in una vilissima tunica, mitto apud vulgus, quod 15 vilius tunica, sed apud quosdam graves homines; quos ego cum recordor in re inani frigida adsidua tam insatiabiliter desidere, capio aliquam voluptatem, quod hac voluptate non capior. Ac per hos dies libentissime otium meum in litteris conloco, quos alii otiosissimis occupationibus 20 perdunt. Vale.

76. (BOOK 9. 7.)

As Romanus is building at Baiae, so Pliny on the Lago di Como is enlarging two villas there, very different in their situation but equally attractive to their master.

C. PLINIUS ROMANO SUO S.

Aedificare te scribis. Bene est: inveni patrocinium; aedifico enim iam ratione, quia tecum. Nam hoc quoque

non dissimile, quod ad mare tu, ego ad Larium lacum.
Huius in litore plures villae meae, sed duae maxime ut
delectant ita exercent.   Altera inposita saxis more Baiano 5
lacum prospicit, altera aeque more Baiano lacum tangit.
Itaque illam tragoediam, hanc appellare comoediam soleo;
illam, quod quasi cothurnis, hanc, quod quasi socculis
sustinetur.   Sua utrique amoenitas et utraque possidenti
ipsa diversitate iucundior.   Haec lacu propius, illa latius 10
utitur: haec unum sinum molli curvamine amplectitur, illa
editissimo dorso duos dirimit: illic recta gestatio longo
limite super litus extenditur, hic spatiosissimo xysto leniter
inflectitur: illa fluctus non sentit, haec frangit: ex illa
possis despicere piscantes, ex hac ipse piscari hamumque 15
de cubiculo ac paene etiam de lectulo ut e naucula iacere.
Hae mihi causae utrique quae desunt adstruendi ob ea quae
supersunt.   Sed quid ego rationem tibi? apud quem pro
ratione erit idem facere.   Vale.

77. (BOOK 9. 13.)

Pliny describes the debate which he raised in the senate on the case of
Certus the enemy of Helvidius, the opposition with which he was met,
the great effect of his concluding speech, and the punishment and death
of Certus.

C. PLINIUS QUADRATO SUO S.

Quanto studiosius intentiusque legisti libros quos de
Helvidi ultione composui, tanto impensius postulas ut
perscribam tibi quaeque extra libros quaeque circa libros,
totum denique ordinem rei, cui per aetatem non interfuisti.
Occiso Domitiano statui mecum ac deliberavi esse magnam 5
pulchramque materiam insectandi nocentes, miseros vindi-
candi, se proferendi.   Porro inter multa scelera multorum
nullum atrocius videbatur, quam quod in senatu senator
senatori, praetorius consulari, reo iudex manus intulisset.
Fuerat alioqui mihi cum Helvidio amicitia, quanta potuerat 10

esse cum eo qui metu temporum nomen ingens paresque
virtutes secessu tegebat, fuerat cum Arria et Fannia, quarum
altera Helvidi noverca, altera mater novercae. Sed non ita
me iura privata ut publicum fas et indignitas facti et exempli
15 ratio incitabat. Ac primis quidem diebus redditae libertatis
pro se quisque inimicos suos, dumtaxat minores, incondito
turbidoque clamore postulaverat simul et oppresserat. Ego
et modestius et constantius arbitratus immanissimum reum
non communi temporum invidia, sed proprio crimine urgere,
20 cum iam satis primus ille impetus defremuisset et languidior
in dies ira ad iustitiam redisset, quamquam tum maxime
tristis amissa nuper uxore, mitto ad Anteiam (nupta haec
Helvidio fuerat), rogo ut veniat, quia me recens adhuc luctus
limine contineret. Ut venit, 'destinatum est' inquam 'mihi
25 maritum tuum non inultum pati. Nuntia Arriae et Fanniae'
(ab exilio redierant): 'consule te, consule illas, an velitis
adscribi facto, in quo ego comite non egeo; sed non ita
gloriae meae faverim, ut vobis societate eius invideam.'
Perfert Anteia mandata, nec illae morantur. Opportune
30 senatus intra diem tertium. Omnia ego semper ad Corellium rettuli, quem providentissimum aetatis nostrae sapi-
entissimumque cognovi; in hoc tamen contentus consilio
meo fui, veritus ne vetaret: erat enim cunctantior cautiorque.
Sed non sustinui inducere in animum quo minus illi eodem
35 die facturum me indicarem quod an facerem non deliber-
abam, expertus usu de eo quod destinaveris non esse con-
sulendos quibus consultis obsequi debeas. Venio in senatum,
ius dicendi peto, dico paulisper maximo adsensu. Ubi
coepi crimen attingere, reum destinare, adhuc tamen sine
40 nomine, undique mihi reclamari. Alius 'sciamus, quis
sit de quo extra ordinem referas;' alius 'quis est ante
relationem reus'? alius 'salvi simus, qui supersumus.'
Audio inperturbatus, interritus: tantum susceptae rei honestas valet tantumque ad fiduciam vel metum differt, nolint

homines quod facias, an non probent. Longum est omnia 45
quae tunc hinc inde iacta sunt recensere. Novissime consul
'Secunde, sententiae loco dices, siquid volueris.' 'Permis-
eras' inquam 'quod usque adhuc omnibus permisisti.'
Resido: aguntur alia. Interim me quidam ex consularibus
amicis secreto curatoque sermone quasi nimis fortiter 50
incauteque progressum corripit, revocat, monet ut desistam;
adicit etiam 'notabilem te futuris principibus fecisti.'
'Esto' inquam, 'dum malis.' Vix ille discesserat, rursus
alter 'quid audes? quo ruis? quibus te periculis obicis?
quid praesentibus confidis, incertus futurorum? Lacessis 55
hominem iam praefectum aerarii et brevi consulem, praeterea qua gratia, quibus amicitiis fultum!' nominat quendam,
qui tunc ad orientem amplissimum et famosissimum exercitum non sine magnis dubiisque rumoribus obtinebat. Ad
haec ego 'omnia praecepi atque animo mecum ante peregi, 60
nec recuso, si ita casus attulerit, luere poenas ob honest-
issimum factum, dum flagitiosissimum ulciscor.' Iam
censendi tempus. Dicit Domitius Apollinaris, consul de-
signatus, dicit Fabricius Veiento, Fabius Maximinus, Vettius
Proculus, collega Publici Certi, de quo agebatur, uxoris 65
meae, quam amiseram, vitricus, post hos Ammius Flaccus.
Omnes Certum nondum a me nominatum ut nominatum
defendunt crimenque quasi in medio relictum defensione
suscipiunt. Quae praeterea dixerint, non est necesse narrare; in libris habes. Sum enim cuncta ipsorum verbis 70
persecutus. Dicunt contra Avidius Quietus, Cornutus
Tertullus: Quietus, iniquissimum esse querellas dolentium
excludi, ideoque Arriae et Fanniae ius querendi non aufer-
endum, nec interesse, cuius ordinis quis sit, sed quam
causam habeat: Cornutus, datum se a consulibus tutorem 75
Helvidi filiae petentibus matre eius et vitrico; nunc quoque
non sustinere deserere officii sui partes, in quo tamen et suo
dolori modum inponere et optimarum feminarum perferre

modestissimum adfectum, quas contentas esse admonere
80 senatum Publici Certi cruentae adulationis et petere, si
poena flagitii manifestissimi remittatur, nota certe quasi
censoria inuratur. Tum Satrius Rufus medio ambiguoque
sermone 'puto' inquit 'iniuriam factam Publicio Certo,
si non absolvitur: nominatus est ab amicis Arriae et
85 Fanniae, nominatus ab amicis suis. Nec debemus solliciti
esse: iidem enim nos, qui bene sentimus de homine, et
iudicaturi sumus: si innocens est, sicut et spero et malo
et, donec aliquid probetur, credo, poteritis absolvere.' Haec
illi, quo quisque ordine citabantur. Venitur ad me: con-
90 surgo, utor initio quod in libro est, respondeo singulis.
Mirum qua intentione, quibus clamoribus omnia exceperint
qui modo reclamabant: tanta conversio vel negotii digni-
tatem vel proventum orationis vel actoris constantiam
subsecuta est. Finio: incipit respondere Veiento: nemo
95 patitur: obturbatur, obstrepitur, adeo quidem ut diceret
'rogo, patres conscripti, ne me cogatis inplorare auxilium
tribunorum.' Et statim Murena tribunus 'permitto tibi,
vir clarissime Veiento, dicere.' Tunc quoque reclamatur.
Inter moras consul citatis nominibus et peracta discessione
100 mittit senatum ac paene adhuc stantem temptantemque
dicere Veientonem reliquit. Multum ille de hac (ita vocabat)
contumelia questus est Homerico versu

ὦ γέρον, ἦ μάλα δή σε νέοι τείρουσι μαχηταί.

Non fere quisquam in senatu fuit, qui non me com-
105 plecteretur, exoscularetur certatimque laude cumularet, quod
intermissum iam diu morem in publicum consulendi susceptis
propriis simultatibus reduxissem, quod denique senatum
invidia liberassem, qua flagrabat apud ordines alios, quod
severus in ceteros senatoribus solis dissimulatione quasi
110 mutua parceret. Haec acta sunt absente Certo: fuit enim
seu tale aliquid suspicatus sive, ut excusabatur, infirmus.
Et relationem quidem de eo Caesar ad senatum non

remisit; obtinui tamen quod intenderam. Nam collega
Certi consulatum, successorem Certus accepit, planeque
factum est quod dixeram in fine, 'reddat praemium sub 115
optimo principe, quod a pessimo accepit.' Postea actionem
meam, utcumque potui, recollegi, addidi multa. Accidit
fortuitum, sed non tamquam fortuitum, quod editis libris
Certus intra paucissimos dies inplicitus morbo decessit.
Audivi referentes hanc imaginem menti eius, hanc oculis 120
oberrasse, tamquam videret me sibi cum ferro imminere.
Verane haec adfirmare non ausim; interest tamen exempli
ut vera videantur. Habes epistulam, si modum epistulae
cogites, libris quos legisti non minorem; sed inputabis
tibi, qui contentus libris non fuisti. Vale.   125

78. (BOOK 9. 15.)

Pliny has sought leisure in the country, but does not find much satisfaction there either in his studies or in the duties of a country
gentleman.

C. PLINIUS FALCONI SUO S.

Refugeram in Tuscos, ut omnia ad arbitrium meum
facerem. At hoc ne in Tuscis quidem: tam multis undique
rusticorum libellis et tam querulis inquietor, quos aliquanto
magis invitus quam meos lego; nam et meos invitus. Re-
tracto enim actiunculas quasdam, quod post intercapedinem 5
temporis et frigidum et acerbum est. Rationes quasi absente
me negleguntur. Interdum tamen equum conscendo et
patrem familiae hactenus ago, quod aliquam partem praediorum, sed pro gestatione percurro. Tu consuetudinem
serva nobisque sic rusticis urbana acta perscribe. Vale.   10

79. (BOOK 9. 21.)

Pliny begs a pardon from Sabinianus for a freedman of the latter
who had offended him.

C. PLINIUS SABINIANO SUO S.

Libertus tuus, cui suscensere te dixeras, venit ad me ad-
volutusque pedibus meis tamquam tuis haesit. Flevit
multum, multum rogavit, multum etiam tacuit, in summa
fecit mihi fidem paenitentiae. Vere credo emendatum,
5 quia deliquisse se sentit. Irasceris, scio, et irasceris merito,
id quoque scio: sed tunc praecipua mansuetudinis laus,
cum irae causa iustissima est. Amasti hominem et, spero,
amabis: interim sufficit ut exorari te sinas. Licebit rursus
irasci, si meruerit, quod exoratus excusatius facies. Remitte
10 aliquid adulescentiae ipsius, remitte lacrimis, remitte indulgentiae tuae: ne torseris illum, ne torseris etiam te.
Torqueris enim, cum tam lenis irasceris. Vereor ne videar
non rogare, sed cogere, si precibus eius meas iunxero.
Iungam tamen tanto plenius et effusius, quanto ipsum acrius
15 severiusque corripui destricte minatus numquam me postea
rogaturum. Hoc illi, quem terreri oportebat, tibi non idem.
Nam fortasse iterum rogabo, impetrabo iterum: sit modo
tale ut rogare me, ut praestare te deceat. Vale.

80. (BOOK 9. 23.)

Pliny, hearing that his name is coupled with that of Tacitus, and also
known on its own merits, is delighted with these assurances that his
literary fame is fairly established.

C. PLINIUS MAXIMO SUO S.

Frequenter agenti mihi evenit ut centumviri, cum diu se
intra iudicum auctoritatem gravitatemque tenuissent, omnes
repente quasi victi coactique consurgerent laudarentque;
frequenter e senatu famam, qualem maxime optaveram,

rettuli: numquam tamen maiorem cepi voluptatem, quam 5
nuper ex sermone Corneli Taciti. Narrabat sedisse secum
circensibus proximis equitem Romanum : hunc post varios
eruditosque sermones requisisse ' Italicus es an provincialis?':
se respondisse ' nosti me, et quidem ex studiis': ad hoc
illum ' Tacitus es an Plinius?'. Exprimere non possum, 10
quam sit iucundum mihi, quod nomina nostra quasi litterarum propria, non hominum, litteris redduntur, quod uterque
nostrum his etiam ex studiis notus, quibus aliter ignotus est.
Accidit aliud ante pauculos dies simile. Recumbebat
mecum vir egregius, Fadius Rufinus, super eum municeps 15
ipsius, qui illo die primum venerat in urbem ; cui Rufinus
demonstrans me ' vides hunc?' Multa deinde de studiis
nostris. Et ille ' Plinius est' inquit. Verum fatebor,
capio magnum laboris mei fructum. An, si Demosthenes
iure lactatus est, quod illum anus Attica ita noscitavit, 20
οἷτός ἐστι Δημοσθένης, ego celebritate nominis mei gaudere
non debeo? Ego vero et gaudeo et gaudere me dico.
Neque enim vereor ne iactantior videar, cum de me aliorum
. iudicium, non meum profero, praesertim apud te, qui nec
ullius invides laudibus et faves nostris. Vale. 25

81. (BOOK 9. 33.)

The story of the boy and the dolphin at Hippo.

C. PLINIUS CANINIO SUO S.

Incidi in materiam veram, sed simillimam fictae dignamque
isto laetissimo altissimo planeque poetico ingenio, incidi
autem, dum super cenam varia miracula hinc inde referuntur.
Magna auctori fides. Tametsi quid poetae cum fide? Is
tamen auctor, cui bene vel historiam scripturus credidisses. 5
Est in Africa Hipponensis colonia mari proxima: adiacet
navigabile stagnum: ex hoc in modum fluminis aestuarium
emergit, quod vice alterna, prout aestus aut repressit aut

impulit, nunc infertur mari, nunc redditur stagno. Omnis
hic aetas piscandi navigandi atque etiam natandi studio
tenetur, maxime pueri, quos otium lususque sollicitat. His
gloria et virtus altissime provehi: victor ille qui longissime
ut litus ita simul natantes reliquit. Hoc certamine puer
quidam audentior ceteris in ulteriora tendebat. Delphinus
occurrit et nunc praecedere puerum, nunc sequi, nunc circumire, postremo subire, deponere, iterum subire trepidan-
temque perferre primum in altum, mox flectit ad litus
redditque terrae et aequalibus. Serpit per coloniam fama:
concurrere omnes, ipsum puerum tamquam miraculum
aspicere, interrogare, audire, narrare. Postero die obsident
litus, prospectant mare et siquid est mari simile. Natant
pueri, inter hos ille, sed cautius. Delphinus rursus ad tempus,
rursus ad puerum. Fugit ille cum ceteris. Delphinus,
quasi invitet revocet, exilit mergitur variosque orbes implicat
expeditque. Hoc altero die, hoc tertio, hoc pluribus, donec
homines innutritos mari subiret timendi pudor. Accedunt
et adludunt et appellant, tangunt etiam pertrectantque
praebentem. Crescit audacia experimento. Maxime puer
qui primus expertus est adnatat, insilit tergo, fertur re-
ferturque, agnosci se et amari putat, amat ipse: neuter
timet, neuter timetur: huius fiducia, mansuetudo illius
augetur. Nec non alii pueri dextra laevaque simul eunt
hortantes monentesque. Ibat una (id quoque mirum)
delphinus alius, tantum spectator et comes: nihil enim
simile aut faciebat aut patiebatur, sed alterum illum ducebat
reducebatque, ut puerum ceteri pueri. Incredibile, tam
verum tamen quam priora, delphinum gestatorem collu-
soremque puerorum in terram quoque extrahi solitum
harenisque siccatum, ubi incaluisset, in mare revolvi. Constat Octavium Avitum, legatum proconsulis, in litus educto
religione prava superfudisse unguentum, cuius illum novi-
tatem odoremque in altum refugisse nec nisi post multo

dies visum languidum et maestum, mox redditis viribus
priorem lasciviam et solita ministeria repetisse.   Confluebant
omnes ad spectaculum magistratus, quorum adventu et 45
mora modica res publica novis sumptibus atterebatur.
Postremo locus ipse quietem suam secretumque perdebat.
Placuit occulte interfici ad quod coibatur.   Haec tu qua
miseratione, qua copia deflebis, ornabis, attolles ! quamquam
non est opus adfingas aliquid aut adstruas : sufficit ne ea 50
quae sunt vera minuantur.   Vale.

82. (BOOK 9. 36.)

How Pliny spends his day in his Tuscan villa.

C. PLINIUS FUSCO SUO S.

Quaeris quem ad modum in Tuscis diem aestate disponam.
Evigilo cum libuit, plerumque circa horam primam, saepe
ante, tardius raro ; clausae fenestrae manent.   Mire enim
silentio et tenebris ab iis quae avocant abductus et liber et
mihi relictus non oculos animo, sed animum oculis sequor, 5
qui eadem quae mens vident, quotiens non vident alia.
Cogito, siquid in manibus, cogito ad verbum scribenti emen-
dantique similis, nunc pauciora nunc plura, ut vel difficile
vel facile componi tenerive potuerunt.   Notarium voco et die
admisso quae formaveram dicto : abit rursusque revocatur 10
rursusque dimittitur.   Ubi hora quarta vel quinta (neque
enim certum dimensumque tempus), ut dies suasit, in xystum
me vel cryptoporticum confero, reliqua meditor et dicto.
Vehiculum ascendo : ibi quoque idem quod ambulans aut
iacens : durat intentio mutatione ipsa refecta.   Paulum 15
redormio, dein ambulo, mox orationem graecam latinamve
clare et intente non tam vocis causa quam stomachi lego ;
pariter tamen et illa firmatur.   Iterum ambulo, ungor,
exerceor, lavor.   Cenanti mihi, si cum uxore vel paucis,

20 liber legitur: post cenam comoedus aut lyristes: mox cum
meis ambulo, quorum in numero sunt eruditi. Ita variis
sermonibus vespera extenditur et quamquam longissimus
dies cito conditur. Non numquam ex hoc ordine aliqua
mutantur. Nam si diu iacui vel ambulavi, post somnum
25 demum lectionemque non vehiculo, sed quod brevius, quia
velocius, equo gestor. Interveniunt amici ex proximis oppidis partemque diei ad se trahunt interdumque lasso mihi
opportuna interpellatione subveniunt. Venor aliquando, sed
non sine pugillaribus, ut, quamvis nihil ceperim, non nihil
30 referam. Datur et colonis, ut videtur ipsis, non satis
temporis, quorum mihi agrestes querellae litteras nostras
et haec urbana opera commendant. Vale.

83. (BOOK 9. 37.)

Pliny excuses himself from being present at Paulinus' inauguration as
consul, as he is engaged in rearranging the terms of tenancy on his
estates.

C. PLINIUS PAULINO SUO S.

Nec tuae naturae est translaticia haec et quasi publica
officia a familiaribus amicis contra ipsorum commodum
exigere, et ego te constantius amo, quam ut verear ne aliter
ac velim accipias, nisi te kalendis statim consulem videro,
5 praesertim cum me necessitas locandorum praediorum plures
annos ordinatura detineat, in qua mihi nova consilia sumenda
sunt. Nam priore lustro, quamquam post magnas remis-
siones, reliqua creverunt: inde plerisque nulla iam cura
minuendi aeris alieni, quod desperant posse persolvi; rapiunt
10 etiam consumuntque quod natum est, ut qui iam putent se
non sibi parcere. Occurrendum ergo augescentibus vitiis
et medendum est. Medendi una ratio, si non nummo, sed
partibus, locem ac deinde ex meis aliquos operis exactores
custodes fructibus ponam. Et alioqui nullum iustius genus
15 reditus, quam quod terra caelum annus refert. At hoc

magnam fidem, acres oculos, numerosas manus poscit. Experiendum tamen et quasi in veteri morbo quaelibet mutationis auxilia temptanda sunt. Vides quam non delicata me causa obire primum consulatus tui diem non sinat; quem tamen hic quoque ut praesens votis gaudio gratulatione 20 celebrabo. Vale.

84. (BOOK 9. 39.)

Pliny gives his architect a commission to rebuild a temple of Ceres on one of his estates, and to add porticoes near it.

C. PLINIUS MUSTIO SUO S.

Haruspicum monitu reficienda est mihi aedes Cereris in praediis in melius et in maius, vetus sane et angusta, cum sit alioqui stato die frequentissima. Nam idibus Septembribus magnus e regione tota coit populus, multae res aguntur, multa vota suscipiuntur, multa redduntur. Sed 5 nullum in proximo suffugium aut imbris aut solis. Videor ergo munifice simul religioseque facturus, si aedem quam pulcherrimam extruxero, addidero porticus aedi, illam ad usum deae, has ad hominum. Velim ergo emas quattuor marmoreas columnas, cuius tibi videbitur generis, emas 10 marmora, quibus solum, quibus parietes excolantur. Erit etiam vel faciendum vel emendum ipsius deae signum, quia antiquum illud e ligno quibusdam sui partibus vetustate truncatum est. Quantum ad porticus, nihil interim occurrit, quod videatur istinc esse repetendum; nisi tamen ut formam 15 secundum rationem loci scribas. Neque enim possunt circumdari templo: nam solum templi hinc flumine et abruptissimis ripis, hinc via cingitur. Est ultra viam latissimum pratum, in quo satis apte contra templum ipsum porticus explicabuntur; nisi quid tu melius inveneris, qui 20 soles locorum difficultates arte superare. Vale.

85. (TRAI. 1.)

Pliny congratulates Trajan on his succession to the empire.

C. PLINIUS TRAIANO IMPERATORI.

Tua quidem pietas, imperator sanctissime, optaverat ut quam tardissime succederes patri. Sed di immortales festinaverunt virtutes tuas ad gubernacula rei publicae, quam susceperas, admovere. Precor ergo ut tibi et per te generi
5 humano prospera omnia, id est digna saeculo tuo, contingant. Fortem te et hilarem, imperator optime, et privatim et publice opto.

86. (TRAI. 2.)

Pliny thanks Trajan for having granted to him (although childless)
the rights of a father of a family.

C. PLINIUS TRAIANO IMPERATORI.

Exprimere, domine, verbis non possum quantum mihi gaudium attuleris, quod me dignum putasti iure trium liberorum. Quamvis enim Iuli Serviani, optimi viri tuique amantissimi, precibus indulseris, tamen etiam ex rescripto
5 intellego libentius hoc ei te praestitisse, quia pro me rogabat. Videor ergo summam voti mei consecutus, cum inter initia felicissimi principatus tui probaveris me ad peculiarem indulgentiam tuam pertinere; eoque magis liberos concupisco, quos habere etiam illo tristissimo saeculo volui,
10 sicut potes duobus matrimoniis meis credere. Sed di melius, qui omnia integra bonitati tuae reservarunt : maluerunt hoc potius tempore me patrem fieri, quo futurus essem et securus et felix.

87.   (TRAI. 65.)

Pliny asks Trajan whether foundlings are to be considered the property
of those who have been at the expense of bringing them up.

C. PLINIUS TRAIANO IMPERATORI.

Magna, domine, et ad totam provinciam pertinens quaestio
est de condicione et alimentis eorum quos vocant θρεπτούς.
In qua ego auditis constitutionibus principum, quia nihil
inveniebam aut proprium aut universale quod ad Bithynos
referretur, consulendum te existimavi, quid observari velles, 5
neque putavi posse me in eo quod auctoritatem tuam pos-
ceret exemplo esse contentum.   Recitabatur autem apud me
edictum quod dicebatur divi Augusti ad Anniam pertinens;
recitatae et epistulae divi Vespasiani ad Lacedaemonios et
divi Titi ad eosdem [Achaeos] et Domitiani ad Avidium 10
Nigrinum et Armenium Brocchum proconsules, item ad
Lacedaemonios.   Quae ideo tibi non misi, quia et parum
emendata et quaedam non certae fidei videbantur, et quia
vera et emendata in scriniis tuis esse credebam.

88.   (TRAI. 66.)

Trajan can find no general rescript of his predecessors on the subject
of the foregoing letter; but himself decides in favour of the children's
freedom.

TRAIANUS PLINIO.

Quaestio ista quae pertinet ad eos qui liberi nati expositi,
deinde sublati a quibusdam et in servitute educati sunt saepe
tractata est, nec quicquam invenitur in commentariis eorum
principum qui ante me fuerunt, quod ad omnes provincias
sit constitutum.   Epistulae sane sunt Domitiani ad Avidium 5
Nigrinum et Armenium Brocchum, quae fortasse debeant
observari, sed inter eas provincias de quibus rescripsit inter-

missa est Bithynia. Et ideo nec adsertionem denegandam ii-
qui ex eius modi causa in libertatem vindicabuntur puto
10 neque ipsam libertatem redimendam pretio alimentorum.

89. (TRAI. 74.)

Pliny sends to Trajan one Callidromus who had escaped to Bithynia
after a long slavery in the court of Parthia.

C. PLINIUS TRAIANO IMPERATORI.

Appuleius, domine, miles, qui est in statione Nicomedensi,
scripsit mihi quendam nomine Callidromum, cum detineretur
a Maximo et Dionysio pistoribus, quibus operas suas loca-
verat, confugisse ad tuam statuam perductumque ad magis-
5 tratus indicasse servisse aliquando Laberio Maximo captum-
que a Susago in Moesia et a Decibalo muneri missum
Pacoro, Parthiae regi, pluribusque annis in ministerio eius
fuisse, deinde fugisse atque ita in Nicomediam pervenisse.
Quem ego perductum ad me, cum eadem narrasset, mitten-
10 dum ad te putavi; quod paulo tardius feci, dum requiro
gemmam, quam sibi habentem imaginem Pacori et quibus
ornatus fuisset subtractam indicabat. Volui enim hanc quoque, si inveniri potuisset, simul mittere, sicut glebulam misi,
quam se ex Parthico metallo attulisse dicebat. Signata
15 est anulo meo, cuius est aposphragisma quadriga.

90. (TRAI. 96.)

Pliny asks how he ought to deal with the Christians, describes the
method which he has hitherto followed, relates what he has been able to
learn of their life and observances, and adds that, though the evil has
spread rapidly, it may be, and is being, checked.

C. PLINIUS TRAIANO IMPERATORI.

Sollemne est mihi, domine, omnia de quibus dubito ad te
referre. Quis enim potest melius vel cunctationem meam

regere vel ignorantiam instruere? Cognitionibus de Christi-
anis interfui numquam: ideo nescio quid et quatenus aut
puniri soleat aut quaeri.   Nec mediocriter haesitavi, sitne 5
aliquod discrimen aetatum, an quamlibet teneri nihil a robus-
tioribus differant; detur paenitentiae venia, an ei qui omnino
Christianus fuit desisse non prosit; nomen ipsum, si flagitiis
careat, an flagitia cohaerentia nomini puniantur.   Interim *in*
iis qui ad me tamquam Christiani deferebantur hunc sum 10
secutus modum.   Interrogavi ipsos an essent Christiani: con-
fitentes iterum ac tertio interrogavi supplicium minatus: per-
severantes duci iussi.   Neque enim dubitabam, qualecumque
esset quod faterentur, pertinaciam certe et inflexibilem obstinationem debere puniri.   Fuerunt alii similis amentiae, quos, 15
quia cives Romani erant, adnotavi in urbem remittendos.
Mox ipso tractatu, ut fieri solet, diffundente se crimine
plures species inciderunt.   Propositus est libellus sine auctore multorum nomina continens.   Qui negabant esse se
Christianos aut fuisse, cum praeeunte me deos appellarent et 20
imagini tuae, quam propter hoc iusseram cum simulacris
numinum adferri, ture ac vino supplicarent, praeterea male
dicerent Christo, quorum nihil posse cogi dicuntur qui sunt
re vera Christiani, dimittendos esse putavi.   Alii ab indice
nominati esse se Christianos dixerunt et mox negaverunt; 25
fuisse quidem, sed desisse, quidam ante triennium, quidam
ante plures annos, non nemo etiam ante viginti.   Hi quoque
omnes et imaginem tuam deorumque simulacra venerati sunt
et Christo male dixerunt.   Adfirmabant autem hanc fuisse
summam vel culpae suae vel erroris, quod essent soliti stato 30
die ante lucem convenire carmenque Christo quasi deo
dicere secum invicem seque sacramento non in scelus aliquod obstringere, sed ne furta, ne latrocinia, ne adulteria
committerent, ne fidem fallerent, ne depositum appellati ab-
negarent: quibus peractis morem sibi discedendi fuisse, rur- 35
susque *coeundi* ad capiendum cibum, promiscuum tamen et

innoxium; quod ipsum facere desisse post edictum meum,
quo secundum mandata tua hetaerias esse vetueram. Quo
magis necessarium credidi ex duabus ancillis, quae ministrae
40 dicebantur, quid esset veri et per tormenta quaerere. Nihil
aliud inveni quam superstitionem pravam immodicam. Ideo
dilata cognitione ad consulendum te decucurri. Visa est
enim mihi res digna consultatione, maxime propter peri-
clitantium numerum. Multi enim omnis aetatis, omnis
45 ordinis, utriusque sexus etiam, vocantur in periculum et
vocabuntur. Neque civitates tantum sed vicos etiam atque
agros superstitionis istius contagio pervagata est; quae
videtur sisti et corrigi posse. Certe satis constat prope iam
desolata templa coepisse celebrari et sacra sollemnia diu
50 intermissa repeti pastumque venire victimarum, cuius adhuc
rarissimus emptor inveniebatur. Ex quo facile est opinari,
quae turba hominum emendari possit, si sit paenitentiae
locus.

91. (TRAI. 97.)

Trajan approves of Pliny's conduct. The Christians are to be pun-
ished if convicted, but they are not to be sought for, they are to be
pardoned if they sacrifice, and no anonymous charge against them is to
be admitted.

TRAIANUS PLINIO.

Actum quem debuisti, mi Secunde, in excutiendis causis
eorum qui Christiani ad te delati fuerant secutus es. Neque
enim in universum aliquid quod quasi certam formam habeat
constitui potest. Conquirendi non sunt: si deferantur et argu-
5 antur, puniendi sunt, ita tamen ut qui negaverit se Christia-
num esse idque re ipsa manifestum fecerit, id est supplicando
dis nostris, quamvis suspectus in praeteritum, veniam ex
paenitentia impetret. Sine auctore vero propositi libelli *in*
nullo crimine locum habere debent. Nam et pessimi exem-
10 pli nec nostri saeculi est.

Clarendon Press Series

SELECTED LETTERS

OF

PLINY

WITH NOTES FOR THE USE OF SCHOOLS

BY THE LATE

CONSTANTINE E. PRICHARD, M.A.

Formerly Fellow of Balliol College

AND

EDWARD R. BERNARD, M.A.

Formerly Fellow of Magdalen College

NEW EDITION

PART II. — NOTES, &c.

Oxford

AT THE CLARENDON PRESS

M DCCC XCVI

London

HENRY FROWDE

Oxford University Press Warehouse
Amen Corner, E.C.

New York

MACMILLAN & CO., 66 FIFTH AVENUE

NOTES.

Ep. 2.—Some editors think that the book which Pliny alludes to in this letter is a copy of a speech which he made before the Centumviri, the court in which he pleaded in behalf of Attia Viriola who claimed to inherit her father's property. He mentions this speech in Ep. 62 'Dedimus vela indignationi, dedimus irae, dedimus dolori: et in amplissimâ causâ, quasi magno mari, pluribus ventis sumus vecti.' His friends, he says, considered this to hold the chief place among his speeches, as the De Coronâ among those of Demosthenes. Unfortunately, except the Panegyric on Trajan, we have no specimen of Pliny's orations.

4. Eodem ζήλῳ, 'with so strong an emulation,' i.e. of Demosthenes.

5. Demosthenen semper tuum. Calvum nuper meum; 'Demosthenes who has always been your model, Calvus whom I have lately taken as mine.'

C. Licinius Macer Calvus is mentioned by Cicero (who was twenty-four years older) as a young orator who would have been eminent for eloquence if he had lived, but he died in his thirty-fifth or thirty-sixth year. Cicero thought his style exact and polished, but wanting in force, and fitted for a learned audience, not for the multitude. Pliny would hardly have joined him with Demosthenes if he had agreed with this estimate; and Quintilian speaks of it as appearing to many too unfavourable, since Calvus could be forcible as well as elegant; 'est et sancta et gravis oratio, et castigata, et frequenter vehemens quoque' Quintil. Inst. Orat. 10. 1. Cic. de Claris Orator. 81; Fam. 15. 21. Smith's Biog. Dict.

6. Dumtaxat figuris orationis; 'at least in the rhetorical forms of the speech.' 'Figurae' are not merely what we call figures of speech, metaphors, or ornaments, but include also the forms in which the sentences were cast, and even their arrangement; answering partly to Aristotle's σχήματα τῆς λέξεως, Poet. 19. 7, Rhet. 3. 8, 1; or more properly to his λέξις, Rhet. 2. 9. Repetition of words, exclamations, questions, apostrophes, examples, in fact all methods of enforcing the subject and moving the hearer, are spoken of as 'figurae' by Quintilian and Cicero. Demosthenes is particularly powerful in the use of such turns of expression. Quintil. Inst. Orat. 9. 1. Cic. de Orat. 3. 52 and 53.

7. Aequus, sc. 'Jupiter.' Virg. Aen. 6. 129.

9. In contentione dicendi, 'in a vehement style of address.' 'Contentio sermonis' is opposed to 'lenitas.' 'Tu iamdiu multo dicis remissius et lenius quam solebas; neque minus haec tamen tua gravissimi sermonis lenitas, quam illa summa vis et contentio probatur' Cic. de Or. 1. 60. 'Contentiosa oratio,' Bk. 2. 19, is different, and means a contentious speech.

12. ληκύθους, lit. flasks for oil or artists' colours. Hence λήκυθοι and the Latin equivalent 'ampullae' were used for rhetorical ornaments and exaggerations which writers and speakers employed to deck their language. Cp. Cic. Att. 1. 14, and Hor. Ep. 6. 3, 14. Pliny calls these ornaments **Marci nostri** ληκύθους because Cicero in the passage quoted had confessed to their use.

14. **Nec est quod putes.** Arrianus is not however to think that, because he makes this stipulation in favour of ornament, he therefore wants 'venia' instead of 'emendatio.'

15. **Quo magis intendam limam tuam,** 'that I may urge you to more searching criticism;' lit. 'that I may give more force to your file.' 'Lima' is a common metaphor for care in polishing verse or prose. Martial (speaking of Pliny's criticism on his book) says,

> 'Quem censoria cum meo Severo
> Docti lima momorderit Secundi' Mart. 5. 80.

17. **Fortasse errori nostro,** 'what is perhaps my folly,' namely his intention to publish.

18. **Album calculum adiicere,** 'to approve.' Cp.

> 'Mos erat antiquis niveis atrisque lapillis,
> His damnare reos, illis absolvere culpae'
> Ov. Met. 15. 41.

3 **Ep. 3. 1. Suburbanum,** sc. 'rus vel praedium.'

3. **Euripus.** This name, specially applied to the strait between Euboea and Boeotia, was used both in Greek and Latin of any narrow canal or conduit, though Cicero implies that in his time this use was thought grandiloquent. 'Ductus vero aquarum, quos isti nilos et euripos vocant' Cic. Leg. 2. 1.

4. **Serviens lacus.** 'Serviens' carries out the metaphor of subiectus. Here it means 'yielding itself to the view,' and so serving to enhance the attractions of the villa. Cp. 'Piscinam quae fenestris servit et subiacet' Bk. 5. 6, and 'Diversis servit sua terra fenestris' Stat. Silv. 2. 2, 75.

5. **Gestatio.** This was an avenue for exercise on horseback, in a carriage, or in a litter. It was sometimes covered. Cp.

> 'Porticus in qua
> Gestetur dominus quoties pluit' Juv. 7. 178.

6. **Triclinia illa popularia, illa paucorum,** 'those dining-rooms for large parties, and the others for small ones.' 'Triclinium' was extended to mean the room for dining in, as well as the couch for dining on. 'Popularia' in this sense is justified by the similar use of 'populus' simply to express a large number. Cp. 'Populo natorum . . . meorum,' Ov. Met. 6. 198, quoted by Gierig.

7. **Possidentne te,** sc. cubicula. He means, 'do you stay at home and only move from the blue bed to the brown?'

15. **Exclude.** So Keil for 'excude' which has no MSS. authority. The expression is either borrowed from birds hatching their young (Lucr. 5. 799), or = 'claude.' Cp. 'Excludit (sc. claudit) volumen Genethliacon Lucani' Stat. Silv. 2. Praef.

18. **Tu modo .... fueris.** 'I pray you to endeavour to rate yourself at that value, which others will certainly put upon you, if only first of all you attain it in your own estimation.' An obscure and fancifully turned entreaty that Caninius will rely on his ability to command literary success.

Ep. 4. 4. **In proximo,** 'close by.' 'Proximum' governed by various **4** prepositions is frequent in Pliny to express proximity. Cp. Epp. 20. 38, and 41. **12**

5. **Pugillares,** sc. 'tabulae.' The word 'pugillares,' a name frequently given to tablets covered with wax, is derived from 'pugillus' (handful), because they were small enough to be held in the hand.

Ep. 5. 1. Mirum est ..... non constet; 'it is wonderful what a **5** rational account may be given of single days spent in the city, while it cannot be of a number of days together.' Cp. 'Confido laetioris stili constare rationem' Ep. 32. 38.

10. **In Laurentino meo,** in his Laurentine villa, described Ep. 21.

19. **Quam multa invenitis,** 'how many topics you suggest.'

Ep. 6. 3. **Euphrates:** see Life of Pliny, p. ix. **6**

15. **Latitudinem,** 'copiousness.' There seems to be a play on the sound and etymology of Plato's name (πλάτος).

24. **Etiam cum persuaserit.** His mode of convincing is so attractive that one wishes him to go on even after one is convinced.

31. **Officio.** Pliny was 'Praefectus aerarii' in the year 99, the second year of Trajan, and it is to the engagements of this office that he here alludes.

32. **Subnoto libellos,** 'I make comments on petitions.' Libellus is frequently used in this sense :—

> 'Sed iam supplicibus Dominum lassare libellis
>   Desine'   Mart. 8. 31.

Pliny uses it elsewhere as a writ of accusation. Ep. 68. 68.

Conficio tabulas, 'I make up (the public) accounts.' The treasury had been successively under the care of praefects, then of some of the praetors, and afterwards of the quaestors again, which was a return to the older system of the republic. Nero chose praefects for the office in order to have men of greater experience than the quaestors, who might be only twenty-five years of age.

33. **Inlitteratissimas litteras,** 'with nothing literary about them.' Cp. 'Rationes legebam invitus et cursim, aliis enim chartis, aliis sum litteris initiatus' Ep. 48. 28.

33. **Invideo aliis bono:** see on Ep. 18. 3.

Ep. 7. Pliny mentions Corellius elsewhere with the highest respect and **7** affection, as his adviser, friend, and guide, who had introduced him into public

5

life, and, though much older than himself, had shewn the warmest interest in his success. On two occasions he relates that he had recourse to him for advice in important professional matters, esteeming him one of the most experienced and wisest lawyers of his time. From this letter we learn that Corellius survived Domitian (who was murdered Sept. 17, A.D. 96), and he afterwards spoke highly of Pliny to the emperor Nerva. On his deathbed he mentions Pliny to his daughter as one of the friends she could most rely on, and both she and her aunt Corellia found him ready to do them kindness. Epp. 40 and 64.

1. **Si iactura dicenda est.** The word 'iactura' from its application to everyday losses of money, property, &c., had material associations, which to Pliny's refinement made it unsuitable to use of the death of such a friend as Corellius.

4. **Utcumque:** see on Ep. 46. 7.

12. **Tot pignora, sc. filiam, uxorem, &c.** In post-Augustan Latin 'pignora' was applied to all near relations, not merely to children, as the English phrase 'pledges.' Cp. Paneg. 37.

21. **Isti latroni,** Domitian, whose cruelty became more atrocious in the few last years of his reign. See Merivale, c. 62.

29. **Fecisset quod optabat;** i.e. he would have helped to kill Domitian. 'Si,' as here, is often omitted before a supposition. The subjunctive is used here because the supposition is false or imaginary. See the distinction between the sense of the indic. and subj. (when 'si' is omitted), as explained by Madvig, § 442 a, Obs. 2.

39. **Hispulla,** possibly Calpurnia Hispulla, aunt of Pliny's wife Calpurnia (Ep. 41), in which case there would have been a connection as well as a close friendship between Pliny and the house of Corellius.

46. **Valetudinem,** *ill* health.

Superstitibus suis, abl. abs.

54. **Quae audierim nunquam,** 'such as I have never heard.' The subjunctive is used thus, in relative propositions, to complete the idea of a certain quality. Here the adjective 'nova' partly expresses the idea; 'quae audierim' is subjoined in order to define it more precisely. Observe that in the next sentence the indic. is used (**quae audivi**), because it is not a quality or a class, but particular things that are signified. See Madvig, § 364.

We may remark that Pliny seems to have considered it praiseworthy in Corellius to escape continued suffering by suicide. The practice had become quite common at this time; but it would be a mistake to think that it was countenanced by the Stoics. Mr. Merivale remarks that 'we need not pass too austere a judgment on the sick and aged who thus courted present relief from suffering, and even made their escape from a painful existence with a show of dignity and fortitude. But we must guard ourselves against confounding such ordinary mortals with the genuine patriots and sages, who proved themselves generally superior to this morbid intemperance.' It was, he thinks, a mere fashion, the result of satiety and weariness, or, at best, of false reasoning, not of political indignation and hopelessness. See Merivale's Hist. Emp. c. 62.

Ep. 8. 1. Magnum proventum poetarum, 'a great crop,' or **8** 'abundance, of poets.' The original use of the word is of the growth of corn, fruits, or increase of animals;

> 'Proventuque oneret sulcos, atque horrea vincat'
>
> Virg. Georg. 2. 518.

The number of persons who employed or amused themselves with literature at Rome, in the time of Pliny, is very remarkable. The Roman nobles were highly educated, and the jealousy of the Emperors, depriving the aristocracy of active interest in public affairs, turned their thoughts the more towards literary exertion. Almost every distinguished man among them wrote either prose or verse; and as the remembrance of freedom became fainter, the style of these compositions improved in a certain artificial polish and exactness, while they became less vigorous and daring in thought. Mr. Merivale contrasts in this respect the writings of the Flavian age (A.D. 70-96) with those of the previous generations; Hist. Emp. c. 54 and c. 64.

2. Quo non recitaret aliquis. The subj. is the proper mood of dependent relative clauses, (1) when a *quality* is to be expressed, belonging to the subject of the principal sentence, as 'non is es qui gloriere;' (2) when it is stated that there is, or is not, something of which the relative clause may be asserted, as 'nemo est orator qui se Demosthenis similem esse nolit' Cic. de Opt. Gen. Or. 2. Madvig, §§ 364, 365.

It was the custom of poets and historians at Rome to read their works aloud to a select circle of friends in their own houses, or to larger audiences in public rooms hired for the purpose. Pliny makes frequent allusions to these recitations, and considered it a duty of friendship to attend them. It was not so usual to recite orations, and he excuses himself on one occasion for thus reading a speech which he had previously delivered, in order to profit by the remarks of the hearers before publishing it. Bks. 7. 17 and 8. 12. Juvenal speaks bitterly of the tediousness of some of the poets (1. 1-13); and elsewhere of the interest felt when eminent authors, like Statius, recited:

> 'Curritur ad vocem iucundam et carmen amicae
> Thebaidos, laetam fecit quum Statius urbem'
>
> Juv. 7. 82.

3. Proferunt se, 'bring themselves forward.' Used by Seneca of self-taught men, 'quibus ex se ipsis impetus fuit, qui seipsos protulerunt' Ep. 52. Also by Pliny, 'materiam se proferendi' Ep. 77. 7, 'an opportunity for bringing himself into notice.' And by Tacitus, 'Montanum, quia protulerit ingenium extortem agi' Ann. 16. 29.

Stationibus, places of public resort, for conversation or amusement. 'Domos stationesque circumeo' Bk. 2. 9.

'Convictus, thermae, stationes, omne theatrum
De Rutilo' Juv. 11. 4.

13. **Noninnum.** M. Servilius Nonianus was celebrated both as an historian and an orator. When relating his death (A.D. 60), Tacitus speaks of him as 'diu foro, mox tradendis rebus Romanis celebris et elegantia vitae' Ann. 14. 19. Quintilian, who had heard him, considered him a man of marked genius ; but his style, though rich, was somewhat too diffuse for history : 'Clari vir ingenii, et sententiis creber, sed minus pressus quam historiae auctoritas postulat' 10. 1. He was consul A.D. 35, under Tiberius.

16. **Quia non perdiderit.** The subj. does not necessarily follow 'quia.' It expresses not the actual or objective cause of the complaint, but the idea which was the ground of it, and is used here with a delicate irony : 'they complain that they have lost a day on the ground that—they have not lost it.'

20. **Ut non simul et nos amet.** 'Ut non' is used thus after negative propositions to denote an inevitable consequence. 'There is no one who loves literature, but he must also love me.' 'Ruere illa non possunt, ut haec non eodem labefacta motu concidant' Cic. pro L. Man. 7. Madvig. § 440. 3.

24. **Non auditor . . . . creditor,** 'to have been there not to listen but to put them under an obligation.' Pliny shows more delicacy than Juvenal, who wants an equivalent for his attendance : 'Nunquamne reponam' Juv. 1. 1.

9 **Ep. 9.** Junius Mauricus, to whom this letter is addressed, was (like his brother Arulenus Rusticus) a man of courage and independence of character. He was one of the set of good men banished by Domitian at the close of his reign, when his brother Rusticus was put to death. Even towards Vespasian he had shown his boldness, in requesting that the emperor's journals might be inspected in order to bring the informers to justice. He returned from banishment in the reign of Nerva, and used similar freedom towards him. 'Quo viro nihil firmius, nihil verius' is Pliny's description of him (Ep. 42. 9). This letter and another (Ep. 22), answering an enquiry made by Mauricus for a tutor for his brother's orphan children, show the care with which he attended to their interests.

8. **Aruleno Rustico.** Rusticus is mentioned by Tacitus in his account of the murder of Thrasea by Nero, as then an ardent young man who would have interposed his veto, as tribune, on the decree of the senate condemning Thrasea, unless the latter had forbidden him, as it would only have led to his own destruction. In the civil wars that followed Nero's death, Rusticus was praetor when Vespasian's forces advanced on Rome, and being sent by Vitellius to offer them conditions of peace, was wounded and nearly killed. With others of the best men in Rome he was put to death by Domitian, for writing in praise of Thrasea. For a general view of the sufferings of Pliny's friends see on Ep. 28.

12. **A vobis,** the brothers above mentioned, Junius Mauricus and Arulenus Rusticus.

13. **Brixia**, Brescia, eighteen miles west of the Lago di Garda (Benacus).

Nostra Italia, sc. 'Italia transpadana,' Pliny's native country. Cp. 'Veronensibus nostris' 6. 34.

16. **Equestris ordinis princeps**, 'a chief man of the equestrian order.' It does not appear to denote an office. The term 'princeps iuventutis' was different, and was given at this time to princes of the emperor's family Tac. Ann. 1. 3.

Adlectus. The word was used technically of persons chosen to fill up vacant places in the senate or other orders.

17. Praetorios. 'men of the rank of praetor;' not necessarily who had held the office of praetor. The ornaments and rank of praetor, sometimes of consul or of quaestor, were granted occasionally as honorary distinctions. Such distinctions gave the right of a seat in the senate. Cp. 'ornamenta praetoria' Bk. 7. 29. Tac. Ann. 12. 21.

18. **Huic nostrae … dignitati**, 'this (shall I call it parade or) dignity of mine:' namely, that of senator. Pliny was unwilling to own to himself how little of its ancient power the senate now retained, and threw himself into his duties as heartily as if the republic still existed. The senate had been thinned by the cruelties of Nero, and by the civil wars that followed. Vespasian, after the example of Augustus and Claudius, caused an enquiry to be made into the fortunes and characters of the senators, degrading some and appointing others, and he extended this measure also to the knights. Many of his new senators were provincials, a class of men who had been first admitted by Julius Caesar. Such persons resided at Rome, and were not usually allowed to return home without express leave. Such measures were exceedingly useful, both in interesting the provinces in the affairs of government, and in infusing new blood into the senate, since the provincial senators were men of simpler habits than the Roman nobles. Tac. Ann. 3. 55; 11. 25. Suet. Vesp. 11.

20. **Municipio Patavino**, 'the free town of Padua,' best known as Livy's birthplace. Pliny's remarks on the character of the inhabitants of North Italy is interesting, as from his writings he appears himself to have retained many of the pure and simple tastes which marked his countrymen.

Loci mores, exemplified by the noble Thrasea Paetus, also a native of Padua. Tacitus calls him 'virtus ipsa' Ann. 16. 21.

27. **Iam pro se**, &c. 'Iam' is the emphatic word. He already holds a distinguished position, and will give you no trouble in assisting him to obtain office.

31. **Nescio an adiiciam**, 'I think I *may* add.' See Madvig, § 453.

32. **Cum imaginor**, 'when I picture to myself.' The word is used several times by Pliny, but is not common in earlier writers. Epp. 18. 19 and 54. 11.

35. **Census**. For admission both to the equestrian and senatorian rank a certain fortune was necessary. For the knights it was 400 sestertia, for the senators it was fixed by Augustus at 1200 sestertia, i.e. 1,200,000 sestertii.

'Si quadringentis sex septem millia desunt
Plebs eris'   Hor. Ep. 1. 1. 58.

37. Ilis, sc. posteris.

38. Condicionibus, alliance in marriage. Cp. 'Inter altissimas condiciones' Ep. 6. 28.

Hic quoque ponendus est calculus, ' this too must be taken into account:' literally, 'this counter must be placed.' 'Parem calculum ponere,' 'to pay an equivalent' Ep. 45. 1. 'Omnes, quos ego movi, calculos pone' Bk. 2. 19, 'take into account every argument that I have suggested.'

43. Onerare, ' to overload.'

10   Ep. 10. 1. Promittis; understand 'te venturum esse.' The ellipsis is not unusual. 'Ad cenam alio promisi foras' Plaut. Stich. 4. 2. 16. 'Ad cenam mihi promitte' Phaedr. 4. 24. 15.

4. Nam hanc quoque . . . . . ferculo, 'you will have to reckon in your account this too (nivem), which melted in the dish.'

5. Betacei. Properly an adjective, but used, like 'malvaceus' from 'malva,' as a diminutive substantive for 'beta.' Perhaps agreeing with 'pedes' understood : 'beet-root.'

6. Bulbi, edible roots (as onions and others); it is uncertain of what exact kind.

Audisses comoedos vel lectorem. Such amusements at meals were common among the Romans, and with Pliny himself. 'Cenanti mihi, si cum uxore vel paucis, liber legitur: post cenam comoedus aut lyristes' Ep. 82. 19.

'Ecce inter pocula quaerunt
Romulidae saturi quid dia poemata narrent'   Pers. 1. 30.
But see on Ep. 24. 36.

8. Gaditanas, ' dancers from Cadiz.'

13. Incautius, ' with less constraint.'

Mihi semper excusa. ' don't come near me again.'

11   Ep. 11. Erucius, to whom this letter is addressed, is probably Sextus Erucius Clarus, of whom Pliny speaks in the highest terms in Bk. 2. 9. The family of the Clari at this time were eminent not only in rank, but also for virtue and talents. The uncle of Sextus was Septicius, to whom Pliny dedicates his letters (1. 1), 'the most truthful, single-minded, candid, faithful of men;' and Marcius the father of Sextus was a man of uprightness and ability; Bk. 2. 9. Sextus himself, for whom Pliny obtained from Trajan the 'latus clavus,' giving him admission into the senate, was praefect of the city and twice consul: he was remarkable for his devotion to ancient literature. A. Gellius, 6. 6; 13. 17, quoted in Smith's Dict. Biog. This accomplished family formed part of that circle of literary friends in which Pliny lived: they seem moreover to have been generally men of high character in public and private.

1. Hunc dico nostrum, ' I mean my friend Pompeius;' perhaps inserted because there were others of the same name. Nothing more is known of

the works of Saturninus than may be gathered from this letter, but there are epistles addressed to him, Bk. 5. 21 ; 7. 7 and 15 ; 9. 38.

5. Sive meditata sive subita proferret, 'whether he spoke from preparation or extempore.'

6. Aptae crebraeque sententiae. 'Sententia' had a technical meaning in writers upon style, and is defined by the author of the treatise 'ad Herennium' (c. 2) as 'Oratio sumpta de vita, quae aut quid sit, aut quid esse oporteat in vita, breviter ostendit,' hence the phrase 'maxima sententiarum,' 'a maxim.' Quintilian classes 'sententiae' among the 'lumina' of a speech, and from his examples it appears that he means not only general maxims, but other pointed sayings, briefly expressed. The orators of this age, he says, were too fond of filling their speeches with these 'sayings,' which should be more sparingly used. 'Ego vero haec lumina orationis velut oculos quosdam esse eloquentiae credo. Sed neque oculos esse toto corpore velim, ne caetera membra officium suum perdant : et, si necesse sit, veterem illum horrorem dicendi malim, quam istam novam licentiam. Sed patet media quaedam via' Quint. 8. 5.

7. Antiqua : opposed to modern or newly coined words. The older words were considered more expressive (propria) than modern ones ; as the use of words of Saxon origin in English instead of those of Latin origin is thought a mark of vigour.

9. Si retractentur, 'if they should be afterwards read ;' literally, 'handled again.' The orations of Pompeius were pleasant both to hear and read.

13. Contionibus, speeches related (or invented) in his history ; orationibus, those which he himself delivered in pleading.

14. Pressior . . . . adductior, 'more brief, compressed, and concise.'

16. Catullus aut Calvus. For Calvus as an orator, see note on Ep. 2. 5. Nothing but a few small fragments of his poems remain : but in spite of Horace's sneer,

'Nil praeter Calvum et doctus cantare Catullum'
Sat. 1. 10. 19.
they were highly esteemed by the ancients for grace and wit.

Catullus was a contemporary of Calvus, having been born at Verona, five years before him, B.C. 87.

18. Data opera, 'on purpose.'

21. Metro solutum ; i. e. they had the elegance of Plautus or Terence, without the metre.

22. Qui illa aut componat, 'because he either composes them or,' &c. The subjunctive in the relative proposition expresses the reason.

25. Antequam scribam. The subjunctive is found with 'antequam' in speaking of a thing which *usually* happens before something else. 'Qui quotidie antequam pronuntient, vocem excitant' Cic. de Or. 1. 59. So 'antequam scirem' may be explained in the second line of this letter. Madvig. § 360 c.

26. **Non tamquam eundem.** There is always something fresh about him.

28. **An . . . . . conquireremus?** 'An' cannot introduce (like 'num' or 'nonne') a simple independent question. Here it introduces a question of a 'supplementary kind, an inquiry what must be the case otherwise, in case some objection is made to the foregoing,' i.e. in this instance to the assumption that an author's being alive ought not to stand in the way of his honour. See Madvig. § 453. 'An' may therefore be rendered 'or.'

30. **Imagines.** Not only were statues of public men frequent in cities and private houses in Italy (cp. Bk. 1. 17), but the great men of literature were honoured in a similar way. Caligula (Suet. Calig. 34) thought of banishing the busts of Virgil and Livy from *all* libraries, which proves that they must have been common.

12 **Ep. 12.** Tranquillus, to whom this letter is addressed, is the historian Caius Suetonius Tranquillus, author of the lives of the Caesars. He was younger than Pliny, perhaps by ten years or more; his father fought at the battle of Bedriacum, at which Otho was defeated, A.D. 69. The son was a literary man, and shunned public offices; at least we hear of his declining a military tribuneship which Pliny could have procured him (Bk. 3. 8). The latter speaks of him, in a letter to Trajan, as a man of the highest integrity and of learning. Trai. 95. He was the author of a number of works on antiquities, biography, and criticism, and as 'Magister Epistolarum' under Hadrian, had access, no doubt, to important documents for his biographical work. Smith's Dict. Biog.

3. καὶ γάρ. Hom. Il. 1. 63.

4. **Refert tamen . . . . somniare,** 'but it is a material point whether it is your habit to dream things that will turn out true or exactly the reverse.' The ancients had a superstition that some dreams were to be interpreted by contraries: to be beaten or killed portended sometimes a piece of good fortune. Apul. Met. 4. p. 155. quoted by Corte.

7. **Iuni Pastoris,** perhaps that Pastor, to whom Mart. Ep. 9. 23 is addressed.

8. **Socrus,** Pompeia Celerina (Ep. 1. 4), mother of Pliny's first (or second) wife, not of Calpurnia. See on Ep. 41.

9. **Eram acturus adulescentulus.** He began to plead in his nineteenth year; and from what he says below, this dream must have related to one of his early causes.

Quadruplici iudicio, 'the four courts.' These formed the tribunal mentioned a few lines below as the iudicium centumvirale, the court in which Pliny usually practised, and which he calls his 'arena.' It was under the presidency of the praetor, and was divided into four sets of 'iudices' ('concilia' or 'iudicia'), who however sometimes sat together in one building and heard the same causes. From other letters of Pliny we learn that these causes were often on trifling or uninteresting matters of business; frequently concerning wills. Cicero (de Or. 1. 38) mentions a number of the kinds of cases tried before the 'centumviri.' They differed from the other judges in being a definite body or 'collegium,' and are said to have derived their name from being chosen three from each of the thirty-five tribes, making 105 originally. Augustus however enlarged the court, and it contained 180 judges. Very young men appear to have practised in it, and Pliny complains of the way in which the pleadings were conducted. He however continued to plead in it occasionally in the time of Trajan, or perhaps later, and was pleased with the crowded audiences which listened to him. Ep. 20 and 62. Smith's Dict. Antiq.

11. Caesaris. Domitian.

Quae singula, 'which separately,' i.e. any one of which.

13. εἶς οἰωνός. Hom. Il. 12. 243.

14. Nam mihi patria. &c. He felt his loyalty as much engaged to the cause of Pastor, as to his country.

20. Stropham, 'excuse.' 'Remotis strophis ac fucis' Sen. Ep. 26.

Agamque .... possis. 'I will so plead your cause (asking that your suit may be delayed) that you may be able to plead it yourself at the time you wish to.'

21. Est enim ... fuit, 'your case certainly is different from mine :' no delay was possible in the court in which I pleaded ; it is in yours (istud).

Ep. 13. 4. Praevaricatio. Observe that 'praevaricatio' is the predicate. 13 The word means the betrayal of his cause by an advocate, and was used most properly of the accuser, but also of the defendant. Pliny frequently uses it in its proper sense, as in Bk. 3. 9 'Accidit enim res contraria et nova, ut accusatore praevaricationis damnato rea absolveretur.' Cicero (Fam. 8. 11) uses 'praevaricator publicae causae' for one who culpably neglects public interests. It is derived from 'varus,' and a ploughman who makes a crooked furrow is said 'praevaricari' by Pliny the elder, who adds 'inde translatum hoc crimen in forum' H. N. 18. 49. Cp. expression borrowed from turf phraseology 'not to run straight.'

9. Auctoritatibus, 'on the support of authorities, such as Lysias,' &c. Instr. ablative.

10. Lysiae. Lysias is likened to Cato by Cicero (Brut. 16), who says of both, 'Acuti sunt, elegantes, faceti, breves.' He wrote a great number of orations for others to use, of which two only are said to have been unsuccessful. He was born at Athens B.C. 458. Thirty-five of his orations are extant, besides fragments of others. Of those of Cato, which were almost equally numerous, only fragments remain. Cicero, who had read more than 150 of them, praises them highly, especially for vigour and weight, but says that even in his time few persons read, or even knew them at all, and admits a certain roughness of style in them. Brut. 17. Smith's Dict. Biog.

11. Sano : used here in its concessive sense, 'it is true that.'

12. Hyperiden. He was a friend of Demosthenes ; only fragments of his orations are extant.

13. Pollionem. C. Asinius Pollio, the friend of Horace and Virgil, had

a high place among Roman orators ('Insigne moestis praesidium reis' Hor. Od. 2. 1, 13). Quintilian praises him for imagination, diligence, vigour and skill, but places him far below Cicero in the brilliant and pleasing qualities of style 'nitore et iucunditate.' He died in the eightieth year of his age, A.D. 4. None of his works remain.

Caelium. M. Caelius Rufus was a younger contemporary of Cicero, having been born B.C. 82, the same year and day as Licinius Calvus. He was a man of talent and eloquence, but extravagant and unprincipled. He was defended by Cicero (pro Caelio) when accused of attempting murder, and was afterwards one of Cicero's correspondents (Fam. 8). Seneca calls him 'orator iracundissimus' (de Ira 3. 8); and the author of the Dial. de Orat. (21) ranks him with Caesar, Calvus, and others, as an orator, although considering him wanting in grace. His speeches have not come down to us. Smith's Dict. Biog.

23. **Inconprehensibilis et lubricus,** 'hard to lay hold of, and slippery in argument.'

27. **In quibus . . . . indicatur,** 'in which a short, bare notification of certain charges is expressed under mere heads.' He refers to Cicero's answer to Postumius. After saying 'Respondebo igitur Postumio primum,' Pro Mur. 27 sub. fin., he omits all the particulars of his recrimination. The speech for Varenus is lost.

Subscriptio was properly the signing of the name of the plaintiff, or a party in the suit, to the charge: then, the accusation itself. The verb is used in its proper sense in Ep. 44. 24, 'cum caeteris subscripsit centumvirale iudicium,' where see note.

30. **Se . . . perorasse,** 'that he had pleaded out the whole cause alone, in the ancient manner.' Until the time of Pompey there was no restriction on the time a speaker might employ. 'Nemo inter paucissimas horas perorare cogebatur, et liberae comperendinationes erant, et modum dicendi sibi quisque sumebat, et numerus neque dierum neque patronorum finiebatur' Dial. de Orat. 38. Pliny complains (Ep. 52) that speeches had become too short, in his time. Cicero's speech for Cornelius is lost, except fragments.

31. **Ne dubitare possimus . . . coartasse,** 'so that we cannot doubt that he compressed.'

36. **Actio** is the speech as delivered in court. **Oratio** the speech as planned and composed before delivery.

39. **Extemporales figurae,** 'extemporaneous turns of expression.' 'Figurae' used as in Ep. 2. 6. 'Extemporalis' is used by Quintilian, but not by Cicero.

41. **Quemnam? recte admones: Polyclitum esse dicebant.** Cicero pretends to interrupt himself, and to ask his solicitor who the statuary was. In Verr. 2. 4, 3.

60. **Iugulum statim video,** &c. This is mentioned by Quintilian as a common metaphor among pleaders. 'Caeterum allegoria parvis quoque ingeniis, et quotidiano sermoni, frequentissime servit: nam illa, in agendis

causis iam detrita, *pedem conferre*, et *iugulum petere*, et *sanguinem mittere*, inde sunt : nec offendunt tamen' Quint. 8. 6.

73. **Eupolide.** The lines quoted are taken from a play called Δῆμος. Eupolis was a contemporary of Aristophanes, who is the **comicus alter** mentioned below. Hor. Sat. 1. 4, 1. Aristoph. Ach. 531.

95. Ἀμετροεπῆ, 'unbridled in talk :' the epithet of Thersites, Hom. Il. 2. 212.

Hunc, Ulysses ; Il. 3. 222.

97. Ille, Menelaus ; Il. 3. 214.

101. At introduces an objection, as before.

Ep. 14. Catilius Severus was great-grandfather of the Emperor M. **14** Aurelius. He aimed at the empire for himself, and in consequence of expressing discontent at the adoption of Antoninus Pius by Hadrian, was removed from the office of praefect of the city by the latter. He had before been consul, A.D. 120. Smith's Dict. Biog.

2. **Aristonis.** Aristo was an eminent lawyer in the time of Trajan, and his works are often mentioned by Ulpian.

4. **Litterae ipsae,** 'literature itself.'

11. **Quam pressa et decora cunctatio,** 'how chastened and becoming is his caution.' 'Periculum observandum pressiore cautela' Apul. Met. 1. 5.

18. **Nihil ad ostentationem ... refert,** 'does nothing with regard to ostentation as a motive.'

21. **Ex istis qui,** &c., professed philosophers. 'Praeferre,' to advertise. 'Modestiam praeferre' Tac. Ann. 13. 45.

Habitu, sc. ' barba, pallio, baculo.'

27. **Cesserit.** For mood and tense see Madvig, § 350 b.

28. **Ut .... transmittat,** 'how he bears.' 'Ecquid denique secessus, voluptates regionisque abundantiam inoffensa transmitteres' Ep. 54. 6. ' Omne hoc tempus inter pugillares et libellos iucundissima quiete transmisi' Ep. 75. 1.

Observe that the English idiom is the converse of the Latin : we speak of passing through an illness, they spoke of letting it pass them.

38. **Impetu quodam.** Cp. note on the fashion of suicide, Ep. 7.

49. **Confusioni,** 'disturbance' of mind. It is thus used in Tac. Hist. 3. 38, and Plin. Panegyr. 86 'Quam ego audio confusionem tuam fuisse, cum digredientem prosequereris.'

Ep. 15. The office of tribunes of the people continued to exist at Rome **15** till the fifth century of our era. Augustus and his successors, however, by assuming it themselves, made the other tribunes comparatively powerless. Tacitus indeed mentions the case of Arulenus Rusticus, in Nero's reign, and of Vulcatius in the first year of Vespasian, showing that the power of 'interceding' by veto, in the Senate, still remained. Tac. Ann. 16. 26; Hist. 4. 9. Cp. 'Ne me cogatis inplorare auxilium tribunorum' Ep. 77. 96.

4. **In ordinem cogi,** 'to be treated with contempt ;' literally, 'be reduced to the position of a common person.' The phrase, properly applicable to the

tribune, is here applied to his office, which makes it impossible to translate the passage literally. Cp. 'Decemviri querentes se in ordinem cogi' Liv. 3. 51.

10. **Clepsydra,** an 'hour-glass,' a vessel used for measuring time by water. See note on 'binas vel singulas' Ep. 52. 18.

13. **Aestus,** 'perplexity,' disturbance of mind. 'Explica aestum meum' Bk. 9. 34. 'Magno curarum fluctuat aestu' Virg. Aen. 8. 19.

15. **Eiurato magistratu,** 'by resigning my office.' Cp. 'Adactus Silanus eiurare magistratum' Tac. Ann. 12. 4. The word also means to decline, or protest against, an authority.

19. **Quam personam tibi inponas,** 'what character you take on yourself.' The word originally means a mask used by actors to speak through 'a personando:' hence 'a character in a play.'

Quae sapienti . . . perferatur, 'which a wise man should fit on with the view of wearing it to the end of the piece.' **Ita** is the emphatic word.

16 **Ep. 16.** 4. **Gloriae suae,** arising not so much from the victory of his army over Vindex (see on 57. 15) as from his refusal of the empire, which was both then and afterwards offered to him ; see below 'cum principis noluisset.' Lord Orrery, in his observations, draws an ingenious parallel between Verginius and Monk Duke of Albemarle.

3. **Perinde felicis,** 'and as happy as he was great.'

5. **Historias,** such as those of Cluvius Rufus mentioned Bk. 9. 19.

Posteritati suae interfuit, 'was himself witness of his fame among posterity.' 'Posteritas' = 'posteritatis memoria' Bk. 5. 8. This pregnant sense of the word is determined by 'certus posteritatis' Ep. 74. 2, and confirmed by 'sola posteritatis cura' Tac. Hist. 2. 53.

7. **Cum principis noluisset.** His two refusals are mentioned Tac. Hist. 1. 8; 2. 51.

9. **Optimum,** Nerva.

13. **Citra dolorem;** lit. 'this side of,' hence 'without attaining,' or 'amounting to;' cp. 'peccavi citra scelus' Ov. Trist. 5. 8, 23.

15. **Acturus gratias,** as was usual on assuming office. Pliny's Panegyric on Trajan was delivered by him on the occasion of his consulship, A.D. 100. 'Officium consulatus iniunxit mihi ut reipublicae nomine principi gratias agerem' Ep. 32. 1.

16. **Et seni et stanti.** Both datives are governed by **elapsus est,** and explain why he failed to hold the book.

23. **Laudator eloquentissimus.** The exquisite conclusion of the life of Agricola by Tacitus justifies his fame in this respect. But this letter is worthy of comparison with that conclusion as regards grace and tenderness, and suggests the belief that Pliny must have written these lines with the thoughts and rhythm of the 'laudatio' of Verginius by Tacitus still fresh in his memory.

27. **Non solum** publice quantum. Either supply 'sed etiam privatim,'

or render thus: 'my affection for him was not merely commensurate with my admiration for his *public* conduct.'

32. **Ad omnes honores accucurrit.** Every candidate for office expected his friends, as a matter of course, to attend him at the election. This attendance was chief among the 'officia' or duties of compliment which friendship enjoined, such as 'officium togae virilis,' 'nuptiarum,' and the rest. While the elections were held in the Campus Martius the duty of these attendant friends consisted of three parts: first, they forwarded the candidate's election by recommending him as 'testes' or 'suffragatores;' secondly, they voted for him themselves; thirdly, they accompanied him to the Capitol, where some form of inauguration was observed. The third book of Varro, De Re Rust. is represented as a conversation among the friends of a candidate for the aedileship, who are waiting close by for the result of the election. After the transference of the elections to the Senate, the custom of complimentary attendance on candidates still survived, and at length the 'suffragatores' became so clamorous as to compel resort to the ballot. Ep. 34.

36. **Quinqueviros.** Commissions were appointed under this name for various purposes in the time of the republic and the empire. The number five seems to have been adhered to because found convenient in case of a division of opinion among the commissioners.

40. **Tibi mandarem,** sc. 'excusandi officium.'

44. **Vivit:** see on Ep. 74. 3, and compare the Positivist conception of immortality.

Ep. 17. This letter is a pendant to Juvenal's fifth Satire. It is a general **17** confirmation of the facts which are there dwelt upon with the minuteness of satire.

2. **Familiaris.** This word has not here a general reference, but describes Pliny's relations with this particular acquaintance.

5. **Minuta,** scraps, such as 'semesus lepus,' 'minor altilis,' Juv. 5. 107.

19. **In ordinem redigenda est.** The phrase is transferred from the constitution of the state to that of the human soul. Appetite must be stripped of its authority, must obey instead of commanding. Cp. 'in ordinem cogi' Ep. 15. 4.

Ep. 18. 1. **Hominem te patientem;** accus. of exclamation, Madvig, **18** § 236.

3. **Invidebis;** constructed by Pliny with a dat. of the person, and an abl. of the thing. So 'invideo aliis bono' Ep. 6. 43. The abl. marks that in respect of which the envy is felt, and sometimes has a preposition prefixed, as 'nisi in hoc Crasso inviderem' Cic. de Or. 2. 56. It is evident that an accus. of limitation would answer the same purpose, hence we find 'invidit collibus umbras' Virg. Ecl. 7. 58. Also the dat. of the person may be exchanged for the accus. which appears in fact to have been the more ancient usage. Quint. Inst. Or. 9. 3.

18. **Praesumo.** This word and its derivatives, in the sense of

'anticipation,' do not belong to classical usage, which preferred 'prae-cipio.'

19   Ep. 10. 2. Ego ... debco, 'there is no one I had rather be in debt to.'

4. Beneficiorum larga materia. The commander of an army had in his patronage the appointment of military tribunes, six to each legion. That these appointments were canvassed for appears from a similar request in favour of Calvisius, Bk. 4. 4.

5. Longum praeterea tempus, during which many tribuneships would fall vacant, as they were only held for six months; cp. 'semestri tribunatu,' l. c.

8. Voconius. Pliny's anxiety for the interests of Voconius led him afterwards to solicit for him from Trajan a seat in the Senate. Trai. 4.

12. Flamen, not one of the 'flamines maiores,' as their office lasted for life.

18. Epistulas quidem scribit; this then was a recognised branch of literature.

Musas ipsas Latine loqui; an adaptation of the eulogy of Plautus recorded by Quint. Inst. Or. 10. 1 'Licet Varro dicat Musas, Aelii Stolonis sententia, Plautino sermone locuturas fuisse, si Latine loqui vellent.'

20. Vincitur, sc. in amando.

21. Trium liberorum ius. The Leges Julia, B.C. 18, and Papia Poppaea, A.D. 9, encouraged marriage and the nurture of children to supply the ravages of the civil wars. They were wide and various in their provisions, and we may probably attribute to them most of the disabilities which we find imposed upon 'caelibes' and 'orbi.' Lipsius, in a learned excursus on Tac. Ann. 3. 25, divides the 'praemia πολυπαιδίας' into several heads. (1) 'Ut in petitione candidati praeferentur, quibus liberi plures.' (2) 'Ut iidem praeferantur in sorte provinciarum.' (3) 'Ut praeeant in omni magistratu;' i.e. seniority between magistrates of equal rank was determined by this test. (4) 'Ut in honoribus petendis gratia sit annorum iis qui liberos habent.' So Calestrius Tiro, Bk. 7. 16, though not of full age for the tribunate of the people, was qualified by the possession of children. (5) 'Ut qui plures liberos habet a cura tutela ceterisque muneribus immunis sit.' All the above privileges and immunities were summed up in the expression 'ius trium liberorum.' The senate, and afterwards the emperors, granted this right to distinguished persons. We find that Pliny obtained it for himself Ep. 86, and for Suetonius, Trai. 95. The reply of Trajan in the latter case illustrates the words parce et cum delectu in this letter.

23. Tanquam eligeret; sc. 'ipse eligeret.'

20   Ep. 20. 1. Centumviralibus causis: see on Ep. 12. 9.

7. Expresse; 'expressus' and its adverb 'expresse' are terms of art in general, and as such are applied to very different branches of art, such as sculpture, painting, rhetoric, and elocution. There seems to be no one English word which can follow 'expressus' through all these various applications. The predominant sense is that of 'distinctness as the result of pains

18

bestowed.' Thus, in reference to statues, Ep. 26. 2, 'expressum' may almost be translated 'bold.' Again in Ep. 48. 10, where the metaphor is from painting, 'expressius ad exemplar,' 'more vividly true to the original.' Again, in this passage 'expresse' means 'with point and clearness,' as also 'expressa' Bk. 4. 27; a meaning closely connected with that which it bears in reference to elocution, namely distinctness and beauty of articulation.

8. **Auspicari.** An instance of that decay of language by which a special expands to a general sense. Here 'auspicari' means simply 'to begin.' Cp. 'auspicabar in Virginem desilire' Sen. Ep. 83.

16. **Actoribus** similes. The pleaders were paid by their clients, just as the audience were by the pleaders. This, though illegal, was most frequent, as we learn from Bk. 5. 4 and 9 and 13. Pliny however says, 'in causis agendis non modo pactione, dono, munere, verum etiam xeniis semper abstinui' Bk. 5. 13.

Manceps, the distributor of the 'sportulae.'

17. **Sportulae.** This word was now applied to any kind of gratuity for whatever purpose, and was no longer restricted to favours from 'patroni' to 'clientes.' For 'sportulae' given with a similar object, cp. Juv. 13. 32.

19. Σοφοκλεῖς **vocantur.** This refers to the 'auditores,' who were called Σοφοκλεῖς from σοφῶς, the usual exclamation of applause, and 'laudiceni,' because that applause was given, not for the speaker's eloquence, but for the dinner which they expected from him.

25. **Numerosa** in this sense belongs to the silver age. In Cicero and Ovid it always means 'rhythmical.'

34. **Corrogaret;** opposed to 'conduceret.' *He* only invited his audience, and did not pay them.

Ex Quintiliano. Quintilian was born at Calagurris in Spain, about A.D. 40. He was educated in Rome, where he was a disciple of Domitius Afer, as we learn from this letter and other sources. He revisited Spain, but came back to Rome in the train of Galba. He began to practise at the bar, but was yet more distinguished as a teacher of rhetoric. Vespasian gave him a salary from the imperial exchequer, not however large enough to justify Juvenal in describing him as the possessor of 'tot saltus' Juv. 8. 188, an exaggeration which is also inconsistent with Pliny's offer (Bk. 6. 32) of £400 towards his daughter's wedding outfit. Quintilian's great extant work is 'De Institutione Oratoria Libri XII,' which for matter and style deserves more attention than it generally receives.

36. **Domitium Afrum,** an orator who flourished under Tiberius and his successors. He died in the reign of Nero. Quintilian often refers to him. 'Eorum (sc. oratorum) quos viderim, Domitius Afer et Iulius Africanus longe praestantissimi.'

38. **Ex proximo,** 'from close by.' See on Ep. 4. 4.

43. **Hoc artificium,** forensic oratory.

45. **Fracta pronuntiatione;** in which the words were broken or mutilated, as in singing.

47. **Plausus**, in the proper sense, 'clapping of the hands.' The applause of which Pliny has been complaining was given by cheers and shouts.

21 **Ep. 21.** We learn from Bk. 9. 40 that Pliny generally spent the winter in his Laurentine, and the summer in his Tuscan villa. In the winter it was desirable to be near Rome on account of 'necessitas agendi, quae frequens hieme.'

3. **Litoris spatium**, the extent of shore belonging to the estate. 'Litus' sometimes stands for the seaside estate itself; 'de electione litorum' Tac. Ann. 3. 63.

5. **Salvo iam et composito die**, 'while the day is still in your possession and in its vigour.' Cp. 'virum aetate composita' Tac. Ann. 13. 1. The only difficulty in assigning to 'compositus' the sense here given, is that the word naturally contrasts itself with youth and dawn, not, as in this passage, with age and decline. But when 'compositus' has once been established in its sense of 'mature,' 'vigorous,' it is plain that it may be equally well contrasted with either extreme, morning or evening, of life or of the day. The context clearly forbids a comparison with Virg. Aen. 1. 374.

8. **Utrimque**, whether you come by the 'Via Laurentina' or the 'Via Ostiensis.'

9. **Iunctis**, 'for harnessed horses,' contrasted with 'equo.' From this contrast we infer the meaning 'et iunctos et solutos' Ep. 36. 8, 'both harness and saddle nags.'

14. **Non sumptuosa tutela**, 'and does not cost much to keep up.' Observe the descriptive abl., for which see Madvig. § 272 and § 287, Obs. 2. The gen. might have been used, as the words here do *not* describe the constitution of the villa with reference to its external parts.' For 'tutela' in this sense cp. 'ut villarum tutela non sit oneri' Plin. N. H. 18. 5.

16. **Porticus**, plur. two porticoes, placed thus ⟨ D, the area being the space of ground between them. The likeness of the letter D means simply a semicircle.

18. **Specularibus**, windows of 'lapis specularis,' mica, which was split into thin plates for the purpose.

19. **Contra medias.** The entrance to the 'cavaedium' was opposite the middle of the two semicircular porticoes, so that in approaching it from the 'atrium' you passed through the convex side of the first portico exactly in the middle, then crossed the area between the two, and found the entrance of the 'cavaedium' opposite to you in the middle of the concave side of the further portico.

24. **A tergo.** If the visitor turned quite round after entering the dining-room, a beautiful vista was presented to him. The eye passed through the 'cavaedium' and one portico, then across the area, through another portico, and an 'atrium,' and finally rested on the woods and hills which stretched inland.

26. **A laeva**, on the left of the dining-room as you enter; i.e. on its south or south-east side.

Retractius paullo: it did not project so far seawards as the dining-room, hence the **angulus** mentioned below.

33. **Exceptis qui.** The corner would be sheltered on every side except the south-west, which was the rainy quarter.

Serenum: cp. 'aperta serena' Virg. G. 1. 393.

38. **Dormitorium membrum**, a bed-chamber.

Suspensus et tubulatus: see on Ep. 30. 8. The 'tubi' were earthenware pipes for conveying hot air.

41. **Plerisque tam mundis**; supply 'cellis' or 'cubiculis.' The substantive is omitted, as the context leaves no doubt of the sense. There may be truth in Buchner's explanation that these rooms, although not large enough for 'cubicula,' were yet too good to be called 'cellae;' hence the omission. Here again is a descriptive abl. connected with the words 'reliqua pars.'

49. **Baptisteria**, baths large enough for immersion, but not for swimming. For the latter purpose the sea was close at hand, and therefore the 'piscina' of cold water usually placed in the 'cella frigidaria' was unnecessary.

51. **Hypocauston**: see on Ep. 30. 8.

Propnigeon, a passage leading from the 'cella frigidaria' to the furnace.

52. **Duae cellae**; the 'tepidarium,' called 'cella media' Bk. 5. 6, and the 'caldarium.' There were thus three principal apartments in a complete bath, 'frigidarium,' 'tepidarium,' 'caldarium,' besides necessary adjuncts, such as an 'unctorium' and a 'propnigeon.' It is not clear whether the 'tepidarium' contained a tepid bath, or whether it was merely a warm room to sit in.

54. **Sphaeristerium**: see Ep. 24. 29. As the exercise of ball play immediately preceded the bath, this was the natural place for the 'sphaeristerium.'

59. **Apotheca**; here was kept the wine in 'amphorae' (in bottle). The 'apotheca' was generally, as here, on the first-floor, and near the baths, that the wine might benefit by the smoke of the furnace. 'Dolia' (wine in cask) were kept in the 'cella vinaria' on the ground-floor. See Becker's Gallus, Sc. 9, Exc. 4.

62. **Gestatio**, an avenue or drive running round the garden.

66. **Vinea**; the vine was sometimes allowed to run wild on the ground without supports, 'vignes courantes.' This was one of the five recognised methods of cultivation. See Pliny N. H. 17. 6.

69. **Hac . . . facie**. 'this view,' i. e. of the garden.

71. **Vestibulum**; in town houses this was merely the vacant space before the door, but in a villa perhaps there may have been something of a porch.

72. **Cryptoporticus.** The usual portico had a wall on one side, and an open row of columns on the other; but the 'cryptoporticus' was completely walled in.

Propo publici operis. It almost rivalled the splendid works of this kind which then existed in the Forum and Campus. The 'cryptoporticus' of this villa seems to have run out from it at right angles on its north or north-western side, and to have been carried on parallel with the coast, which may be supposed to have run from N.W. to S.E. The Xystus lay between it and the sea, and on the inland side was the garden. It could not well have been on the south-eastern side, as we are told above that that was appropriated to the slaves.

74. **Alternis**, 'alternately.' The meaning seems to be that the windows towards the sea were in groups of two or three (' plures '); that the opposite wall had but single windows corresponding to these groups, and even these single windows were not opposite to each group, but only to every other group.

77. **Xystus**, a terrace with flower-beds and ornamental shrubs. Vitruvius notices the different senses of the word in Greek and Latin respectively. 'Ξυστός enim Graeca appellatione est porticus ampla latitudine in qua athletae per hiberna tempora exercentur. Nostri autem hypaethras ambulationes xystos appellant' Vitr. 6. 10. The name is derived from the smooth floor, ξύω.

89. **In capite xysti deinceps cryptoporticus**; 'at the head of the terrace and then at the head of the covered walk.' 'Cryptoporticus' is a gen. governed by 'in capite.' The terrace and portico were parallel and conterminous, both being closed by the wall of the garden-house (horti diaeta), which cut straight across them. 'Deinceps' in this passage means little more than 'deinde,' and has not its usual sense of 'one after another.'

91. **Heliocaminus**, a room exposed on every side to the sun, and therefore suitable for winter use without artificial warmth.

93. **Zotheca**. This name was originally applied to cages or closets for keeping fatted poultry. Hence it was transferred to small rooms for purposes of study or retirement.

96. **A tergo villae**; those of which he speaks below, ' nunc continua, nunc intermissa tecta villarum.'

102. **Andron**, an alley or passage running between the wall of the bedchamber and that of the garden. An ' andron ' in the Greek sense would, of course, have been far from contributing to the quiet of the room. This word, like ' xystus ' above, is noticed by Vitr. 6. 10, as having acquired a different sense in the phraseology of Roman architecture.

109. **Abesse**. This suite of rooms was removed from the villa by the whole length of the ' cryptoporticus.'

112. **Haec utilitas**, sc. ' villae.'

114. **Sunt enim in summo**, 'for they are surface springs.' ' Putei' were wells in which the water lay deep: but the shallow wells here described were properly called ' fontes.' The substantive ' summum ' is frequently used for the surface of water, and here for the surface of the ground in which the water appears.

119. **Quem . . . discernit,** ' between which and my house there is only one villa.'

122. **Calfacere dissuadeat**; poetical or loose syntax for ' ne calfacias dissuadeat.' ' Suadeo ' with the infin. is frequent in Virgil.

Ep. 22. 1. Praeceptorem. The education of the higher classes was **22** generally conducted at home by a private tutor, until the boys were fit to join the classes of the professors. The ' praeceptor ' here intended is a *public* teacher. So in speaking of a similar request made by the daughter of Corellius on behalf of her son, Pliny says, ' iam studia extra limen proferenda sunt, iam circumspiciendus rhetor Latinus ' Bk. 3. 3. Pliny himself had attended the public lectures of Quintilian; and it was that which he now recalled with pleasure.

2. **Fratris tui liberis**, the sons of Arulenus Rusticus (probably) by his wife Gratilla. Editors previous to Keil printed Gratilla for Galla, Ep. 44. 2. In that case it was necessary to assume that Asudius Curianus there mentioned must have been born to Gratilla by a former husband, before her marriage with Rusticus, so that even in that case Asudius Curianus could not have been one of these ' liberi.' Rusticus had also left a daughter under the care of Mauricus, for whom Pliny was commissioned to find a husband. See Ep. 9, note.

3. **Illam dulcissimam aetatem**, sc. ' pueritiam.'

Resumo is used of the ' Pleasures of Memory,' as ' praesumo ' of the ' Pleasures of Hope.' See on Ep. 18. 18.

6. **Coram multis ordinis nostri**; who came, for their own profit, as the father of Julius Naso came to Quintilian's lecture room, or to hear their son's performances. Cp.

' Quae pater adductis sudans audiret amicis ' Pers. 3. 47.

9. **Probe,** ' probitate illaesa.'

10. **Profitentur.** A word which in Cicero's time required an accusative to explain its sense, now by itself conveyed an unmistakable meaning. This alone would be sufficient evidence of the progress of education in Rome between the two dates.

15. **Dicerem tui**; a far-fetched conceit. He would call them Mauricus' children, if he did not think that he loved them better as his lost brother's children, than he would do if he regarded them as his own.

Ep. 23. 1. Assem para: see on ' circulator ' Ep. 37. 26. **23**

Auream; so Apuleius calls the Ass of his romance ' aureus,' superior to all others.

3. **Verania Pisonis.** ' Piso's wife.' Cp. ' Liceat tumulo scripsisse Catonis Marcia ' Lucan 2. 343.

Graviter iacebat. In the looser style of this period an adverb is used with ' iaceo,' which properly belongs to the synonym ' aegroto.'

4. **Adoptavit.** A mutiny in Germany caused Galba to adopt Piso as his son and colleague. Only four days intervened between his adoption and the outbreak of Otho's conspiracy, in which both Galba and Piso were slain.

Regulus, M. Aquilius, the foremost of that crowd of 'delatores,' which gathered round the bad emperors. He was a creature of Domitian, and is accordingly flattered by Martial in four epigrams, which chiefly relate to his escape from the fall of a portico. Pliny in sketching this man's character unconsciously gives us a foil to his own. He was utterly wanting in Pliny's high qualities of honour, liberality, humanity, and truthfulness. Bk. 1. 5 gives an amusing account of his apprehension after the loss of his patron Domitian. For the rise and influence of the delatores, see an admirable sketch in Merivale, Hist. Emp. c. 44.

5. **Inpudentiam**: cp. 'hominem te patientem' Ep. 18. 1.

10. **Climactericum**. All multiples of 7 and 9 were called climacteric years, and thought dangerous to life. $7 \times 9 = 63$ was therefore the grand climacteric, cp. Gell. 3. 10. Regulus employed the term in his jargon to frighten Aurelia.

29. **Scholastica lege**. A common and erroneous interpretation is 'like an idle fellow,' which gives 'tertiam' no more sense than 'aliam.' This is much too pointless for our author's style. There must be an allusion to some unknown precept of the schools, perhaps one requiring that a thesis should be illustrated by at least three instances; cp. Ep. 31, which is in fact a theme on the subject 'alia clariora, alia maiora,' illustrated by *three* incidents from the life of Arria the elder.

30. **Ornata**, adjectival, not participial, in sense; 'a lady of rank.'

Aurelia: we learn from another source also that she was an object of attention to 'captatores.' Juv. 5. 98.

42. **Consuleret quam cito**, 'was inquiring how soon.'

43. **Aliena testamenta**, 'other people's wills.'

Inprobissimum genus falsi, 'a most impudent kind of trickery.' 'Falsum' was a wider word than 'forgery,' embracing also base coinage, and, as we learn from this passage, undue influence.

46. **Ipsis quorum sunt illa**. This is put thus emphatically to mark how Regulus reversed the natural order of things. Usually the testator dictated to some one else the terms of his will; but here we find Regulus dictating them to the testator. 'Dicto' is the technical word for such transactions. Cp. 'rivalis dictabitur heres' Juv. 6. 218.

24 **Ep. 24. 8. Sera**, 'too late.'

11. **Lectulo**; not in bed, but on his writing couch. They used for the purposes of study, not chairs and desks, but a couch, 'lectus,' 'lectulus,' 'lecticula.' Cp. 'iacere in lectulo suo compositus in habitum studentis' Ep. 46. 21.

12. **Calceos**; always worn in public with the toga. They covered the whole foot, while the 'soleae,' worn at other times, were merely sandals.

21. **Hoc** is explained by **ne praecipere videatur**.

25. **Lyrica**. Four mutilated lyrical fragments bearing the title 'Vestricius Spurinna De contemptu Saeculi' were discovered and edited by Barthius in 1613. They are probably early forgeries suggested by this passage, and

so composed as to accord with what is here said of Spurinna. See Wernsdorf's Poet. Lat. Min., vol. 3.

26. **Gratiam cumulat.** This makes it probable that Spurinna's verses were somewhat free in their tone. Elsewhere (Bk. 4. 14) we find that Pliny considered such freedom not only consistent with purity of life, but also, as it were, an agreeable relief.

27. **Nuntiata est;** a slave watched the 'solarium' or the 'clepsydra,' and announced the expiration of each hour.

29. **Movetur pila;** as was usual before bathing. Old men commonly played with the 'follis,' a larger and lighter ball, requiring less exertion than the 'pila.'

34. **Puro,** 'plain,' without ornament. Spurinna's simple and refined taste preferred this to the more admired 'caelatum' or 'asperum argentum.' See Becker's Gallus, Sc. 2. n. 12.

35. **Corinthia;** vessels made of the rare and costly Corinthian bronze. Even Pliny had nothing in his villa of this material, and when he bought a 'Corinthium signum,' placed it in a temple as 'dignum deo donum' Ep. 26. 17. The secret of manufacturing Corinthia had long been lost, hence their value.

Adficitur; a word of strong emotion, here contrasted with the *moderate* pleasure signified by 'delectatur.' Cp. 'delectare oculos imperitorum' Ep. 26. 12.

36. **Comoedis.** We have frequent mention in these letters of entertainments performed during dinner. At some houses ballet dancers ('Gaditanae') were introduced, Ep. 10. 8; or clowns ('scurrae vel moriones') strayed about the room, Bk. 9. 17. But persons of a higher taste, such as Pliny and his friends, diverted themselves with more instructive amusements, 'ut voluptates quoque studiis condiantur.' They resorted to standard authors, from which history was read by the 'lector,' poetry sung to music by the 'lyristes,' or some passage of comedy rendered memoriter by the 'comoedus.' Chosen slaves were trained for these several duties. Cp. for 'lector,' Cic. Fam. 5. 9; for 'comoedus,' Ep. 50. 8.

Ep. 25. 3. Indicis partibus. The words 'titulus' and 'index,' with **25** reference to books, have two distinct senses. It cannot be said that the one sense is always represented by 'titulus,' and the other by 'index,' but at least the meanings themselves are clearly separate, by whichever name either may be designated. There was first the title written on the strip of paper or parchment, and affixed to the outside of the roll, and this was usually called 'titulus;' secondly, there was the table of contents, found in some books, written inside the book, probably at the beginning, and this is the usual sense of 'index,' or 'indices.' Such were the indices composed by Pliny the elder for his Natural History, and by Gellius for his Noctes Atticae. It is easy to see that from such an index of the contents of one book might grow an index describing, as in this letter, all the works of one author, or even an index of the works of various authors of the same class, such as that alluded to by Seneca, 'sume in manus indicem philosophorum' Sen. Ep.

39. Cp. also Quint. Inst. Or. 10. 1. Salmasius' Prolegomena to Solinus contain much that is valuable on this subject.

7. **Pomponi Secundi**; a general and a poet, whom Quintilian pronounced to have excelled in tragedy all his contemporaries. Pliny the elder speaks of this life of Pomponius, N. H. 14. 7.

12. **Drusi Neronis**, stepson of Augustus and brother of the emperor Tiberius. He died at the age of twenty-nine, after a brilliant campaign in Germany

Germaniae latissime victor. Although ' victor' here retains its original subst. meaning and construction, governing the genitive, yet we find the adverb ' latissime ' affixed to it. It is a stronger case than 'minime largitor dux' Liv. 6. 2, where ' largitor' loses its independence and adheres closely to ' dux.' Cp. ' populum late regem ' Virg. Aen. 1. 21.

14. **Studiosi tres**; three books of the ' Studiosus,' a title of a work of the same nature as the ' Orator ' of Cicero.

In sex volumina. ' Liber' and ' volumen ' were originally synonymous, both meaning a single roll of MSS. Subsequently ' volumen ' only was retained for this meaning, while the extent of the ' liber ' was fixed by the limits of the subject and the design of the author, not by the accidental size of the roll on which he wrote. Hence, as here, one ' liber ' might extend through two rolls, ' volumina ;' or again, one ' volumen ' might embrace all the forty-eight books of Homer's works. Ulp. Dig. 32. 50.

16. **Dubii sermonis**, ' on bad grammar.' For this sense of ' dubius' cp. ' dubio de petasone' Mart. 3. 77. Pliny the elder himself, in his only extant work, speaks of ' libellos quos de Grammatica edidi ' Plin. N. H. Praef.

18. **A fine . . . . Bassi**, 'a continuation of the history of Aufidius Bassus.'

22. **Scrupulosa** = ' aspera,' troublesome, and therefore easily derived, in this sense, from ' scrupulus,' a sharp pebble. The sense of ' minute,' ' scrupulous,' which this word bears in late Latin seems to require a connection with ' scrupulus ' in a different sense, viz. $\frac{1}{24}$ of an ounce.

27. **Vulcanalibus**, Aug. 23.

Non auspicandi causa. Other people began the use of candle-light on that morning because it was sacred to the god of flame, and then left it off again. But Pliny really began to study before daybreak at that date. The ambitious father, in Juvenal, does not make his son get up to work by candle-light till later in the year, ' post finem auctumni' Sat. 14. 190, where see Mayor's note.

28. **Statim a nocte multa.** At once, before the days really grew short, he took, even in August, a great portion of the night for study ; but in the winter he took as much as five-twelfths of it for that purpose. The Roman days and nights were reckoned from sunrise and sunset respectively; and day and night were each divided into twelve hours, which therefore varied in length at the different seasons with the variations of the days and nights themselves. If we had merely ' sexta,' ' midnight' would be sufficient without

further comment; but for the above reason it is impossible to give English hours corresponding to 'septima' and 'octava' throughout a lapse of time, though if one day only had been specified the calculation might easily be made. The point therefore which we must seize is the proportion of the night which he devoted to study in the winter time, remembering always that it was taken from the end of the night and not from the beginning.

30. **Paratissimi.** 'Paratus' in this author is often a thorough adjective with the sense of 'ready.' Cp. 'parata oblivio mortuorum' Ep. 57. 17.

31. **Ante lucem**: cp. Suet. Vesp. 21.

34. **Cibum**, luncheon, taken about noon.

35. **Facilem**, simple, easy to be got. So 'Afrae aves' are said to be admired, 'quod non sunt faciles' Petr. 93.

43. **Perperam**; used of unconscious mistakes, especially in language. Contrast with the ignorance implied in this word the opposite sense of 'perverse.' See on Ep. 36. 20.

47. **Decem amplius versus**, 'more than ten lines.' 'If a magnitude which is expressed by a numeral is increased by "plus" or "amplius," then either "plus" or "amplius," with or without "quam," is added to the name of the magnitude without any influence on its case, which remains the same which the context would require without the comparative; cp. "plus septingenti capti sunt" Liv. 41. 12,' Madvig, § 305. Observe that in this passage the usual order is transposed, 'decem amplius,' for 'amplius decem.'

48. **Intra primam**; hence we learn that three hours was thought a short time to devote to dinner.

51. **De interioribus**; the actual immersion.

54. **Notarius.** Short-hand was generally used by these secretaries. Cp. 82. 9. A system of Roman short-hand is printed at the end of Gruter's Corp. Inscr. Unlike our own it consisted of abbreviations for prepositions, terminations, &c. thus, I = amus, λ = emus.

56. **Sella**; in the 'sella' they sat upright, but lay at length in the 'lectica.'

59. **Hac intentione**, 'it was by this unremitting application that,' &c.

61. **Opisthographos.** It was usual for less prolific authors to write on one side only of the paper or parchment. Hence the backs of worthless books were used for school exercises, and Martial thus addresses a volume of his, 'Inversa pueris arande charta' Mart. 4. 87.

64. **Largio Licinio**, mentioned, Ep. 20. 33, as the first to collect claqueurs in the law courts.

66. **Nonne videtur.** The knowledge of his public employments would have led us to expect infinitely less results, but the knowledge of his laboriousness to expect even more.

72. **Ego autem tantum**, a verb must be supplied for 'ego' by a reminiscence of soleo ridere si comparer above, 'but am I so earnestly to deprecate comparison,' &c. Pliny's literary industry will not bear comparison with his uncle's, although he has the excuse of many distractions.

Still less can those literary men who have no distractions bear the comparison.

26   **Ep. 26.** 1. **Corinthium** : see on 'Corinthia' Ep. 24. 35.

2. **Festivum et expressum,** 'elegant and bold.' See on 'expresse' Ep. 20. 7.

8. **Cedentes,** 'recedentes a fronte.'

Isto, 'in your direction.'

26. **Ad paucos dies.** 'Ad' with the accus. would naturally fix the date of his coming, 'after a few days,' 'in a few days time;' cp. 'ad praefinitum diem' Ep. 63. 10, 'ad decem annos' Cic. Att. 5. 2. But the context forbids this sense. It must mean 'for a few days stay,' and is a careless expression which may be explained in either of two ways. It may be an abbreviation for 'ad paucos dies commorandum,' in which case 'ad' will really belong to a suppressed gerund; or, as seems more probable, the words 'ad paucos dies,' 'up to, as long as, a few days,' are thrown in as though he had written them 'adfuturum,' instead of 'venturum.'

27   **Ep. 27.** 1. **Silius Italicus.** His great work, an epic of seventeen books on the Second Punic war, is extant, and confirms by its style and matter what is said in this letter of his devotion to Virgil.

5. **Minorem,** Severus by name, as we learn Mart. 9. 87.

12. **Lectulo,** here, as in Ep. 24. 11, not his bed but his couch, as we see from what follows **cum a scribendo vacaret.** There is no reference here to his illness, which came on him after his retirement to Campania.

Semper, non ex fortuna, to be taken with **frequenti.** His chamber was always a place of resort, and that not on account of his wealth.

14. **Maiore cura quam ingenio.** Merivale takes this as the motto of the literature of what he calls the 'Flavian period.' 'Silius writes with all the principles of art in his head, and all the works of the great models ranged in order round his desk' Hist. Emp. c. 64.

18. **Novi principis,** Trajan, who had received at Cologne, A.D. 98, the news of his accession, but did not enter Rome till more than a year had elapsed.

34. **Modo modo,** 'the other day.' The reduplication sharpens the sense from 'lately' to 'quite lately.' Compare the Italian idiom 'ben bene,' &c.

37. **Per summum facinus.** Attempts were made to implicate Piso, proconsul of Africa, in treason against Vespasian; and when these failed he was murdered in his own house by order of Valerius Festus, who commanded the troops stationed in the province. Baebius Massa, often mentioned by Pliny, was the man who pointed out Piso to the assassins. Tac. Hist. 4. 49 and 50.

47. **Quatenus;** this conjunction passes through the meanings, 'as far as,' 'while,' and 'when,' till it = 'quum.' Then, like 'quum,' it comes to stand for 'quoniam,' 'since.' Cp. 'quatenus, heu nefas, Virtutem incolumem odimus' Hor. Od. 3. 24, 30.

49. **Currentem quoque**; this frequent proverbial expression continues the metaphor introduced by **stimulis**. lit. goads.

50. **Ἀγαθὴ δ' ἔρις**, in allusion to Hesiod's distinction between good and bad strife, competition and contention. Hesiod describes the former thus,

> ἥτε καὶ ἀπάλαμόν περ ὅμως ἐπὶ ἔργον ἐγείρει.

> Hes. Op. et Di. 20.

Ep. 28. 2. **In maius.** This phrase (with 'in melius,' 'in peius,' &c.) is **28** frequent in Pliny and writers of his age. Cp. also Sall. Jug. 73, and ἐπὶ τὸ μεῖζον κοσμεῖν, Thuc. 1. 21.

4. **Quum essent philosophi ab urbe summoti.** In A.D. 86 Domitian revived the decrees of Vespasian against the philosophers.

6. **Fui praetor.** He allowed himself to be promoted by Domitian until that emperor's final outbreak of cruelty in the slaughter of Senecio, Rusticus, and the rest. After this he determined to retire into privacy, yet he was obliged to fulfil the remaining term of his office as praetor. 'Provectus ab illo insidiosissimo principe antequam profiteretur odium bonorum, postquam professus est substiti' Plin. Pan. 95.

8. **Mussantibus.** By the whispering murmurs of persons in doubt, 'musso' passes from the sense of murmuring to that of hesitation, which latter is frequent enough; cp. 'Mussat rex ipse Latinus Quos generos vocet' Virg. Aen. 12. 657.

10. **Septem amicis meis.** This seems a convenient opportunity for some account of that great and ill-fated family, of whose virtues and sorrows these letters so often speak. Ep. 31 contains nearly as much as is known of Caecina Paetus and Arria his wife, who perished for his share in the conspiracy of Scribonianus against the Emperor Claudius A.D. 42. They left a daughter, Arria the younger, already married to Paetus Thrasea, afterwards the noblest of Nero's victims, in the narrative of whose death the last extant book of the Annals of Tacitus comes abruptly to a close. Thrasea's widow, Arria the younger, survived to see the disasters of her family, and the final return of happier days under Nerva. The next member of the family is one of whom Pliny writes with more than usual affection, Ep. 67. Thrasea Paetus left one daughter, Fannia, married before his death to Helvidius Priscus, who escaped his father-in-law's fate only by the alternative of banishment, from which he returned with his wife after the accession of Vespasian. Again the same sentence was pronounced, and a second time Fannia followed her husband into exile, 'bis maritum secuta in exsilium est' Ep. 67. 12. The enemies of Helvidius, and his own indiscretion, changed the sentence to that of death; and Helvidius, under Vespasian, met the fate of his father-in-law Thrasea under Nero. Fannia returned to Rome with Helvidius the younger, her husband's son by a previous marriage. This Helvidius was subsequently married to Anteia, who, like her husband, had to deplore a murdered father, Anteius, Tac. Ann. 16. 14. Fannia's troubles were not ended, for Domitian had yet to reign. She furnished Senecio with materials for a life of her husband, and with her

29

mother Arria suffered a third banishment for her share in the matter, while Senecio expiated his by death, 'tertio ipsa *propter* maritum relegata' Ep. 67.13. At the same time, Fannia's stepson Helvidius the younger was condemned on a trifling charge, and this is the Helvidius to whose murder allusion is made in this letter. With him suffered a close friend of the family, Arulenus Rusticus, on the same charge as Senecio, while the wife of Rusticus, Gratilla, and his brother Junius Mauricus were banished. Nerva's accession brought back the exiles, and the gloomy band of mourners which advances from this single family and its connections enables us to conceive what was that laceration of the state which Domitian completed, ' non iam per intervalla et spiramenta sed continuo et velut uno ictu' Tac. Agr. 44. Four widows, Arria, Fannia, Anteia, Gratilla, mourned for husbands, three of them for fathers, who had perished, while Junius Mauricus lamented a brother. In this society Pliny lived, having himself barely escaped, Ep. 68. 65. His bitterness against the delatores, Regulus, Bk. 1. 5, Certus, Ep. 77, in part causes of so much misery, is easy to understand, and is in no way contrary to his usual humanity.

18. **Quum in Syria tribunus militarem**: see Life of Pliny.

19. **Indolis**; the good sense of this word was so nearly universal, that no qualifying adjective was necessary.

32. **Unde coepi.** Cp. l. 1, benigna natura.

29 **Ep. 29.** 3. **Erunt officia antelucana.** 'early visits of compliment will be going on.' 'Officium' was the common name for the various attentions shown by one friend to another, or by a client to his patron, such as the morning salutation. This took place at daybreak; cp. 'Prima salutantes atque altera continet hora' Mart. 4. 8. Such 'officia' were sometimes even 'antelucana'; cp. 'ante lucem ibat ad Vespasianum' Ep. 25. 31.

In **quae incidere**, 'to fall in with which,' i.e. to meet with the persons engaged in them. Pliny is afraid that Catilius' party will be so late, that when he returns home, he will meet with people already beginning the duties of the next day. It will be seen by the illustration which is given, that more is meant by 'incidere' than is actually expressed by the word.

5. **C. Caesar**; in his Anticato, a reply to Cicero's panegyric of Cato. It was a considerable work, and is quoted by Gell. 4. 16 as an authority for the use of *u* in the dative of the fourth declension.

30 **Ep. 30.** 1. **Nec tantum epistula**, 'sed tragoedia.' A letter cannot do justice to it.

3. **Alioqui.** Here we have 'alioqui et qui' 'in other respects, and in that he' or 'especially in that he,' an imitation of the Greek idiom ἄλλως τε καί. 'Alioqui,' 'in other respects,' 'moreover,' is not frequent till the time of Tacitus and Pliny. Besides its strictly adverbial use with adjectives and verbs, it is sometimes prefixed to a whole clause; 'alioqui narrasses mihi' Ep. 72. 2, 'or else you would have told me.'

8. **Fervens pavimentum.** The floor of the 'caldarium' in a Roman bath, and sometimes the floors of passages (' transitu ... qui suspensus' Ep. 21. 38), were heated from beneath by 'hypocausta,' being raised from the

ground on short pillars, 'pilae quae habeant altitudinem pedum duorum' Vitr. 5. 10. This arrangement may still be seen in the walls and floor at Uriconium (Wroxeter). To this invention Seneca refers, Ep. 90, 'Quaedam nostra demum prodisse memoria scimus; ut *suspensuras* balneorum et impressos parietibus tubos, per quos circumfunderetur calor, qui ima simul et summa foveret aequaliter.'

11. **Quasi** introduces either a word or a proposition, and its use implies either that the word is not exactly applicable, or that the proposition is not exactly true. Here of course it is used for the latter purpose.

17. **Focilatus.** 'Focilo' and its compounds belong to late Latin, and, like other Silver Age words, were probably revived from ante-classical usage. 'Foveo' and 'focus' have been suggested as probable roots; but Casaubon derives 'focilo' from 'fauces' by a process exactly the inverse of that by which we obtain the word 'comforter.'

21. **Non . . . iudicio.** He means that masters are murdered not by way of retribution because they have been cruel, but good and bad alike out of pure instinct to crime.

27. **Ut transitum daret.** 'Anteambulones' went before the litter to clear the way. They were not always so gentle as the slave here mentioned. Cp. 'Ferit hic cubito, ferit assere duro Alter' Juv. 3. 245.

Ep. 31. 2. Alia clariora: see on 'scholastica lege' Ep. 23. 29.   **31**

3. **Arriae :** see on Ep. 28. 10.

12. **Vivere filium simulabat.** For fortitude in some respects similar see an elegant version of a Jewish legend, 'The Loan' in Baring-Gould's 'Silver Store.'

21. **Paete non dolet.**

> 'Casta suo gladium cum traderet Arria Paeto,
>> Quem de visceribus traxerat ipsa suis,
>> Si qua fides, vulnus quod feci non dolet, inquit,
>> Sed quod tu facies hoc mihi Paete dolet.'

Mart. 1. 14.

24. **Matrem agere,** 'to act the mother.' Cp. 'Etiam quum amicum imperatoris ageret' Tac. Hist. 1. 30.

26. **Fuerat Paetus in partibus,** 'Paetus had been a partisan,' i.e. in the conspiracy. Cp. 'militum acerrimos ducere in partes' Tac. Ann. 15. 51.

30. **Calcietur.** 'Calceo' is the usual pres. ind. act. from which would be formed 'calceetur,' but the double *e* is avoided by the substitution of *i*.

33. **Apud Claudium ;** when they came to trial before the emperor.

Profiteretur indicium, 'turned king's evidence,' as we should say. Cp. 'Summum supplicium decernebatur ni professus indicium foret' Tac. Ann. 6. 3. The phrase literally means 'to volunteer information.'

34. **Ego, inquit, te audiam.** 'Audiam' is pres. subj. not fut. ind. 'Am I to (let myself) listen to you.' 'The subj. is used in inquiries as to what is (or was) to be done, when it is intended to indicate that something will

not be done (or has not been done).' 'Illius stultitia victa ex urbe rus tu habitatum migres?' Ter. Hec. 4. 2. 13. 'Ego te videre noluerim' Cic. ad Q. F. 1. 3. Madvig, § 353. Also cp. 'Numeros reipublicae summam' Ep. 66. 3.

Cuius in gremio. The meaning is, 'you who could bear to survive your husband's death.' The disjointed mode of expression, et vivis, is a witness to the genuineness of the words.

38. Filiam tuam mori mecum. Twenty-four years later, as Thrasea foresaw, a decision had to be made on this point, which resulted in his persuading Arria the younger to survive him for the sake of their daughter Fannia; Tac. Ann. 16. 34.

45. Impegit. Pliny's admiration for this ferocious attempt forms a pendant to Seneca's observation, Ep. 70, in which, among anecdotes of hideous suicides, he remarks, 'cui difficilis occasio (mortis) est, is proximam quamque pro optima arripiat, sit licet inaudita, sit nova.'

49. Circumfert, sc. 'celebrat,' occurs three times in the letters in this unusual sense.

32 Ep. 32. 2. Principi gratias: see on Ep. 16. 15.

11. E specula. Fires were lighted on 'speculae' for military purposes; cp. Lucan 6. 276. But Pliny is probably thinking of a lighthouse or Pharos, such as stood on the rock of Capreae, Suet. Tib. 74.

15. Codicillos, waxed tablets used for short notes to persons near at hand. The following passage seems to imply that letters sent to a distance, 'epistolae,' were not written on 'codicilli;' ' adeo tecum sum, ut dubitem, an incipiam non epistolas, sed codicillos tibi scribere' Sen. Ep. 55 sub fin. 'Epistolae,' were therefore probably written on paper whenever it was unlikely that the tablet would be returned. So we find Pliny using paper, 'charta adhuc superest' Ep. 30. 23.

15. Libellos, bills publicly circulated as opposed to private notes of invitation. In the dialogue de Oratoribus, attributed to Tacitus, the giver of a recitation is said 'libellos dispergere.'

33. Hac severitate aurium lactor. Here is the result of Quintilian's teaching. Pliny, like his master, earnestly desired to bring about a reform in the public taste, hitherto devoted to the stilted and florid rhetoric in which Seneca and Lucan excelled. The criticism on Seneca, Quint. Inst. Or. 10. 1, is the best comment on this passage, and is as well worth reading as the rest of that celebrated chapter.

34. Theatra, the audiences. Cp. 'Theatra tota reclamant' Cic. de Or. 3. 50.
Male, to be taken with 'canere.'

38. Constare rationem: see on Ep. 5. 1.

43. Iusta possessione, 'the ground which they might fairly occupy,' such as panegyric. The double regimen of 'decedere' is uncommon, though its use in these two senses, 'to make way for,' and 'to retire from,' with the dat. and abl. severally, is common enough. Cp. 'sanctis decedere Divis' Cat. Pel. 62; 'decedere instituto suo' Liv. 37. 54.

Ep. 33. 1. **Adsumo te in consilium**: a technical phrase, used **33** especially of the imperial 'consiliarii.' See on Ep. 42. 1.

3. Sollicitant; here as elsewhere = 'alliciunt,' which seems to point to a community of derivation for the two words, either real or supposed.

4. Iungendi. Cp. 'Si Libyam remotis Gadibus iungas' Hor. Od. 2. 2, 10.

6. Procuratore. One steward would be quite sufficient, and fewer 'subagents' or 'clerks,' 'actores,' would be required for contiguous estates, than for such as lay entirely separate from each other. There is no mention of a 'villicus' or farm-bailiff, as this estate seems not to have been farmed by the owner, but let out to 'coloni.'

7. Unam villam colere. It would be sufficient to have a house of residence, 'villa urbana,' on one of the two estates. The other might simply be kept up as a 'villa rustica' for the habitation of agents and slaves.

9. Atriensium: the 'atriensis' and the slaves under him had to keep in order the house and furniture.

Topiariorum. fancy gardeners, whose art consisted in training and clipping into shapes and patterns ('litteras quae nomen domini dicunt;' 'bestiarum effigies' Bk. 5. 6) those evergreen plants which then formed the chief ornaments of Italian gardens. Cp. 'topiarium laudavi: ita omnia convestit hedera qua basim villae, quae intercolumnia ambulationis ut,' &c. Cic. ad Q. F. 3. 1. See Becker's Gallus, Exc. 2, Sc. 5.

17. Materiam, timber for building, not wood for fuel; in which sense always 'lignum,' from 'lego' or 'ligo.'

20. Pignora, the farm stock, live or dead, on which distraint was made. This would include the slaves belonging to the 'coloni.'

Reliqua, arrears.

23. Instruendi; 'they therefore (the 'coloni,') must be provided with slaves at so much higher a price than usual, because good slaves.' The 'coloni,' though attached to the land, and themselves to some extent under servile disabilities, were nevertheless tenants paying rent and possessing property of their own in stock and slaves. See Smith's Dict. Ant. art. 'Colonus,' and Daubeny's Roman Husbandry, Lect. 2.

Quod frugi. Pliny has no 'servi vincti' to give them. This class of slaves being untrustworthy worked in fetters and were confined in a sort of prison. He must therefore buy 'servi soluti' of good character, and these will cost a great deal, and add greatly to the expense of entering upon the property.

25. Sestertio tricies. A million of sesterces is regularly expressed by 'decies centena millia sestertium' (Abbreviated gen. plur. for 'sestertiorum.') But instead of this we commonly find the abbreviated expression, 'decies sestertium' (generally reversed, 'sestertium decies'), and so on for larger numbers. In such expressions 'sestertium,' which is properly a gen. plur., is treated as a neuter subst. sing. Madvig, Suppl. **2.** From this imaginary subst. we here have 'sestertio,' abl. of price.

C

26. **Hac paenuria colonorum.** Since the 'coloni' were inseparable from the soil, their condition affected the value of the estate.

30. **Aliquid tamen fenero.** He had some little money out at interest, and therefore says above, '*prope* totus.'

31. **Non secus ac mea.** Cp. his letter to her, 'Non, mehercule tam mea sunt quae mea sunt, quam quae tua' Bk. 1. 4.

34   **Ep. 34. 2. Lex tabellaria.** Cicero mentions four such leges, by which vote by ballot was gradually sanctioned in the various functions of the comitia; namely, the election of magistrates, the iudicia publica, and the enactment and repeal of laws. The dates of these laws range between 139 and 107 B.C. and Cicero pro Sest. 48, in speaking of the 'Lex Cassia,' confirms what is here said of the contentions which the question called forth. When the election of magistrates was transferred by Tiberius to the senate, the ballot was laid aside till the date of this letter.

6. **Contionum**, open meetings, as opposed to legally constituted assemblies.

16. **Sub quo militaverat ;** military service was a necessary qualification of all candidates for office.

20. **Annos arguebat**, under the 'leges annales,' which fixed the age necessary for each office.

31. **Ut in reciperatoriis iudiciis.** 'Reciperatores,' generally three in number, were appointed by the praetor to decide on some issue of fact which required no knowledge of law ; Sigonius de Iud. 1. 22. Hence there was no reason against these being picked out on the spot from persons present in court, instead of being taken from a fixed list as the 'iudices' were. So we find Cicero, Verr. 2. 3, 59 and 60, complaining of Verres for not naming 'reciperatores de conventu.' The point of comparison between the senate on this occasion and 'reciperatores' lies in the words **repente apprehensi.**

35   **Ep. 35. 1. Decessisse.** We have reason to believe that Martial lived till the close of the year 100 A.D.

3. **Fellis**, 'bile,' the emblem of bitterness. Pliny seems to have in his mind Martial's own criticism, Mart. 7. 25, which enumerates the same ingredients, 'sal,' 'fel,' and 'candor,' as necessary for epigrams that were meant to be read.

Candoris, kindness of heart. Ovid credits Salanus with 'candor' for his sympathy with him in his exile, although their acquaintance was but slight. Ov. Pont. 2. 5, 5. Sincerity was not necessarily implied in the word, and indeed candour, in the English sense, could not possibly have been attributed to the sycophant Martial.

4. **Prosecutus eram.** 'Prosequor' is only twice used in these letters in the sense 'to accompany,' but very frequently in its idiomatic sense, 'to compliment with,' followed by such ablatives as 'libello,' 'legatis,' 'suffragio.' It seems to be used of such attentions as could not be claimed or even expected, and intimates that the benefactor went as it were out of his way, and *followed up* the friend whom he wished to honour. This sense of

'prosequor' was so clearly understood, that the verb occurs without an explanatory abl. Ep. 46. 6, and Suet. Dom. 9.

12. **Tenerem.** Cp. 'Numeros memini si verba tenerem' Virg. Ecl. 9. 45.

19. **Hoc.** Observe that 'studeo' begins to take an accus. together with its proper dat.

20. **Arpinis.** So Juvenal, 8. 237, calls Cicero himself 'Arpinas,' from Arpi his birthplace.

Ep. 36. 1. Regulus. See note on Ep. 23. 4. 36

Hoc uno malo, &c.; 'the only misfortune that I grudge him, and I doubt if he thinks it a misfortune.' Lord Orrery takes Pliny to task for a want of humanity in disbelieving Regulus' grief. But Pliny is justified by the use which the father is said to have made of his son's name in his perjuries. Ep. 23. 17.

4. **Emancipavit,** 'set him free from the patria potestas.' The boy's mother had left her property to him on the condition that Regulus should first do this. It was worth his doing, because he thus retained his wife's property in the family. It might therefore be said that his son had been sold by him (*mancipatum*) for this consideration, rather than gratuitously emancipated. 'Mancipatus' is coupled with 'venditus' Cic. Phil. 2. 21.

5. **Ex moribus hominis,** 'with an allusion to the character of the man' (Regulus).

8. **Et iunctos et solutos.** See note on Ep. 21. 9.

9. **Luscinias.** Pet birds were kept not by children only, but also by empresses and poets. Cp. Plin. H. N. 10. 59 and 60; and the elegant poem of Statius on the death of his parrot, Stat. Silv. 4. Also cp. the famous 'Passer' of Catullus, Cat. 2.

14. **In Regulo demerendo.** Regulus was now 'orbus,' and therefore an object of interest to legacy-hunters.

18. **Tempore;** this refers to the season of the year, which was trying to his visitors.

20. **Perverse;** generally opposed to 'recte,' 'against right and reason,' so much against them that the wrongdoing seems the result of wilfulness rather than ignorance. Hence the notion of wilfulness now dominant in the English word 'perverse.'

Ep. 37. 6. Auditorio; the name of the place put for the persons 37 occupying it, as 'theatra' Ep. 32. 34. Cp. English use of 'pit' and 'gallery.'

7. **De vita eius.** This is simple narration. But **de vita pueri,** which follows, is the scornful reflection of the narrator interrupting himself.

8. **Exemplaria mille.** Whether this be or be not taken literally, it marks the great facility with which copies of books could be made; and harmonizes with our accounts of the low prices at which they could be obtained, e.g. the first book of Martial's Epigrams for five denarii = 3s. 1½d.

9. **Decurionibus.** See note on 'Duumviratus' Ep. 42. 4.

14. **'Αμαθία μὲν θράσος,** Thuc. 2. 40.

16. **Latus**; here as elsewhere in the sense of 'lungs,' 'power of voice.'

20. **Herennius.** See note on Ep. 69. 10.

Catonis illud. Pliny might have heard this from his master Quintilian, who quotes it Inst. Or. 12, 1. Quintilian says that if the orator be not a good man to begin with, then the art of his instructor 'comparat haec arma latroni non militi.'

26. **Circulator.** From 'circulus,' a ring of gazers or listeners, are derived 'circulari,' to collect a crowd, and 'circulator,' one who attracts or addresses a crowd. The name was generally applied to conjurors, snake-charmers, and cheap-jacks. They had then, as now, a ready volubility; cp. Sen. Ep. 40, 52, where 'circulor' has its secondary meaning 'to exercise the trade of a circulator.' These performers seem sometimes to have related stories; cp. Ep. 23. 1, where 'assem para' is a parody of the cry of a 'circulator' before beginning his performance.

27. **Ut ait Demosthenes:** Dem. de Cor. 90. The sense is, 'if Lepidus has had to read the work, he will have declaimed it with as much want of feeling as Aeschines showed in speaking of the calamities of his country.'

30. **Sed a puero;** a good instance of Pliny's way of concluding his letter with an epigram.

38 **Ep. 38.** 1. **Nos**; Pliny and Sabinus.

14. **Cavit enim.** Sabina is the nominative to 'cavit,' she who chose her heirs discreetly. 'Elegerit,' instead of elegit, would have allowed of an indefinite nominative to 'cavit,' and made the sentence (what it now is not) a general observation on the security insured by a good choice.

39 **Ep. 39.** 9. **Praetextatus,** added to mark the boy's age.

11. **Mediolani,** at Milan. Milan, at this time a place of importance, rose to great splendour two centuries later as the residence of the emperor Maximian, and is celebrated by Ausonius as the seventh in importance of the cities of the Empire.

13. **Intererat.** 'When it is declared what might or ought to happen, but does not happen (with possum, debeo, &c.) the indic. is commonly made use of, and in the imperfect tense, if in regard to present time' Madvig, § 348, 1.

21. **Mercedibus,** the teacher's pay.

29. **Religio recte iudicandi.** 'scrupulousness in making a right choice.' Cicero's derivation of 'religio' from 'relego' is probably correct, and 'scrupulousness' is often, as here, an adequate translation of the word without throwing in any sense of obligation. The sense given is confirmed by the occurrence of two other compounds of 'lego' immediately below, 'neglegentes,' 'diligentes.'

43. **Quae ad te convenit;** for similar attentions paid to another man of letters cp. the 'frequens cubiculum' of Silius, Ep. 27. 12.

49. **Hinc,** 'from this part of the country.' He classes the Tuscan villa from which he writes in the same region with Rome, by comparison with the distant Comum.

50. **Quam fiduciam.** This, like the close of Ep. 37, is one of those epigrammatic surprises which stamp Pliny's prose as well as Martial's verse with the character of 'Flavian polish and refinement.'

In conclusion it will be worth while to put together what can be gathered from this letter respecting education *in the provinces.*

Schools of two separate kinds were in existence, firstly, government schools, not uncommon ('multis in locis'); and secondly, schools established by public subscription where sufficient money could be raised to engage a teacher. We do not hear of teachers starting schools on a private venture. They expected to be engaged ('conduci') with a certain payment guaranteed. If there was a good school in any place, boys came from a distance and took lodgings in the place to attend it.

Pliny's views set forth in this letter attest not only his generosity and interest in education, but a shrewd judgment in the matter quite on a level with modern opinion. He sees the danger of bad appointments likely to arise from fixed payments and centralization, and he also sees the necessity of some subsidy to encourage local effort.

We must add to the list of his benefits to Comum the establishment of a public library, and an endowment for the support of a certain number of free-born children. Bk. 1. 8.

Ep. 40. 5. **Corelli filiam**; perhaps the first cousin of Pliny's second **40** wife Calpurnia. See note on the following letter. For Corellius see note on Ep. 7.

15. **Contra,** 'just the other way.'

16. **Penitus inspexi.** Pliny uses the same phrase with reference to Euphrates, Ep. 6. 4; and of Trajan, Pan. 83.

17. **Nihil a me**; supply 'habuit.'

21. **Suffragator et testis.** Cp. 'Testes et laudatores dabat, vel eum sub quo militaverat, vel cum cui quaestor fuerat, vel utrumque si poterat. Addebat quosdam e suffragatoribus: illi graviter et paucis loquebantur' Ep. 34. 15. Though this description refers to an earlier state of things, yet no doubt something of the same order was observed in the time of Pliny.

In inchoandis deductor. See note on Ep. 16. 32.

26. **De bonis iuvenibus.** Pliny was, at the time mentioned, thirty-five years of age, and therefore in the period of 'iuventus,' which succeeded 'adolescentia,' and was reckoned to begin at about the age of thirty.

36. **Cornutum.** Ep. 48 tells us all we know of Cornutus.

41. **Nova lis.** 'Nova' is limited by **ut.**

Foeminae. The action, whatever it was, was of a kind not usually brought against a woman.

Ep. 41. This letter is addressed to Calpurnia Hispulla, daughter of **41** Calpurnius Fabatus, and aunt of Calpurnia, Pliny's second (or third) wife, whom Hispulla had brought up. The fact of her having been brought up by her aunt makes it probable that her mother, as well as her father, must have died when she was a child; and hence we may conclude with Mommsen

(Onomast. Keil's second ed.) that Pompeia Celerina, whom Pliny speaks of as his 'socrus' (Bk. 1. 4.), was not the mother of Calpurnia, but of a former wife of Pliny.

We find Calpurnia hastening to comfort her aunt Hispulla at the death of Fabatus, Hispulla's father, Trai. 120. There is a letter addressed to Fabatus, Bk. 4. 1.

12. **In proximo.** See on Ep. 4. 4. For further proofs of Pliny's conjugal affection see Epp. 54 and 56.

14. **Format,** 'sets them to music.'

26. **Invicem,** 'in turn,' i.e. first a wife for Pliny, then a husband for Calpurnia.

42   **Ep. 42. 1. In consilium adsumptus.** The emperors had a limited number of advisers, whom they summoned for consultation, just as inferior officers, e.g. praetors and proconsuls summoned their 'consiliarii.' The famous 'Council of the Turbot' (Juv. 4. 73 sqq.), whether real or fictitious, testifies to the existence of this custom, which is said to have been instituted by Augustus. Pliny was often summoned ('frequenter in consilio fui' Ep. 13. 51), as for instance in the trial of Atticinus, Bk. 6. 22, and that of Ariston, with others, Bk. 6. 31. See Merivale, Hist. Emp. c. 67.

2. **Vienneuses,** 'the people of Vienne.' Vienna, now Vienne, is situated on the Rhone, not far below Lyons. It was a city of great importance under the Empire, and the site of a flourishing Christian church. The remains of a large amphitheatre still confirm what is here said of the taste of the inhabitants for spectacles. This amphitheatre was probably the scene of many martyrdoms during the great persecution by Aurelius, A.D. 177.

4. **In duumviratu.** The provincial towns were governed by senators ('decuriones'), who elected duumvirs from their own body. The duumvirs united in their persons the functions separately exercised at Rome by the consuls and praetors. The duumvirs were originally elected by the people in each place; but the transference of the Roman comitia to the senate was followed by a similar change in the provinces. Smith's Dict. Ant. art. 'Colonia.'

8. **Cum sententiae perrogarentur.** Cp. 'Parum est ut censentes audias, nisi et perroges' Pan. 60. 'Perrogo'='deinceps rogo,' to ask in order. Here the opinions of the 'consiliarii' were asked all the way down in order as they sat.

9. **Iunius Mauricus.** See note on Ep. 28. 10 sub fin.

11. **Etiam Romae.** These performances had been fostered to excess by Domitian. See Merivale, Hist. Emp. c. 62.

Pliny's assent to the sternness of Mauricus is somewhat inconsistent with what he says to Maximus, Ep. 63, although it be in accordance with his judgment on the Circenses, Ep. 75. See also note on Ep. 64. 13.

14. **Veiento;** his power as a creature of Domitian was so great, that a mere look from him was a boon; Juv. 3. 185. He is recorded as present

with Catullus at the 'Council of the Turbot,' see below, and he still sat in the senate under Trajan, Ep. 77. 64.

16. **Luminibus orbatus.**

'Et cum mortifero prudens Veiento Catullo
Qui nunquam visae flagrabat amore puellae' Juv. 4. 113.

23. Nobiscum **cenaret.** The moderation which Nerva prescribed to himself in regard to this great criminal seems to have marked his dealings with the class (cp. Ep. 77); and the victims of the delators were probably little satisfied with the amount of favour which they (the delators) experienced from him. Merivale, Hist. Emp. c. 63.

Ep. 43. 1. **Scripseram tibi,** viz. in Ep. 54.   **43**

6. **Iratum principem.** 'Iratum' is the predicate.

7. **Fefellit.** Cp. 'Nec vixit male qui vivens moriensque fefellit' Hor. Ep. 1. 17. 10.

9. **In senatu.** The emphasis is on these words.

Ep. 44. 1. **Legatum mihi obvenit.** This is that legacy of Curianus **44** which is mentioned towards the close of the letter. It gave Pliny satisfaction because it was a recognition of his honourable conduct in regard to the former legacy, that of Galla, the story of which he proceeds to relate first.

6. **Praeiudicio,** 'by my first giving judgment in his favour.' An opinion given and acted upon by Pliny would have great weight in the centumviral court, in which he was a distinguished pleader. This sense of 'praeiudicium' is quite distinct from the technical sense which it sometimes has of 'a previous trial to clear the way for the determination of the main issues.'

9. **Non satis honestum;** too like the conduct of a 'captator,' a legacy-hunter.

14. **Minorem,** in moral worth. If Curianus could trust to Pliny's honour to judge his own case, why should Pliny distrust himself?

16. **Secundum,** 'in favour of,' for the validity of the will.

22. **Consilii;** i.e. Pliny and his two assessors.

24. **Cum ceteris subscripsit.** Those who brought an action, both plaintiff and counsel, were required to put their names to the notice of action; hence 'subscribere iudicium' or 'subscribere' mean to go to law with a man. 'Subscribere **cum ceteris**' is an unusual construction, to be explained by the sense of the word which = 'certare.' 'Certare' could of course be constructed with 'cum' and abl. Elsewhere we find 'subscribere in aliquem' Cic. Q. F. 3. 3, or a dative following, 'cras subscribam homini dicam' Plaut. Paen. 3. 6, 5.

25. **Centumvirale iudicium :** see note on Ep. 12. 9.

30. **Gratillae amicitia.** Domitian had killed Rusticus, and banished his wife Gratilla. Notorious intimacy with them might have exposed the litigators to a like fate.

32. Ex **parte quarta.** Curianus sought to have his mother's will set aside as 'inofficiosum,' wanting in that provision which a parent is morally

bound to make for a child. This could be done under 'Lex Falcidia' in any case where the natural heirs were not made at least 'heredes ex quadrante,' i. e. did not at least receive a fourth part of the inheritance. If Gratilla had made such a provision, Curianus would have had no ground for action. Or again, she might have made him 'heres ex asse,' but might have exhausted the property by legacies out of it so as to leave him in effect but one fourth of the whole. For this also he would have had no remedy.

34. **Ex asso**, 'to the whole inheritance.' In divisions of property the 'as' was taken to represent the whole.

38. **Biennium.** Two years undisturbed possession gave the possessor a title by 'usus' to real property. Pliny's 'coheredes' had enjoyed their shares of the property as long as he had his, but notice of action had been served on them but not on him.

44. **Antiquum.** The word occurs in Cicero in the same good sense, but Pliny's frequent and habitual use of it is characteristic of his mind, which clung to the old memories of the state, and the forms in which they survived. Cp. Bk. 2. 11, 18, where he couples 'pulcrum' with 'antiquum.' The parenthesis **nisi forte**, &c. refers to 'antiquum.'

45 **Ep. 45.** 1. **Turdos**, fieldfares, which were not taken wild when in season, but kept and fed for the table all the year round in 'ornithones.' Even in Varro's time they were sold when fat for about three denarii apiece.

Parem calculum, 'which I cannot match in value.' The Romans learnt to compute by the help of 'calculi,' small stones placed in an 'abacus' or tray, with different compartments for units, tens, and hundreds. Pliny varies his use of the same metaphor of 'calculi' in Bk. 2. 19, and Ep. 9. 38, where see note.

2. **Urbis copiis**, 'city commodities.' His Laurentine villa was only seventeen miles from the city, so that it would be natural for him to send a present of some city luxury to a friend residing further from Rome than himself. The fact that Ostia was the usual market-town of the villa (Ep. 21. 118) presents no real difficulty ; and the conjecture 'ullis' for 'urbis' has no MS. authority.

4. **Sollertiam Diomedis.** Diomede's advantageous exchange of his own brazen armour for the golden armour of Glaucus (Hom. Il. 6. 236) gave rise to the proverb χρύσεα χαλκείων.

46 **Ep. 46.** 4. **Veritate promptissimus.** This abl., unlike the two preceding ablatives, is 'abl. of respect.' **Natura** and **usu** are 'abl. of the means.' 'Veritas' here means a true and accurate statement of the matter on which he was consulted. There is no occasion or authority for reading 'varietate' with Gierig.

6. **Prosecutus.** See note on Ep. 35. 4.

7. **Utcumque** ; properly a relative conjunction meaning 'however' or 'whenever,' and followed by a verb. But in this passage it stands alone with an indefinite meaning, and is in fact an adverb. Like 'quandoque,' 'utcumque' reaches this indefinite sense by an ellipse, which may perhaps in this

passage be thus filled up, 'hoc, utcumque id fiat, tolerabile est.' He admits that it is endurable, though he does not clearly see *how* it can be so. For the use cp. 'Excepto quod adhuc utcumque valemus' Ov. Ep. ex Pont. 4. 14. 3.

14. **Acerba**, 'untimely.' The sentence is an apology for applying this epithet to the death, not of a child but of a grown man.

21. **Lectulo.** See note on Ep. 24. 11.

22. **Habitum**, 'attitude.'

Scrinium; not a desk to write upon, but a box to hold what was written.

30. **Frustra**; in preparing materials for another volume, which he was prevented from writing.

Ep. 47. In a bantering humour he personifies the epigrams in which he **47** had promised the appearance of Suetonius' book, and speaks of his verses as having given bail for its appearance, and being called upon in legal form to answer their obligation. For Suetonius see on Ep. 12.

2. **Appellantur.** 'Hendecasyllabi' is the nominative to this verb, and also to 'cogantur,' since 'scripta' must evidently be supplied as an accus. after ad exhibendum.

3. **Ad exhibendum formulam accipere**, to undergo legal proceedings, such as to make them bring the 'scripta' into court. These 'formulae' were drawn to suit every variety of case, and from them the plaintiff chose that which suited him, and inserted his own particulars. 'Formulam intendere' was said of the plaintiff, 'formulam accipere' of the defendant. 'Exhibere' is a technical term, meaning 'to bring into court.' The use of the gerund in this passage is remarkable; and, as it stands after 'formulam recipere,' it must be translated 'with regard to bringing them forward.' 'Ad' with the gerund is not employed in final clauses for 'ut' with subj.

6. **Vicisti**, 'you have surpassed.'

8. **Scazontes**, or 'choliambi,' 'limping iambics,' were so called from σκάζω, 'to limp,' and are iambic trimeters with a spondee or trochee in the place of the final iambus. They were invented by Hipponax of Elis, who recorded in this metre his experience of the married state :

Δύ' ἡμέραι γυναικός εἰσιν ἥδισται,
Ὅταν γαμῇ τις κἀκφέρῃ τεθνηκυῖαν.

Scazons were not exclusively employed for satire, witness Catullus' beautiful poem on Sirmio. Cat. 29.

10. **Titulum tuum.** See note on 'indicis' Ep. 25. 3.

Ep. 48. 1. **Municipium**, sc. Comum. **48**

2. **Aemiliae viae curam.** 'Quatuorviri viis curandis' had existed under the republic; but Augustus increased their number, separated the care of the roads within the city from that of the roads without it, and finally gave a lasting dignity to the office by himself undertaking the care of the 'via Flaminia,' and allotting the other 'viae' to men of note.

Under the 'Curatores' were 'mancipes,' who contracted to perform the repairs which the former thought necessary.

7. **Mandatum mihi officium.** Two concurrent inscriptions lead us to suppose that this office was that of 'curator alvei Tiberis et riparum' to which the office of Cornutus might be said to be **par.** Cp. Suet. Aug. 37, where we find the two charges put side by side, 'curam viarum, aquarum, alvei Tiberis.'

10. **Expressius:** see note on Ep. 20. 7.

29. **Aliis litteris;** namely, belles lettres.

31. **Commeatus,** 'leave of absence.'

49   **Ep. 40.** 17. **Acerbum:** see note on Ep. 46. 14.

22. **Ut ... invenit,** 'with the inventiveness which grief gives of all the details of mourning.'

23. **Margarita,** chiefly used for earrings, which were often very costly. 'Margaritarii,' dealers in pearls, are mentioned in extant inscriptions. 'Margarita' and 'margaritum' are various forms of the nom. sing.

28. **Pietatis est totus.** Cp. 'hominum non caussarum toti erant,' Liv. 3. 36. The idiom is classical and frequent, but is more properly used of devotion to persons than to things.

This whole letter will bear comparison for elegance with any in the collection, not excepting Ep. 16.

50   **Ep. 50.** 1. **Tuos,** 'your slaves and freedmen.'

8. **Inscriptio.** This word alludes to the 'titulus' fastened on slaves for sale, describing their age and qualifications. Cp. 'qui titulum illi impegerat,' i.e. the man who had sold him, Sen. Ep. 47.

Comoedus: see note on Ep. 24. 36. Zosimus seems also to have had the qualifications of a 'lyristes.'

21. **Nimis imperat voci,** 'asks too much from his voice.' Cp. 'Alius patrimonio suo plus imperavit quam ferre posset' Sen. Tranq. 4.

23. **Foro Iuli,** Fréjus, on the warm south coast of Gaul, which was even then resorted to by consumptive patients.

29. **Frugalitate.** Pliny's kindness to Zosimus was met by a delicacy on his part which makes this pleasant picture of humanity complete. Paulinus, to whom the letter was addressed, remembered Pliny's conduct in this matter, and at his death left him, 'ius Latinorum suorum,' the claims of a patron over his freedmen, who, though manumitted, yet possessed only the 'Latinitas' or Latin rights under the 'Lex Iulia Norbana,' and hence were called 'Latini.' The position of a patron of 'Latini' was valuable, and gave claim to various services to be rendered by them. Pliny justified the confidence of Paulinus by obtaining from Trajan full citizenship for three of them, Trai. 104.

51   **Ep. 51.** 4. **Ut venissem,** 'when I should have come.'

5. **Graviter iacet:** see note on Ep. 23. 3.

6. **Ne hoc quidem triste.** The probability of his death is not really sad, for it will bring him relief.

Illius utilitatibus, by the consideration of his own gain. 'Utilitates' and 'commoda' are coupled by Cic. de Fin. 1. 10. 'Utilitas,' usefulness;

'utilitates,' gains. For the rule concerning plurals of substantives of abstract meaning, see Madvig, § 50, Obs. 3.

16. **Sine fructu posteritatis**, without producing their legitimate fruit of lasting fame, see on Ep. 16. 5.

17. **Abierunt.** The 'editio princeps' substitutes 'aruerunt,' which would suit the metaphor suggested by various parts of the passage; such as, **in flore primo**; **maturuissent**; **sine fructu.**

Frenos. In the case of those substantives which have more than one plural form, the neuter form is usually confined to poetical use; cp. 'ostreae, ostrea,' and 'sibili, sibila.'

Ep. **52.** 1. **Quaerere:** cp. 'quaerit patria Caesarem' Hor. Carm. 4. 52 5, 15.

M. Regulum: see on Ep. 23. 4.

3. **Quamvis non posset ediscere.** Regulus wrote and prepared his speeches with great care, but never could quite get them by heart, which spoiled their effect.

It will be worth while to examine the history of this passage as an instance of the way in which the text was corrupted for want of a close adherence to MSS. The Medicean MS. read, for 'posset ediscere,' 'posse te discere.' Catanaeus, an early editor, saw this would not do, and cutting 'te' in two, restored 't' to the previous 'posse,' and 'e' to the following 'discere.' But not content with this he introduced 'd,' and printed 'quamvis non posset dediscere.' He then removed the full stop, and took **illud ipsum** and the following sentence as the accusative of 'dediscere,' introducing hopeless confusion, and compelling the reader to take **veniebat** as an impersonal verb. This confusion was perpetuated by Cortius, and all the inferior modern editions, e. g. the Tauchnitz edition.

5. **Circumlinebat**; with paint.

10. **Una dicentibus,** ' to the counsel engaged in the same case;' not, ' on the same side.'

Libera tempora. Cn. Pompeius, by a law passed in his third consulship, defined the proportions of time to be allotted to the accuser and the accused respectively. The enactment was primarily to regulate the trial of Milo then about to take place, Ascon. Arg. Cic. pro Mil. The proportion was apparently that of two to three, and was measured by 'clepsydrae.' But if the plaintiff or prosecutor asked for 'libera tempora,' *unlimited* time, then the same privilege was necessarily granted to the other side.

11. **Audituros corrogabat.** For Pliny's opinion on the custom of inviting or hiring an audience, cp. Ep. 20. 15.

12. **Sub alterius invidia.** Regulus bore all the odium attaching to a protracted trial and a packed audience. Pliny reaped the advantages of unrestricted time for his oratory and a crowd of listeners, in the midst of which he found himself 'caught,' as he expresses it. He had not brought them, but there they were. The remembrance of all this is what leads him to look for Regulus, ' quaerere Regulum,' with a sort of half regret.

18. **Binas vel singulas.** In the trial of Marius Priscus (Bk. 2. 11) Pliny spoke through sixteen clepsydrae, and his speech lasted nearly five hours. As that trial took place in January, these five hours would be equivalent to about four hours of our time. See note on Ep. 25. 28. Hence 'binas vel singulas' would be 'half an hour or a quarter of an hour apiece.'

29. **Fidei,** to the obligation of their duty to their clients.

39. **Communium.** This is the MSS. reading, but 'communia' in the sense of 'public interests' is unparalleled. The earliest editors seem to have either felt the difficulty or to have had another reading before them, as they insert 'civium.' Mommsen's emendation 'amore communi omnium' is probable, and it is easy to imagine that the two latter words may have run into one.

Emendari cupero quae iam corrigere difficile est. Why 'emendare' is spoken of as easier than 'corrigere' may be seen by considering the metaphors involved in them. It is a less matter to remove a few *blemishes* ('mendae'), than to *straighten* throughout a thing which has grown crooked.

41. **Mihi autem;** this sentence explains to Arrianus why he is to take 'no news,' **novi nihil,** for 'good news.'

53 Ep. 53. Pliny practised what Cicero preached, 'nutrices et paedagogi iure vetustatis plurimum benevolentiae postulabunt' Cic. Lael. 20. Nurses have their place both in the epic and the tragic poetry of Greece and Rome.

54 Ep. 54. 3. **In Campaniam,** perhaps to Baiae. Pliny the elder describes the whole coast as possessing 'vitalis ac perennis salubritas.'

E vestigio, 'immediately.'

6. **Ecquid denique.** Pliny is anxious to know if his wife is enjoying the delights of Campania without being retarded in her recovery by indulgence in them.

7. **Transmitto** means to let go by one, yet not so as to miss or neglect. By zeugma it is here joined to both 'secessus' and 'voluptates.'

55 Ep. 55. 6. **Omnium quae decucurri candidatus,** 'candidate for all the offices which I have successively enjoyed.' Compounds of 'curro' may either retain or drop the augment. Cp. 'decursu honorum' Cic. de Or. 1. 1.

12. **Quintilianum:** see on Ep. 20. 34.

13. **Ventitabat** = ἐφοίτα.

15. **In senatu,** where the magistrates were now elected, the result of the election being announced to the people who continued to meet for this purpose long after the loss of their power to elect. The elections retained their original name of 'comitia,' which properly belonged to the popular assembly. Cp. 'E campo comitia ad patres translata sunt' Tac. Ann. 1. 15. This change was made under Tiberius.

24. **Cum fratre,** probably Julius Avitus, whose death is lamented in Ep. 51.

28 **Suffragio meo.** On the importance of influential 'suffragatores' see on Ep. 40. 21.

Ep. 56. 1. **Adfici**: see on Ep. 24. 35.   **56**

3. **In vestigio meo**, in the place where I used to sit or lie. 'Vestigium a Latinis dicitur de loco ubi quis fuerit, licet vestigia eius appareant nulla' Gierig. Cp. 'isdem vestigiis institisti' Pan. 23.

Ep. 57. 1. **Socrus meae**, Pompeia Celerina.   **57**

Villam Alsiensem; near Alsium, a seaside town of Etruria. A list of Pompeia's other villas will be found Bk. 1. 4.

2. **Rufi Vergini.** Ep. 16 is a panegyric of Verginius.

10. **Post decimum mortis annum.** This determines the date of this letter as not earlier than 107 A D. It is therefore (except Bk. 9. 19 referring to the same subject) the latest of the whole series to which a date can be affixed.

11. **Sine titulo.** 'without an epitaph.' For this sense of 'titulus' cp.

> 'Titulique cupido
>
> Haesuri saxis cinerum custodibus' Juv. 10. 243.

15. **Pulso Vindice.** Julius Vindex, propraetor of Gaul, rose against Nero, having first offered the empire to Galba. Verginius commanding in upper Germany marched against the insurgents, and his army engaged and defeated them in spite of an agreement which is said to have been come to between the generals on either side.

16. **Adseruit non sibi.** He proved his disinterestedness by refusing the empire which was offered to him. See on Ep. 16. 4.

17. **Parata oblivio**: see on Ep. 25. 30.

18. **Conditoria** were sepulchres underground, in which dead bodies were placed entire as distinguished from those sepulchres or chambers which contained bones or ashes only. Smith's Dict. Ant. art. 'Funus.'

Ep. 58. 2. **Excepit**; an inverted idiom: 'the story fell in with me,' **58** instead of 'I fell in with the story.'

Passennus Paulus; Pliny's affection and admiration for him is expressed at length Bk. 9. 22.

4. **Municeps Propertii.** Propertius was of Mevania, an Umbrian town.

6. **Prisce iubes**, the first words of the poem of Paulus.

7. **Ego vero non iubeo.** Pliny's gentlemanly feeling was naturally outraged by this vulgar wit of Javolenus. Certain German critics have thought fit to defend Javolenus. One of these critics (who was also a lawyer) is thus amusingly answered by Gierig. 'non carpit noster merita Iavoleni; id unum modo tradit, cum senem dubiae esse sanitatis. Et quis tandem neget ICtos quoque nobiles, urgente senectute, huic naturae humanae imbecillitati esse obnoxios.'

9. **Adhibetur consiliis**, to act as praetor's assessor. See on Ep. 42.

10. **Ius civile respondet.** For the construction of 'respondeo' with an accus. cp.

> 'Seu civica iura
>
> Respondere paras' Hor. Ep. 1. 3, 23.

The Jurisconsulti gave their opinion on points of law in public and in private to those who inquired. There appear to have been two classes of Jurisconsulti, those who held an imperial privilege of being consulted, ' ius respondendi,' and those who did not. The opinions of the former class had of course far greater weight in court.

59 **Ep. 59.** 1. **Avunculi mei.** For an account of the life and studies of Pliny the elder, see Ep. 25.

3. **Inmortalem gloriam.** He expresses the same confidence in the immortality of the works of Tacitus, Ep. 69. 1. We do not know whether Tacitus availed himself of the materials here sent him, as the extant portion of the 'Histories' breaks off ten years before the eruption.

4. **Pulcherrimarum clade terrarum**; 'clade' is an ablative belonging to **occiderit**, denoting the cause of Pliny's death.

Ut populi, ut urbes, 'as nations and cities did (i. e. perish).' Probably this refers to Herculaneum and Pompeii, whose inhabitants are with some affectation styled ' populi.' Some commentators have understood the passage as a comparison of Pliny's fame with that of such a town as Saguntum.

5. **Memorabili casu**, abl. after **victurus**, denoting the cause of his immortality.

12. **Erat Miseni.** Suetonius says of Augustus, 'classem Miseni et alteram Ravennae ad tutelam superi et inferi maris collocavit' Suet. Aug. 49. This arrangement seems to have been permanently maintained, and we find references in Tacitus both to the fleet of the Lower sea at Misenum, and to that of the Higher or Adriatic sea at Ravenna. The promontory of Misenum forms the northern limit of the 'Sinus Cumanus' or bay of Naples.

15. **Usus ille sole, mox frigida.** Cp. 'Post solem plerumque frigida lavabatur' Ep. 25. 39.

Gustaverat, 'had taken some luncheon.' 'Gusto' is used intransitively in this sense.

26. **Liburnicam**, a vessel built in imitation of those used by the Liburnians of Dalmatia. It seems to have had sharp bows and consequent swiftness. Juvenal mentions slaves from the same district. Orelli understands by ' saevis Liburnis' Hor. Carm. 1. 37. 30, the vessels and not the slaves. Whatever the Liburnica was, it is at any rate here contrasted with the larger **quadriremes**, which are launched when the voyage is changed (**vertit ille consilium**) from purposes of curiosity to those of succour.

29. **Rectinae Tasci:** cp. ' Verania Pisonis' Ep. 23. 3.

30. **Subiacebat**, sc. ' monti.'

43. **Stabiis**, Castellamare, a village on the side of the bay opposite Misenum, and looking north-west.

Erat, sc. Pomponianus.

44. **Diremptus sinu medio**, 'separated' from Pliny by the bay which lay between them.

47. **Certus fugae**, 'determined on flight.' The poets and the later prose writers use the genitive even after adjectives not strictly transitive in sense,

46

to denote a certain reference to a thing which is otherwise expressed by the ablative (*with respect to*) alone, or by the ablative with the prepositions 'de' or 'in.' Madvig, § 290 g.

50. **Leniret.** See on Ep. 68. 43.

82. **Is ab eo quem novissime viderat erat tertius,** 'and it was the third day from the last which he had seen.' He had died the day before, but he had not seen daylight since the day before that. Hence Pliny is able to make a sort of quibble on the common phrase 'novissimus dies,' which usually meant the day of a man's death, but in this case must be applied to the day before death, as the day of death was no day at all, **dies alibi, illic nox omnibus nigrior densiorque.** 'Erat' is a conjectural insertion by Mommsen. It makes the construction smoother, and might easily have dropped out after 'viderat.'

Ep. **60.** 4. **Ne pecunias deponant,** i. e. with 'sequestres,' by whom 60 the money was distributed to the voters after the candidate was elected.

7. **Homullus noster;** he is found eating with Pliny, Bk. 4. 9.

8. **Sententiae loco,** 'as a resolution,' literally, 'on the occasion of his opinion.' Each senator was asked in turn for his 'sententia' on the subject under discussion, and if he did not agree with previous speakers, he gave his opinion under the form of a resolution, which was put to the vote at the end of the debate if it seemed likely to command any support.

10. **Sua,** sc. 'principis:' a lax use of 'suus.'

15. **Et erat,** sc. deforme.

17. **Quoque,** sc. 'et quo.' 'Quo'='ut.'

Ep. **61.** 1. **Litteris,** Ep. 59. This letter resumes the narrative broken 61 off in Ep. 59 at the words 'Interim Miseni ego et mater.'

4. **Quamquam animus meminisse horret,** Virg. Aen. 2. 12.

12. **In area domus;** a vacant space left outside a town house (domus). Here it intervened between the house and the sea shore. 'Area' must not be confounded with 'atrium.'

21. **Dies,** 'daylight.'

32. **Processerat litus.** This happened on the other side of the bay also; cp. 'vadum subitum ruinaque montis litora obstantia' Ep. 59. 40.

44. Miseni **quod procurrit,** the promontory of Misenum.

48. Addere gradum, a colloquial phrase for moving quickly forward. Cp. 'in utroque agmine adhortationes erant; adderent gradum' Liv. 3. 27. Like most colloquial expressions it is obscure in its origin, and probably elliptical; perhaps it may have been in full 'addere gradum gradui,' to make one step after another, to put one foot before the other.

54. Consideramus; i for o in the penultimate of the perfect is found both in 'sido' and its compound 'consido.' Hence from 'considi' comes 'consideram.'

Et nox, sc. 'facta est.' 'Et' has a temporal force.

56. Quiritatus, appealing cries. 'Quiritare' and 'quiritatus' are not connected with 'queror,' but, as Varro shows, are derived from the old

formula of appeal to the citizens, 'Porro Quirites,' used by those in danger of injustice or illtreatment. Varr. de Ling. Lat. 5. 7. So in a fragment of Laberius, preserved in Macrob. Sat. 2. 7, we find the words 'Porro Quirites, libertatem perdimus,' put into the mouth of a man who is being scourged.

63. **Illud ... illud**, this part and that part of the town.

71. **Misero**, to be construed with solacio.

74. **Deficit**, the proper word for eclipse. Cp. 'Solis defectiones itemque lunae praedicuntur in multos annos' Cic. de Div. 2. 6.

77. **Utcumque** : see note on Ep. 46. 7.

62   **Ep. 62. 1. Tollite cuncta**, the address of Vulcan to his Cyclopes, Virg. Aen. 8. 439.

3. **Illa arma**, the arms to be made for Aeneas. The comparison is not exact, as Vulcan did not bring the arms, but the order for them.

8. **Intra undecim dies, quam.** This involved idiom requires to be traced carefully. The simplest construction would have been 'undecim diebus postquam.' But sometimes 'post' is transferred to the beginning of the sentence, and the phrase left to stand thus, 'post undecim dies quam' Madvig, § 270, Obs. 4, note ; cp. § 276, Obs. 6. But in the present instance 'post' would not exactly express the meaning of the writer, and 'intra' is substituted for it. Thus 'post' disappears from the sentence, but 'quam,' which belonged to it syntactically, is nevertheless retained, and forced into conjunction with 'intra.' Cp. 'intra quintum quam affuerat diem' Suet. Jul. 35. Such instances of the construction proper to one particle being applied to another, are characteristic of a decaying language.

9. **Quadruplici iudicio** : see note on Ep. 12. 9.

12. **Advocatio**, sc. 'advocati.' Cp. 'cum ingenti advocatione' Liv. 3. 47.

Subsellia, occupied by the audience. The same terms are employed in the description of the court, Ep. 20. 25.

14. **Tribunal**, the raised dais at the further end of the basilica, on which the judges sat. It was sometimes thrown back in the form of an apse, and on the conversion of basilicas into churches became the sanctuary where the altar was placed.

Ex superiore basilicae parte, the galleries, which are somewhat obscurely described by Vitruvius 5. 1. It was difficult for persons in them to hear the proceedings, but easy to look down and see them. They were reached by a staircase from the outside of the building. They were defended by a low balustrade from the hall within, and were probably open to the air, being little more than the roofs of the side aisles.

18. **Duobus consiliis**, by the verdict of two out of the four 'consilia' into which the 180 judges were divided. It appears at first sight that the verdict of two out of the four carried the day in Pliny's favour. But as two points on which he was successful are mentioned below, **victa noverca ... victus Suberinus**, it may be that each of the four 'consilia,' though sitting together, gave its verdict on a different issue in the case, and that

only those two instances are mentioned in which the verdict was favourable.

20. **Isdem iudicibus**, not of course *individually* the same, but judges of different divisions of the *same* centumviral court.

21. **Non ... videretur.** See Madv. § 357. 2, b: 'I use the word chance, but I don't mean to say that it looked like chance.' Perhaps he hints at the possibility of bribery.

40. Ὑπὲρ Κτησιφῶντος, is as much my best as that is Demosthenes' best.

Ep. 63. 1. Recte fecisti: see note on Ep. 42. 11.   63

Veronensibus nostris, 'nostris' because Verona was in 'Italia Transpadana,' 'illa nostra Italia' Ep. 9. 13, in which Comum, Pliny's birthplace, was situated.

2. **Olim amaris**, 'you are now and have long been loved.' This use of 'olim' where Cicero would use 'iamdudum' is characteristic of the Silver Age. Cp.

> 'Sed olim
> Prodigio par est in nobilitate senectus'   Juv. 4. 96,

where see Mayor's note.

The classical uses of 'olim' are as follows: (1) of *past* time—once, formerly; (2) of *future* time—one day, a time will come when; (3) of *repeated* occurrence—now and then.

9. **Africanae**, wild beasts, especially panthers. A 'venatio' was to have been combined with a gladiatorial exhibition, as was done in the Roman 'ludi circenses.' 'Venationes' consisted either of the destruction of criminals by wild beasts, or of the destruction of the beasts by trained 'bestiarii.' Cp. 'aut homo imbecillus a valentissima bestia laniatur, aut praeclara bestia venabulo transverberatur' Cic. Fam. 7. 1.

10. **Ad praefinitum diem**: see note on Ep. 26. 26.

11. **Acceptum fieret**; *passive* of 'acceptum facere,' which means to set down as having been received from a man. The phrase is used of a debt which has been paid or is regarded as paid, as in Bk. 2. 4, 'quicquid mihi pater tuus debuit acceptum tibi fieri iubebo.' Hence the passage above means, 'you have deserved that you should be considered to have fulfilled your promise.' 'Acceptum ferre' differs in sense from 'acceptum facere,' and means to enter as owed on the debit side of one's account book. So the man who scratches out an old debt to himself on the credit side of his book is said 'acceptum facere,' whereas he might be said 'acceptum ferre' when he enters a debt from himself to some one else on the debit side. **Tibi** is 'dativus commodi.'

Ep. 64. 2. Proscribi, 'to be advertised for sale.' This was done then, 64 as now, by putting up on the property a notice (titulus) to that effect. Cp. 'proscribebatur tamen (domus)' Ep. 68. 28.

Pro meo quincunce ex septingentis millibus, 'as my five twelfths out of (a total of) seven hundred thousand sesterces.' In estimating the value of Pliny's share of the land Hermes reckoned the whole estate at two hundred thousand sesterces below its real value, so that Corellia got the part which she bought from him very cheaply.

9. **Corelli Rufi**: see note on Ep. 7.

13. **Ludis meis**; the 'ludi Circenses vel Apollinares' were given by the praetor, in accordance with the 'carmen' which had ordered their institution when the Carthaginians were in Italy, B.C. 212. They were at first vowed afresh every year; but in consequence of a pestilence, B.C. 208, a law was passed 'ut hi ludi in perpetuum in statam diem voverentur' Liv. 27. 23. The appointed day was July 5.

Praesederit. Pliny had probably absented himself to mark his indifference to popular amusements. Cp. 'Circenses erant, quo genere spectaculi ne levissime quidem teneor' Ep. 75. 3.

14. **Circa Larium nostrum.** For 'nostrum' cp. 'huius (Larii lacus) in litore plures villae meae' Ep. 76. 4.

16. **His enim cedere.** 'Cedo' here governs an abl. ('his') besides its usual dative (Corelliae). Cp. 'nisi sibi possessione hortorum cessisset' Cic. pro Mil. 27.

65   **Ep. 65.** This letter shows how Corellia had responded to the liberality which had been shown her.

2. **Ex septingentis**; see note on the preceding letter.

4. **Partem vicesimam.** This succession duty of five per cent. had been imposed by Augustus, and was the only direct tax levied on Roman citizens. It was paid on all inheritances except those which came from a man's nearest relatives, or did not exceed a certain sum. It was collected by 'procuratores,' who in turn farmed it out to 'publicani.' From this passage it seems to have been taken in kind, unless some compromise could be arrived at. The 'publicani' appear to have laid hands on a twentieth part of the estate, and in buying back from them Corellia had become aware of the real value of the property.

66   **Ep. 66. 1. Municipibus nostris**; the people of Comum. In Ep. 3. 1 we learn that Caninius was Pliny's fellow-citizen.

2. **Epulum.** In an inscription found at Milan (Gruter, Insc. 1028), Pliny himself is said to have left funds for a similar purpose.

3. **Numeres.** See note on Ep. 31. 34, and Madvig, § 353.

7. **In alimenta ingenuorum.** He speaks in Bk. 1. 8 of the oration in which he promised this endowment to his countrymen at Comum, and the inscription mentioned above records also his liberality to the free-born youth of Milan. Pliny was in this matter following the example of his master Trajan, who had provided maintenance at his own expense for five thousand children (probably in Rome), Pan. 28. The tablet of Veleia shows that the emperor's liberality also extended to the country towns. The alimentation was continued up to the eighteenth year for males, and the fourteenth for females. The object seems to have been to recruit the free-born population by inducing needy parents not to expose their children, but

to rear them in hope of receiving assistance. It was not merely a provision for orphans, though they may have been included in its benefits. See Merivale, Hist. Emp. c. 63.

S. **Longe pluris**, worth a great deal more than five hundred thousand sestertii.

Actori publico; the clerk who received and disbursed the revenues of a city, just as the 'actores privati' did in the case of private estates. Cp. Ep. 33. 7.

Mancipavi, 'I conveyed.' It was not a real sale, as Pliny only handed it over in order to receive it back.

9. **Tricena milia**. He thus established a perpetual rent-charge on this portion of his estate amounting to thirty thousand sestertii. This made exactly the same provision for the charity at Comum as a direct gift of a capital ('sors') of five hundred thousand sestertii would have done. For the interest of that sum at the usual rate of one-half per cent. per mensem, or six per cent. ('semissium usura'), would have amounted to the same sum, thirty thousand sestertii per annum.

We have in this matter another instance of Pliny's clearsightedness, parallel to that noticed on Ep. 39. The deterioration and even absolute loss of charitable and educational landed endowments in this country is familiar to all students of local history. Pliny's scheme seems free from all objection, as it was calculated to insure the safety of the endowment without breaking up his own estate. 'Vectigales agri' were recognised by the Roman law: the lessees had a right to retain the land so long as they paid the charges due, and this right in the land could probably be disposed of by will. At any rate, in the conclusion of the letter Pliny seems to contemplate the land as remaining in his disposition, though lowered in value by more than the amount of the charge on it, from the fact of its being 'vectigalis.'

16. **Diligentius muneri suo consulere**, 'to be more careful for the security of one's gift than the interests of one's property.' 'Se' and 'suus' sometimes stand in universal assertions (without being referred to a definite subject preceding) in the signification, of 'one's self,' 'one's own,' Madvig, § 490, Obs. 5.

Ep. 67. 1. Fanniae: see note on Ep. 28. 10.

Adsidet: for this special sense, cp. 'nihil scribere adsidenti vacat' Ep. 14. 45.

16. **Mettio Caro**. The share of this man in the death of Helvidius is alluded to in a previous letter, where he is made to speak of Senecio as one of his victims, 'mei mortui' Bk. 1. 5.

17. **Commentarios**; the diaries and note-books of Helvidius. Caesar gave this name of 'commentaries' to his works 'quod nudi essent omni ornatu orationis' Cic. Brut. 75.

21. **Abolitos senatus consulto**. Cp. 'Non in ipsos modo auctores sed in libros quoque eorum saevitum, delegato triumviris ministerio ut monumenta clarissimorum ingeniorum in comitio ac foro urerentur' Tac. Agr. 2.

Sorvavit ; Fannia contrived to preserve one copy.

25. Viri, 'we men.'

30. Novissima, 'the last of the race;' the last, that is to say, endued with the virtues of the race. Cp. 'C. Cassium Romanorum ultimum' Tac. Ann. 4. 34.

38. Ultor reversarum. See Ep. 77. 24.

Non feci tamen paria. Cp. 'parem calculum ponere' Ep. 45. 1.

68 Ep. 68. 5. Curtio Rufo. This story is confirmed by Tac. Ann. 11. 21. Curtius owed his promotion to Tiberius, so the tale was an old one.

6. Obtiuenti Africam, the magistrate in charge of the province.

27. Longior = 'diuturnior,' lasting longer than the sights and sounds which caused it.

28. Monstro. 'Mostellum,' the diminutive of 'monstrum,' also means a 'ghost,' and hence the name of Plautus's comedy, 'Mostellaria.'

Proscribebatur : see on Ep. 64. 2.

30. Athenodorus, said to have been tutor to Augustus. This therefore is another old story, and Lucian also gives a version of it with different names.

39. Auribusque praetendere, sc. 'animum;' i.e. 'animo aures custodire ne vana audiant.' His hands were engaged in writing, so we can neither take 'praetendere' absolutely nor supply 'manum.' 'Praetendere animum auribus' is a bold and poetical expression; but not more so than our own phrase 'to shut one's ear to a story,' which, like the Latin, represents as a physical act that which is really no more than a determination of the mind.

43. Ut paulum expectaret manu significat. 'The *historical* present is conceived and treated with reference to the propositions depending upon it, sometimes as an actual present, sometimes (according to the signification) as a perfect.' Madvig, § 382, Obs. 3. Cp. above dimittit . . . intendit . . . ne fingeret. The sequence of tenses would of course require 'fingat,' 'expectet,' after present tenses which were not historical.

61. In paedagogio. 'Paedagogium' was the name, not of a part of the house, but of the company of young slaves among whom this slave was sleeping. At any rate this is the sense of the word in all the other passages where it occurs.

67. A Caro, one of Domitian's informers, mentioned in the preceding letter. He knew he had made Pliny his enemy by his share in the death of Pliny's friend Senecio, and in the exile of Fannia widow of Helvidius. He would therefore naturally endeavour to put him out of the way.

69. Moris est submittere capillum. For this custom cp.
'Cuius manantia fletu
Ora puellares faciunt incerta capilli' Juv. 15. 136.

74. Ex altera; to fill up the sense supply 'disputa' from disputes above. 'Altera' here stands for 'alterutra,' 'one or the other,' as in Cic. Att. 11. 18 'Quorum fortasse utrumque erit ; alterum certe.' Pliny begs his correspondent to convince him one way or the other.

Ep. 69. 1. **Historias tuas.** The trial of Massa would come within 69
the scope of the 'historiae' of Tacitus properly so called. It occurred in
the reign of Domitian about the time of Agricola's death, as we learn from
Tac. Agr. sub fin. 'Massa Baebius iam tum reus erat.' But inasmuch as
the extant portion of the 'Histories' does not bring us further than the
midst of the reign of Vespasian, we have no means of knowing whether
Pliny's wish was gratified, though we do know that his presentiment was
disappointed.

3. Ab optimo **quoque artifice.** The whole letter is an imitation of
Cicero's letter to Lucceius the historian urging a similar request, Cic.
Fam. 5. 12. Even the illustration from art occurring here is borrowed from
Cicero; cp. 'Neque enim Alexander ille gratiae causa ab Apelle potissimum
pingi et a Lysippo fingi volebat; sed quod illorum artem cum ipsis tum etiam
sibi gloriae fore putabat.'

7. **In publicis actis,** the daily gazette published at Rome under the
empire, otherwise known as 'acta diurna,' or 'diurna.' These gazettes are
spoken of as being read in the armies and the provinces, Tac. Ann. 15. 22.

10. **Herennio Senecione,** put to death by Domitian on various
charges, one of them that of having composed the life of Helvidius Priscus,
Ep. 67. 14. Tacitus pays a tribute to his integrity, 'nos innocenti sanguine
Senecio perfudit' Tac. Agr. sub fin.

11. **Provinciae Baeticae,** Andalusia, the southernmost province of
Spain. It derived its name from the river Baetis (Guadalquivir) which
traverses it from east to west. It is cut off from inland Spain by the Sierra
Morena, and open only on its south-western coast. This fact explains its
connection with Africa under the Empire (cp. 'Priscus ex Baetica ex Africa
Classicus' Bk. 3. 9.) and also, later, under the Vandals and the Moors.
The province seems to have been unlucky in its rulers. Twice after the
trial of Massa they came to Rome with accusations against Classicus,
and against Gallus. In the case of Classicus they prevailed on Pliny to
appear for them again, Bk. 3. 4, and the trial is related at length in the
ninth letter of the same book. In the case of Gallus he resolved to
remain neutral.

12. **Ut bona eius publice custodirentur;** this was to be done in
order that restitution might be made out of them to the provincials.

16. **Ne bona dissipari sinant quorum esse in custodia debent,**
'that they (the consuls) would not allow the property to be made away
with, in charge of which they ought to be.' The antecedent of 'quorum'
is 'bona,' not 'consules,' nor 'ab iis' understood. Either of the latter
antecedents makes the position of 'esse' between 'quorum' and 'in custodia'
extremely harsh and unnatural. If, on the other hand, 'esse in custodia'
be considered as one phrase all is smooth. This explanation (so far as I
am aware, original) is supported by 'cum in eiusdem anni custodia te atque
L. Murenam fortuna posuisset' Cic. pro Mur. 31; 'retinendus est animus
in custodia corporis' Cic. Rep. 6. 15; in which instances the genitives

53

'anni,' and 'corporis,' both express, not that which exercised the 'custodia,' but that *over* which it was exercised. The Medicean reading 'dissipari' may therefore be retained.

'Debent,' 'ought to be,' by the decree of the senate mentioned above, 'ut bona eius,' &c. This decree, it seems, had not been properly attended to by the consuls.

20. **Cui nulla cum provincia necessitudo.** This was in Pliny's early days. Later in life he calls this same province of Baetica 'provinciam quam tot officiis meis devinxerim' Bk. 1. 7.

27. **Impietatis.** The crime of 'maiestas,' high treason, might also be styled 'impietas,' disloyalty. Cp. Pan. 33.

29. **Praevaricationem:** see on Ep. 13. 4.

31. **Privatus.** Nerva was probably at that time in exile at Tarentum, having been banished by Domitian.

36. **Notiora, clariora, maiora.** It is plain by the sense which he attaches to 'maiora,' Ep. 31. 50, 'alia clariora esse alia maiora,' that he does wish the historian to make more of the affair than it deserved, in spite **quamquam non exigo,** &c. He is however not so unblushing as Cicero. Cp. **honeste factis veritas sufficit** with 'amorique nostro plusculum etiam quam concedit veritas largiare' Cic. l. c.

70 **Ep. 70. 2. Vindemias.** Masson thinks that these 'vindemiae' were the 'partes' or proportion of the produce which Pliny had arranged to receive from his tenants in lieu of rent, Ep. 83. 12.

Certatim. by auction.

3. **Invitabat,** sc. 'negotiatores.'

8. **Paria peccata;** a favourite maxim with the Stoics. Cicero states it broadly 'nec minus delinquere eum qui gallum gallinaceum, cum opus non fuerit, quam qui patrem suffocaverit' Mur. 29. Pliny's thought is this: 'if all bad deeds are equally blameable, then all good ones are equally praiseworthy;' hence the importance of accurate justice even towards these dealers.

9. 'Nemo ex hac numero mihi non donatus abibit' Virg. Aen. 5. 305.

18. **Tulerunt,** 'carried off,' as a remission.

20. **Reposuisse:** 'reponere' means to pay, whether it consist in 're-placing' what had been at first received, or in returning an equivalent, as in this place. Cp.

'Semper ego auditor tantum nunquamne reponam?'

> Juv. 1. 1.

Verum, 'right.' Cp.

'Metiri se quemque suo modulo ac pede verum est'

> Hor. Ep. 1. 7, 98.

82. **Una pertica,** 'by one rule.' 'Pertica'='decempeda.'

31. 'Ἐν δὲ ἰῇ τιμῇ Hom. Il. 9. 319.

71 **Ep. 71. 1. Bellum Dacicum.** Caninius' plan seems, from Pliny's observations, **actos bis triumphos,** &c., to have included *both* of Trajan's expeditions, the first A.D. 101-2, and the second A.D. 104-6. The first

campaign was undertaken to avenge the defeat of Fuscus (Juv. 4. 111), and the humiliation of Domitian, who is said to have consented to the payment of a tribute to Decibalus the Dacian king. In the first campaign Trajan penetrated to the heart of Dacia, established a garrison there, and obtained the complete submission of Decibalus. On his return he celebrated a triumph, and received the name of Dacicus.

It was not long before the Dacians, by violating the treaty, provoked a second invasion, which ended in the defeat and death of Decibalus, and the settlement of Dacia as a Roman province. For a full account of the Dacian war, see Merivale, Hist. Emp. c. 63.

4. Inmissa **terris nova flumina.** Decibalus temporarily diverted a river from its course, that he might conceal his treasure in its bed. Trajan repeated the operation to recover the treasure, and this may possibly be the exploit to which Pliny alludes.

Novos pontes; the bridges of boats thrown over the Danube in the first campaign, and the massive permanent bridge constructed in preparation for the second campaign.

5. **Montium abrupta.** These were the great difficulties of a campaign in that region.

Pulsum regia, namely from Zermizegethusa, captured in the first campaign.

6. **Pulsum etiam vita.** Decibalus fell by his own hand at the capture of his hill fort. This completes a noticeable parallel between the Dacian campaign and the late Abyssinian expedition, both being triumphs of engineering skill and of discipline rather than of valour, though the resistance of the Dacian was of course more formidable than that of Theodore. The story of the captive Longinus affords another point of similarity.

12. **Barbara et fera nomina,** such as the names of the king and his capital.

13. **Resultent** = 'abhorreant.' 'Galea resultant' Virg. Aen. 10. 330 means 'they rebound from the helmet.' Here 'resultare Graecis versibus' expresses the stubborn unfitness of Dacian names for Greek metres, with which, as it were, they rebound from them. The **labor** lies in obviating this difficulty, ' ut *non* resultent.'

17. **Non delicata sed necessaria,** 'demanded not by caprice but by necessity.'

18. **Ipso,** sc. ' Trajano.'

Ep. 72. 1. **Clitumnum;** the Clitumnus falls into the Tinia, a tributary 72 of the Tiber. The excellence of the cattle fed on its banks made them in request at great festivals. Virgil mentions them among the glories of Italy: 'Hinc albi Clitumne greges' Georg. 2. 146. The beauty and celebrity of the spot attracted Caligula (Suet. Cal. 43) and Honorius (Claud. Cons. Hon. Sext. 506) to visit it.

5. **Eluctatusque quem facit gurgitem.** Cp. ' Nilus eluctatus ob-

stantia' Sen. Quaest. Nat. 4. 2. Verbs compounded with 'ex' which signify motion, generally take the accusative, rarely the ablative, unless the preposition is repeated before the substantive.

7. **Stipes**, 'small coins.' Seneca, in the passage quoted above, speaks of 'stipes' thrown into the stream by the priests.

8. **Devexitate.** Substantives ending in 'tas' are properly formed from adjectives only, Madvig, § 184. 1. But 'devexus' being adjectival in sense enjoys the privileges of an adjective. So also we have from 'falsus,' 'falsitas,' which has better authority than 'devexitas.' It was by the multiplication of these convenient derivatives that the vocabulary was increased, while the language was enervated.

9. **Fons adhuc et iam amplissimum flumen;** a vivid way of describing the quick transition from a mere spring to a river, which transition was the real marvel of the place; cp. 'Subita et ex abdito vasti amnis eruptio aras habet' Sen. Ep. 41. 'Est,' followed by a comma, suggests itself as an easy emendation for 'et,' and would simplify the sentence.

12. **Illa qua properat ipse,** 'down stream.'

13. **Remis non adiuvetur.** The current is so swift that oars are not required, and indeed cannot be used with advantage. Both 'adiuvetur' and **superetur** have the same nominative, namely Clitumnus, the river itself, which is now in the writer's thoughts though not expressed. Hence **validus** and **adversus** come to be masc., and not neut., in concord with 'flumen.'

15. **Ut flexerint cursum,** viz. either up stream or down stream.

18. **Adnumerat,** 'counts among its *own* charms,' though of course they properly belonged to the dry land.

22. **Sortes.** Lots were also in use at Praeneste and Caere. At the former place they consisted of sticks of oak with characters graven on them, Cic. de Div. 2. 41.

26. **Quod ponte transmittitur,** 'which is crossed (by the visitor) by means of a bridge.' 'Transmittere flumen' means to cross a river, for although 'mittere' has dropped its original meaning and becomes intransitive, ='mitti,' yet the addition of 'trans' enables it to govern an accusative. See Madvig, § 224. Since then 'transmittit flumen' may mean 'he crosses a river,' 'transmittitur flumen' may mean 'a river is crossed (by him).' Finally, the ablative 'ponte' is thrown in to describe the means of crossing; cp. 'In transgressu Euphratis quem ponte transmittebat' Tac. Ann. 15. 7. Or it may be translated simply, 'which is spanned by a bridge.' This would be a corruption of the proper use of 'transmitto,' paralleled by the ambiguous English idiom 'to be crossed by a bridge.'

27. **Infra etiam natare concessum.** The sanitary object of keeping clean springs meant for use was attained under the religious pretext of their sanctity. This was thoroughly in the spirit of the Roman cult as interpreted by Mommsen (vol. i. p. 184). Cp. the offence given by Nero's violation of the much-prized 'Aqua Marcia' Tac. Ann. 14. 22.

28. **Hispellates**; Hispellum was a town about twelve miles from the source of the river.

Ep. 73. 1. **Meorum**, sc. 'libertorum,' slaves whom he had manu- **73** mitted on account of their appearing unlikely to recover.

3. **Facilitas manumittendi.** Manumission by census needed no more than the registration of a slave's name in the list of citizens, with his master's consent.

5. **Servis quoque.** The disposition of their property made by those manumitted before their death would of course hold good; but Pliny allowed as valid even the quasi testamenta of those who died slaves. The property of slaves was called 'peculium,' and though legally it belonged to their masters as much as their persons did, yet usage recognised it as their own. Pliny went beyond usage in allowing them to dispose of it after death. See Dict. Ant. art. 'Servus.'

Ep. 74. 2. **Praesumptione.** See on 'praesumo' Ep. 22. 3. **74**

Certusque posteritatis, 'and assured of posthumous fame.' See on Ep. 16. 5.

3. **Cum,** 'in the enjoyment of.'

5. **Omnes homines**; a reminiscence of the opening of Sallust's Catiline.

9. **Ad vilitatem sui**; 'to holding life cheap,' to being weary of it. Cp. 'En sibi vilis adest invisa luce iuventus' Lucan 4. 276, speaking of the desperate recklessness of soldiers shut up without water. With regard to the substance of the letter it must be remembered that Pliny shared his uncle's cynical unbelief in a future life, expressed by him Hist. Nat. 7. 56, 'puerilium ista deliramentorum avidaeque nunquam desinere mortalitatis commenta sunt.' Immortality had no meaning to our author beyond that of posthumous fame, and to the hope of this he clung, as we see by his earnest request to Tacitus. Ep. 69.

Ep. 75. 4. **Nihil novum.** It is probable that this letter was suggested **75** by Cic. Fam. 7. 1. Cp. 'Quae tamen si videnda sunt, saepe vidisti, neque nos qui spectavimus *quidquam novi* vidimus' Cic. l c.

5. **Tot milia virorum**; cp.

    'Totam hodie Romam Circus capit,'

and foll. Juv. 11. 195.

9. **Favent panno,** 'their interest is in the colours.' Four chariots generally contended in each race, the drivers being distinguished by four colours white, green, red, and blue.

10. **Si in ipso cursu**; he means that if by some miracle the drivers were to exchange tunics in the middle of the race, the spectators' interest would go with the colour, and they would transfer their applause from the one chariot to the other.

Ep. 76. 1. **Inveni patrocinium**; I have found authority to defend **76** me from the charge of folly and extravagance. Our proverb, 'Fools build houses for wise men to live in,' was represented in Latin by 'aliena insania frui,' and this, says Pliny the elder, is the best thing to do, if you want a country house, Plin. N. H. 18. 5.

10. **Latius utitur,** sc. 'lacu,' 'enjoys a *wider* view of the lake,' which compensates for its not being quite so near the water.

13. **Spatiosissimo xysto;** a descriptive ablative governed by 'gestatio' repeated from the preceding clause.

18. **Idem facere,** 'that you are doing the same,' viz. building.

77 **Ep. 77. Quadrato suo,** a young man of ability and promise, whom Pliny, according to his custom, encouraged and advised on his entry on public life, Bk. 6. 11.   The generous interest which Pliny took in his numerous young friends of this class is one of the most amiable traits in his character.

1. **De Helvidi ultione.** Helvidius the younger, son of Helvidius Priscus, is alluded to.

8. **Senator senatori.** Certus was so eager to show his devotion to Domitian (cp. 'cruentae adulationis') that he took on himself to arrest Helvidius, instead of waiting for the proper officers.   Cp. 'Nostrae (sc. senatoriae) duxere Helvidium in carcerem manus' Tac. Agr. 45.

12. **Cum Arria et Fannia.** See on Ep. 28. 10.

16. **Dumtaxat** = γε.

20. **Defremuisset.** 'De' in composition sometimes introduces the sense of 'leaving off:' cp. 'despero.'

22. **Amissa nuper uxore,** his first wife.   See on Ep. 86. 10.

28. **Societate;** for the abl. see on Ep. 18. 3.

30. **Ad Corellium rettuli.** Cp. 'Nihil nisi ex consilio meo facit' Ep. 40. 30.

41. **Extra ordinem,** 'unconstitutionally.' The proper course would have been to present a distinct accusation in legal form ('referre'), and this it appears had to be authorized by the emperor.   Cp. 'Relationem quidem de eo Caesar ad senatum non remisit' line 112. Pliny's object in his motion was to obtain a 'relatio.'

42. **Qui supersumus,** 'who survive' the cruelty of Domitian.

47. **Sententiae loco.**   The consul reminds him that he will be allowed to speak before the votes are taken, to which Pliny angrily replies that that will be no extraordinary favour.   On 'sententiae loco' see on Ep. 60. 8.

50. **Curato,** 'earnest,' lit. 'taken pains with.' Cp. 'curatissimis precibus' Tac. Ann. 1. 13.

53. **Malis,** the adjective.

60. **Omnia praecepi,** &c. Virg. Aen. 6. 105. On the sense of 'praecepi' see on Ep. 18. 18.

63. **Censendi,** for giving opinions ('sententiae') before voting. Cp. l. 47. The other matters ('alia' l. 49) had been despatched.

64. **Fabricius Veiento.** See on Ep. 42. 14.

76. **Helvidi filiae,** one of the two Helvidiae, whose subsequent death in childbed is deplored by Pliny, Bk. 4. 21.   Their mother Anteia had married

58

again, and a guardian was therefore required for her children by Helvidius the younger, namely a boy and two girls.

93. **Proventum**, 'success.' Cp. 'Studia hilaritate proveniunt' Bk. 8. 19, where 'provenire' means ' to advance' and so 'to prosper.'

99. **Discessione**, 'the division,' which took place by the senators cross-ing the floor to join either one or another party.

103. **Ὦ γέρον**, words of Diomede to Nestor, from Hom. Il. 8. 102.

113. **Collega Certi consulatum, successorem Certus accepit.** Vettius Proculus, colleague of Certus in the prefecture of the treasury, was now named for the consulship instead of Certus. Certus thus lost the con-sulship promised him by Domitian (**a pessimo**), and was also superseded (**successorem accepit**) in his office at the treasury. 'Successorem dare alicui' to supersede a man, is not an infrequent phrase.

122. **Interest tamen exempli.** Cp. 'Exempli nonnihil refert' Bk. 8. 22.

124. **Inputabis**, 'you will blame yourself for,' lit. charge to your own account. Though frequent in this sense in later writers, 'imputo' was not thus used in the Augustan age. See Mayor's note on Juv. 5. 14.

Ep. 78. 3. **Tam querulis.** Grumbling was even in those days a **78** farmer's privilege. Cp. 'Querellae rusticorum qui auribus meis post longum tempus suo iure abutuntur' Bk. 7. 30.

6. **Rationes**, the accounts of the estate, to which any but a literary landlord would have given his first attention.

9. **Pro gestatione**, ' by way of exercise,' not really to examine the state of the land. 'Gestatio' is also the name of the place where exercise was taken; cp. 'Hortum et gestationem videt' Ep. 21. 61.

Ep. 79. Two reasons give interest to this letter, firstly, the amiable light **79** in which it exhibits the writer, and secondly its singular parallelism with the Epistle to Philemon. Here we have the language of humane interest in the delinquent, but St. Paul's is the language of brotherly affection.

12. **Tam lenis**, 'kindly as you are by nature.'

Ep. 80. 8. **Italicus es an provincialis.** This distinction was not **80** one of birth, but of residence.

11. **Quasi litterarum . . . . redduntur**, 'as though they belonged not to men but to literary pursuits, are assigned to the studies' (which we severally follow). The next clause, **quod uterque**, &c. is also dependent on **iucundum**, and runs parallel with the clause preceding it. For the idea cp. 'Ut Cicero iam non hominis sed eloquentiae nomen habeatur' Quint. Inst. Or. 10. 1.

Ep. 81. This story, with others to the same purpose, is recorded by Pliny **81** the elder, N. H. 9. 8.

6. **Omnis aetas**, i. e. 'homines omni aetate.'

21. **Si quid est mari simile.** This would include both the lagoon and its estuary.

36. **Incredibile**, because they were supposed to die at once on leaving

the water. So Thetis bids the dolphins (which are to carry her and Achilles to Scyros) to draw up 'pleno in litore,' where the water covers the shore, 'ne nudae noceant contagia terrae' Stat. Ach. 1. 227.

41. **Superfudisse unguentum.** It was customary to consecrate and anoint favourite animals, such as elephants, horses, birds, &c. See Casaubon on Suet. Jul. 81.

48. **Ad quod coibatur,** 'the object of the concourse.'

82 **Ep. 82.** 4. **Quae avocant,** 'which distract one.' Cp. 'Magis mihi vox avocare videtur quam crepitus' Sen. Ep. 56.

6. **Quotiens non vident alia,** 'whenever there is not something else for them to look at.'

7. **Ad verbum scribenti,** 'writing out in full.' He means that he composes mentally with as much care and minuteness as if he were writing and correcting on paper. So Quintilian, speaking of a habit of Cicero's which he is recommending and explaining, says 'Illud quoque *ad verbum* ponere optimum fuerit,' i. e. in all its details; Quint. Inst. Or. 11. 2.

9. **Notarium.** See on Ep. 25. 54.

15. **Intentio,** something stronger than 'attention,' more like 'concentration.' It was stimulated, not arrested, by the change and exercise.

20. **Comoedus.** See on Ep. 24. 36.

Cum meis, sc. 'libertis.' Cp. 'Gymnasium meorum' Ep. 21. 32.

24. **Brevius quia velocius.** Sufficient exercise could be got in less time, on horseback.

28. **Venor,** after the fashion described in Ep. 4.

30. **Colonis.** For their position see on Ep. 33. 23. Villenage in the middle ages was the offspring of the system of 'coloni.' It is not difficult to imagine the topics of their **agrestes querellae.**

83 **Ep. 83.** 1. **Translaticia.** The fundamental application of this word is to things not original, but copied or borrowed, as were legal formulae or the praetor's annual edict. For this sense cp. 'Hoc vetus edictum translaticiumque esse' Cic. Verr. 2. 1. 44; and Cic. Div. 8. 5, where 'haec translaticia' means 'the old story.' Hence it declines into the sense of formal, unmeaning, commonplace, as here. Cp. also 'non translaticia deformitate,' 'no common unsightliness,' Petron. 110.

4 **Nisi.** The use of 'nisi' for 'ni' or 'si non' in this passage is certainly awkward. The negative is thereby removed from **videro,** with which in sense it is closely united; and the clause **nisi te Kalendis,** &c. to which the whole sentence leads up, is introduced by a conjunction ('nisi') which is generally employed to insert an exception. 'Per "nisi" significatur *exceptio* quae ad aliquam sententiam *accedit*' Hand. Turs. sub. voc. 'Nisi,' where the distinction between 'nisi' and 'si non' is clearly laid down. 'Nisi' is nearly coextensive in its use with the English 'unless.'

The sense of the passage may be briefly given thus, (1) you are too kind to insist on this rubbish; (2) I am too dear a friend to be suspected of coldness if I don't ('nisi') come; (3) but above all I am very busy about my farms.

5. **Plures annos ordinatura,** 'which will settle matters for many years to come.' **Necessitas locandorum praediorum** is treated as equivalent to 'locatio praediorum,' and so 'ordinatura' is joined to it, though strictly speaking 'necessitas . . . ordinatura' is nonsense.

7. **Lustro,** the usual term of a Roman lease.

8. **Reliqua,** 'arrears.' Cp. 'Reliqua colonorum minuit' Ep. 33. 20.

10. **Ut qui iam putent.** They think they can't help being bankrupt. Frugality would be only for their creditor's benefit, i. e. their landlord's, and not for their own.

12. **Si non nummo, sed partibus locem,** 'if I let the land not for a fixed rent, but for proportions of the produce.' This was a return to the old system described by Cato as 'politio,' which was in fact the 'metairie' system now prevailing in Italy. See Daubeny's Roman Husbandry, Lect. 2.

13. **Operis exactores.** He would appoint some of his own farm bailiffs to see that he got his due proportion of the produce. This would be a duty exactly analogous to the work of taking tithes in kind before the 'commutation.'

15. **Delicata,** 'capricious,' 'fanciful,' opposed to obligatory. Cp. Ep. 71. 17.

Ep. 84. Mustio, an architect. Cp. inf. 'Qui soles locorum difficultates **84** arte superare.'

2. **In melius.** See on Ep. 28. 2.

6. **In proximo.** See on Ep. 4. 4.

Suffugium aut imbris aut solis. The objective genitive following a verbal substantive has the same meaning as the transitive verb and the accusative; Madv. § 283, Obs. 3. This will apply to 'suffugium' and its genitive, since 'suffugit' is used transitively Lucr. 5. 150.

15. **Quod videatur istinc esse repetendum.** 'Repetendum' has usually been taken to mean the same as 'arcessendum,' and the passage construed thus, 'which seems desirable to be procured from the place where you are.' But this translation entirely omits the force of 're.' 'Repeto' occurs twenty-four times in Pliny's letters, and always in the sense of going *back* to, fetching *back*, or taking up *again*. The only way of giving 'repetendum' an adequate sense is to take the passage thus, 'nothing occurs to me that seems desirable to be taken up into consideration from the spot,' i. e. from the character of the buildings already existing. This interpretation seems to prepare the way more naturally for the clause beginning **nisi tamen.** On the other hand it may be said that 'istinc' must mean 'e loco in quo tu es.' But that 'istinc' for 'illinc' is no solecism appears from 'si quid novisti rectius istis Candidus imperti' Hor. Ep. 1. 6, 67. And cp. 'Nec tantum dicitur pronomen "iste" de eo loco quem alter obtinet quocum aliquis loquitur, sed quicumque intelligitur locus ab eo qui loquitur remotus' Hand. Turs. sub. voc. 'Iste.' Or again, we may suppose Mustius to have lived in the neighbourhood of the temple (though at this time he seems not to have

seen it), or at any rate to have lived nearer to it than the spot from which Pliny was writing.

85 Ep. 85. 2. Patri; Nerva, who had adopted Trajan as his son.

Festinaverunt. Nerva reigned barely a year and a half.

86 Ep. 86. 2. Iure trium liberorum; for an explanation of this see on Ep. 19. 21.

4. Rescripto. By this time the word 'rescriptum' had attained a technical sense, viz. an answer in writing given by the emperor to some magistrate or private person consulting him, which when given carried the force of law. At a later period (in the Institutes of Justinian) it was held that whatever the emperor determined by letter ('rescriptum'), or decided judicially ('decretum'), or declared by edict ('edictum'), was the law of the empire. These three classes of decisions were included under the general name 'constitutiones.' These 'constitutiones' were preserved in the imperial archives even from the time of Augustus, and copies of them more or less complete were also to be found at the seats of provincial government. A careful discrimination was observed between those constitutions which were of universal and those which were of special application. Cp. 'Aut proprium aut universale' Ep. 87. 4.

10. Duobus matrimoniis meis. It appears to be uncertain whether Pliny was married once or twice before his marriage with Calpurnia. We know from Ep. 77. 22 and 65 that the wife who immediately preceded Calpurnia died shortly after the accession of Nerva, and that her step-father's name was Vettius Proculus. Pompeia Celerina, whom Pliny speaks of as his 'socrus' (Bk. 1. 4), was probably the mother of this previous wife, and therefore had married Vettius Proculus as her second husband. See on Ep. 41.

We are then wholly without trace of a marriage on Pliny's part previous to that with the daughter of Pompeia Celerina. Mommsen (Onomasticon, Keil's second ed.), apparently on the strength of this letter only, thinks that two marriages must have been contracted in the reign of Domitian, in which case the 'socrus' mentioned in Ep. 12. 8 must be the mother of a wife married when Pliny was still 'adulescentulus,' who afterwards made way by death for the daughter of Pompeia Celerina.

But the passage before us does not clearly state that the two marriages were contracted in Domitian's time, but only that the fact of his wishing to have children even then is proved by the fact of his not having waited till now to be married, but having married once before, as well as once now, twice in all. We may perhaps suppose that Pliny, like an advocate, gave the sentence an equivocal turn to make his case look better than it was.

12. Futurus essem, sc. 'pater.'

87 Ep. 87. 2. θρεπτούς. These were children exposed by their parents, who had been rescued and brought up by other persons.

3. Constitutionibus. See on Ep. 86. 4.

4. Quod ad Bithynos, to be taken in close connection with **universale**.

Pliny could find no special enactment for Bithynia (**proprium**) nor any universal enactment for the empire which might be applied to the case of the Bithynians.

7. **Exemplo**, 'a precedent.'

10. **Achaeos.** Unless we omit 'Achaeos' 'dein ad' must be inserted before the word, as in the Aldine edition.

Ep. 88. 2. **Sublati.** 'Tollo' has the special sense of taking up new-born **88** children from the ground as a sign that they were to be reared.

7. **Intermissa,** Orelli's emendation for 'inter quas.' Keil's own is more ingenious, 'intra eas provincias de quibus rescripsit inter quas non est Bithynia.'

8. **Adsertionem.** 'Adsero' may be used indifferently with 'in libertatem' or 'in servitutem.' Suet. Vitell. 10; Tib. 2.

10. **Ipsam libertatem.** 'Ipsam' throws an emphasis on 'libertatem,' which may perhaps be rendered by translating the words 'natural liberty.' Their status was already that of freedom itself, and did not, in Trajan's opinion, require to be made so by any payment to their foster parents for the expenses of nurture.

Redimendam, 'requiring redemption.'

Ep. 89. 1. **Nicomedensi.** Nicomedia was the ancient capital of the **89** kings of Bithynia. Two hundred years after Pliny's time it was chosen by Diocletian as the capital of his eastern share of the empire, and was then, according to Gibbon, inferior only to Rome, Antioch, and Alexandria in its extent and populousness.

2. **Cum detineretur.** The bakers to whom he had engaged himself as a journeyman having discovered that he was a runaway slave endeavoured to make him their own slave.

4. **Confugisse ad tuam statuam.** Statues of the emperors shared the right of asylum possessed by temples of the gods. This privilege of sanctuary was much abused, Tac. Ann. 3. 36. It seems to have been the only method of appeal which slaves had in case of ill usage; hence we find a 'constitutio' of Antoninus Pius to the effect that if a slave in a province fled to a temple or a statue to avoid ill treatment, the authorities could compel his master to sell him, and the slave was not to be regarded as a runaway.

6. **Susago.** Susagus was probably a Dacian general who took part in the invasion of Moesia by Decibalus in the first year of Domitian, A.D. 81. This was twenty-three years before the time of Pliny's writing this letter, which would leave room for the many years (**pluribus annis**) mentioned below.

Decibalo. Decibalus was probably not a personal name, but a title, like that of Pharaoh. See Merivale's Hist. Emp. c. 61.

10. **Mittendum ad te putavi.** He thought Trajan would be glad to gather from him information about the state of Dacia and Parthia, both of which he afterwards invaded and conquered.

Feci dum requiro. 'Dum' used of a contemporary action usually takes the present, although the action may be past, and the perfect be used in the leading proposition. Cp. 'Dum obsequor adolescentibus me senem esse oblitus sum' Cic. de Or. 2. 4.

11. **Quibus**; an antecedent for quibus in the gen. case and governed by imaginem must be understood—'an effigy of Pacorus and the ornaments with which,' &c.

14. **Signata est**, sc. glebula, the packet in which the nugget was enclosed.

90   **Ep. 90.** This and the following letter attracted the notice of Christian authors at an early period, and is alluded to by Tertullian, Eusebius and Jerome.

'Nowhere perhaps had Christianity advanced with greater rapidity than in the northern provinces of Asia Minor, where the inhabitants were of very mingled descent, neither purely Greek nor essentially Asiatic, with a considerable proportion of Jewish colonists chiefly of Babylonian or Syrian, not of Palestinian origin. It is here, in the province of Bithynia, that Polytheism first discovered the deadly enemy which was undermining her authority' Milman's Hist. Chr. 2. 6.

Although Paul did not visit Bithynia (Acts 16. 7), yet the province might easily have been evangelized from the neighbouring church of Galatia.

3. **Cognitionibus.** It is manifest, both from this expression and from the executions ordered by Pliny and sanctioned by the emperor, that Christianity was already an offence amenable to capital punishment; and this either under some existing statute, or under the law of the empire, which invested both the emperor and the provincial governor with the arbitrary power of life and death. See Milman, l. c.

8. **Nomen ipsum.** It is evident from Trajan's answer to this enquiry (Ep. 91) that the mere profession and not the practice of Christianity, was the object of punishment. This is a frequent matter of complaint with the Christian apologists. Cp. 'And ye shall be hated of all men for my *name's* sake' Matt. 10. 22.

12. **Iterum ac tertio.** In this repeated questioning may be seen the rudiments of the system of torture afterwards employed to elicit a denial of the faith. Roman law did not accept a *single* confession of a prisoner as proof of guilt, unless the confession was supported by external proof, but required the confession to be repeated. Thus a provision of mercy became a pretext for cruelty.

13. **Duci**, sc. 'ad supplicium,' a common euphemism.

14. **Inflexibilem** obstinationem. Constancy naturally appears obstinacy to spectators who do not see its relation to the object or person external to itself whereon it depends. Pliny most probably, like his uncle (Pliny N. H. 7. 56), could not conceive a future existence possible, and was thus incapacitated for distinguishing between obstinacy and the constancy of Christian hope. So also Marcus Aurelius (11. 3) says the Christians

were ready to die of mere obstinacy, a passage referred to and explained in Smith's Dict. Bible, vol. 2, p. 857 note, art. 'Philosophy.'

Pliny could only see in the conduct of the Christians the violation of the most evident duty, that of passive obedience on the part of subjects towards a beneficent government.

16. **In urbem remittendos**: cp. Acts 25. 12.

17. **Ipso tractatu . . . . crimine.** 'when, as usually happens, the charge became more common, simply from the fact of the matter being dealt with.' 'Crimen' is the charge of being a Christian, which now presented itself as an easy means of gratifying private enmity, even when there was no evidence to bring in support of it.

22. **Ture ac vino supplicarent.** Christians who consented to do this were known in the Church as 'thurificati.' Cp. Cyprian, Ep. 52.

Male dicerent Christo. It was a similar command which about fifty years later drew from Polycarp his dying confession, 'I have now served him eighty-six years, and he has done me no wrong; how can I blaspheme my King and Saviour?'

23. **Quorum nihil cogi.** Verbs which, like 'cogo,' take a double accusative in the active voice may retain one of those accusatives in the passive. Thus, since

> 'Quid non mortalia pectora cogis
> Auri sacra fames? Virg. Aen. 3. 56,

is good syntax, then 'si cogi aliquid consules possunt' Liv. 4. 26, will also stand as good.

30. **Stato die**, namely the first day of the week. This account of the Christian worship corresponds with that given by Justin Martyr, not quite thirty years later, who mentions assemblies for the purpose of worship as being held τῇ τοῦ ἡλίου λεγομένῃ ἡμέρᾳ Apol. 1. 87.

31. **Ante lucem**, before the labours of the day began, which in the case of slave Christians would occupy Sunday as much as any other day. Thus this early hour became the established time for worship, and consequently for the administration of the Holy Communion. The same hour is still regarded as proper for that purpose, an example of how the necessities of an age establish a custom which long survives that age and its necessities.

Carmen, not necessarily either lengthy or metrical. All that 'carmen' implies is 'a set form of words.'

Quasi deo; these words are evidently thrown in by Pliny, and must not be regarded as evidence of the belief of the Church at that time in the Divinity of Christ.

32. **Sacramento.** Waterland, in tracing the history of the various names of the Lord's Supper, refers to this as the earliest application to it of the name 'sacrament.' 'As Pliny is here reporting what the Christians had told him, it is reasonable to judge that they made use of the word "sacrament" to him, which they understood in the Christian sense, however Pliny or Trajan might take it' Waterland on the Eucharist, c. 1.

He says further in support of this interpretation of 'sacramentum' in this place, ' The account given in this passage refers to what the whole assembly were wont to do at the same; they could not all come to receive Baptism, though they might come to receive the Eucharist' Ib. Tertullian, contrasting the commands of the Lord with superadded tradition, employs the word 'sacrament' to denote the Lord's Supper, and also confirms Pliny's account of its being received before daybreak. 'Eucharistiae sacramentum, et in tempore victus, et omnibus mandatum a Domino; etiam *antelucanis* coetibus nec de aliorum manu quam praesidentium sumimus' Tert. de Cor. c. 3, p. 102, ed. Rig.

35. Rursusque coeundi; i. e. for the love feast in the *evening*, now distinct from the Eucharist, which latter was no longer taken ' in tempore victus' at meal-time, Tert. l. c. 'Coeundi' is inserted from the Aldine edition.

36. Promiscuum. 'ordinary,' cp. 'promiscua et vilia,' common and cheap articles,' Tac. Germ. 5. This account of the food at the Agapae was given by the Christians in refutation of the common charge that they ate human flesh; a charge which arose from the language which they employed respecting the Body and Blood of Christ.

38. Hetaerias. Clubs or guilds, for whatever purpose, were looked on as dangerous; cp. Trai. 34 and 93. This being so, the doctrine of the unity of the Church of Christ, and the practice of ' love of the brethren' would, so far as they were understood, appear to the government more formidable than the other features of Christianity.

39. Ministrae, apparently a translation of διάκονοι, deaconesses, a recognised order in the early Church, Rom. 16. 1.

46. Civitates. Here we see ' civitas ' on its way to the exclusive sense of ' city,' which it has reached in modern languages. But in Cicero we find a distinction clearly laid down between ' civitates,' commonwealths of 'cives,' and ' urbes' the places of their habitation. Pro Sest. 42. In Gellius we find note taken of the confusion of the two words, and the use of ' civitas ' ' pro oppido *et* pro hominum multitudine ' Gell. 18. 7.

50. Pastum. It does not appear how the food of victims differed from that of other cattle. They may perhaps have been grazed in the precincts of the temple at the expense of the intending sacrificer.

91 Ep. 91. 2. Neque enim in universum. Trajan refuses to write such a ' rescript' as might be taken for a law of the empire (see on Ep. 86. 4), and confines himself to an approval of Pliny's conduct. Trajan seems to have thought that the new sect would require different treatment according to the political condition of the places in which it appeared; for his point of view was political, and his object rather the peace than the orthodoxy of the empire.

4. Conquirendi non sunt. ' O sententiam necessitate confusam ! Negat inquirendos, ut innocentes; et mandat puniendos ut nocentes ' Tertull. Ap. 2.

8. **Sine auctore.** 'Cum alicui crimen obiicitur praecedere debet in crimen subscriptio' (i. e. the signature of the accuser). Ulpian 48. 2, 7.

10. **Nec nostri saeculi.** Cp. 'Digna saeculo tuo' Ep. 85. 5, and 'Convenientissimum tranquillitati saeculi' Trai. 10.

INDEX OF NAMES.

marry the daughter of Rusticus, Ep. 9.

Minicius Justus, Ep. 64, the husband of the elder Corellia.

Minucius Fundanus, addressed in Ep. 5, loses a daughter, Ep. 49.

Modestus, Ep. 38, a slave of Sabina's, generously treated by Pliny.

Murena, Ep. 77, tribune in 96.

Musonius, C., Ep. 28, a Stoic philosopher, whose acquaintance Pliny made in Syria. He had been banished by Nero, but an exception was made in his favour when Vespasian banished the philosophers, who pushed the Stoic doctrines to an absurd length and aimed at exciting an insurrection. See *Helvidius Priscus* and his fate.

Mustius, Ep. 84, an architect.

Nepos, Licinius, addressed in Epp. 31; 60; often named by Pliny as an upright man and severe praetor.

Nero, see *Drusus.*

Nero, Epp. 25, 27, 46, the nephew Caligula, adopted by Claudius, succeeded the latter in 54, and reigned till 68. His reign marks the lowest point of Roman life, and is one long chronicle of murder, beginning with his relations Britannicus and Agrippina, and ending with all men of superior virtue, such as Thrasea Pactus. Nero was assassinated upon the rising of Vindex and Galba. Literature in his time is represented by Persius, Lucan, and Seneca, but even that distinction became perilous, Ep. 25.

Nerva, M. Cocceius [Epp. 40, 42,

69, note 31], reigned from 96 to 98. He had been consul with Vespasian in 71, with Domitian in 90. Though exiled, his life was spared through Domitian's superstitious belief in an astrologer, who prophesied his speedy death. His reign was marked by the restoration of confidence in the government, but he dealt with the informers much too gently for general approval [Ep. 42]. His adoption of Trajan, a measure which greatly strengthened his position, was immediately due to a revolt of the soldiers, who demanded the punishment of Domitian's murderers.

Nicetes Sacerdos, named Ep. 55 as a teacher of Pliny's in oratory.

Nonianus, M. Servilius, attracts Caligula to his recitation, Ep. 8, note 11.

Nonius Maximus, addressed in Ep. 46.

Octavius Avitus, Ep. 81.

Octavius Rufus, addressed in Ep. 18, a promising poet.

Pacorus, king of Parthia, Ep. 89.

Paetus, (i) Caecina, (ii) Thrasea, both in Epp. 31 and 28, note 10.

Passennus Paulus, interrupted by Iavolenus, Ep. 58, note 2; a distinguished knight who counted Propertius among his ancestors. He was celebrated for his lyric and elegiac verses, and is highly praised by Pliny (Ep. ix. 22). Pliny's warm friendship for Paulus perhaps makes him the more severe upon Iavolenus.

INDEX OF NAMES.

Like our Prince Hal, his youth gave no promise of his future excellence. Rome still possesses some Memorials of him in the Colosseum and the baths which bear his name.

Traianus, M. Ulpius [Epp. 85 to 91], a Spaniard from Italica near Seville, was the first emperor of foreign birth. Born in 52, he reigned from 98 to 117, having been adopted by Nerva in 97. Under so good an administrator, Rome enjoyed a long period of tranquillity: while Trajan increased his military renown by his campaigns in Dacia in the East, where he died.

Trebonius Rufinus [Ep. 42], abolishes the games at Vienne when duumvir.

Tullius, M., see *Cicero*.

Valerius Festus, Ep. 27, note 37.

Valerius Martialis, M., see under *Martialis*.

Veiento, see *Fabricius*, and Ep. 42, note 14.

Velleius Blaesus, Ep. 23, a victim to Regulus' cupidity.

Verania, Ep. 23, another of Regulus' victims.

Vergilius, Ep. 27, venerated by the poet Silius Italicus, was born at Mantua in 70, d. 19, B.C.

Verginius Rufus, described Ep. 16, his monument still unfinished, Ep. 57.

Verus, addressed in Ep. 53.

Vespasianus, T. Flavius Sabinus [Epp. 9, 25, 87], born A.D. 9, reigned from 70 to 79. He was sent by Nero as his best general in 66 to conduct the Jewish war, and in 69 found himself strong enough to crush Vitellius by the help of Mucianus, governor of Syria, whose services he never forgot. Vespasian brought to Rome a respite from persecution, while his example is said to have done more towards purifying Roman morals than all the laws that were ever enacted.

Vettius Proculus, Ep. 77, stepfather of Pliny's wife, defends his colleague Certus.

Vitellius, A., mentioned, Ep. 27, as the friend of Silius Italicus, was emperor in 69. Supported by the German legions to which Galba had appointed him, his lieutenants overthrew Otho; but Vitellius' incapacity for anything but gluttony led to his speedy dethronement in favour of Vespasian.

Vindex, Ep. 57, note 15.

Voconius, see *Romanus*.

Xerxes, the story of his weeping over the mortality of his army used as the theme for moralising, Ep. 27.

Zosimus, Ep. 50, a freedman for whom Pliny asks a favour of one of his friends.

THE END.

Clarendon Press Series.

Latin Educational Works.

GRAMMARS, LEXICONS, &c.

Allen. *Rudimenta Latina.* Comprising Accidence, and Exercises of a very Elementary Character, for the use of Beginners. By J. BARROW ALLEN, M.A. . . . . [Extra fcap. 8vo, 2s.

—— *An Elementary Latin Grammar.* By the same Author. *One hundred and seventeenth Thousand.* . . . [Extra fcap. 8vo, 2s. 6d.

—— *A First Latin Exercise Book.* By the same Author. *Seventh Edition.* . . . . [Extra fcap. 8vo, 2s. 6d.

—— *A Second Latin Exercise Book.* By the same Author. *Eighth Edition.* . . . . [Extra fcap. 8vo, 3s. 6d.

[*A Key to First and Second Latin Exercise Books: for Teachers only, price 5s.*]

Fox and Bromley. *Models and Exercises in Unseen Translation.* By H. F. FOX, M.A., and T. M. BROMLEY, M.A. [Extra fcap. 8vo, 5s. 6d.

[*A Key to Passages quoted in the above: for Teachers only, price 6d.*]

Gibson. *An Introduction to Latin Syntax.* By W. S. GIBSON, M.A. [Extra fcap. 8vo, 2s.

Jerram. *Reddenda Minora.* By C. S. JERRAM, M.A. [Extra fcap. 8vo, 1s. 6d.

—— *Anglice Reddenda.* FIRST SERIES. [Extra fcap. 8vo, 2s. 6d.

—— *Anglice Reddenda.* SECOND SERIES. [Extra fcap. 8vo, 3s.

—— *Anglice Reddenda.* THIRD SERIES. [Extra fcap. 8vo, 3s

Lee-Warner. *Hints and Helps for Latin Elegiacs.* By H. LEE-WARNER, M.A. . . . . [Extra fcap. 8vo, 3s. 6d.

[*A Key is provided: for Teachers only, price 4s. 6d.*]

Lewis. *An Elementary Latin Dictionary.* By CHARLTON T. LEWIS, Ph.D.. . . . . [Square 8vo, 7s. 6d.

—— *A Latin Dictionary for Schools.* By the same Author. [Small 4to, 18s.

Lindsay. *A Short Historical Latin Grammar.* By W. M. LINDSAY, M.A. . . . . [Crown 8vo, 5s. 6d.

Nunns. *First Latin Reader.* By T. J. NUNNS, M.A. *Third Edition.* [Extra fcap. 8vo, 2s.

Ramsay. *Latin Prose Composition.* By G. G. RAMSAY, M.A., LL.D. *Third Edition.* Extra fcap. 8vo.

Vol. I. *Syntax, Exercises with Notes, &c.,* 4s. 6d.
Or in two Parts, 2s. 6d. each, viz.
Part I. *The Simple Sentence.* Part II. *The Compound Sentence.*

.˙. *A Key to the above, price 5s. Supplied to Teachers only, on application to the Secretary, Clarendon Press.*

Vol. II. *Passages of Graduated Difficulty for Translation into Latin, together with an Introduction on Continuous Prose,* 4s. 6d.

Ramsay. *Latin Prose Versions.* Contributed by various Scholars. Edited by G. G. RAMSAY, M.A., LL.D. . . . [Extra fcap. 8vo, 5s.

Sargent. *Easy Passages for Translation into Latin.* By J. Y. SARGENT, M.A. *Seventh Edition.* . . . . . . [Extra fcap. 8vo, 2s. 6d.
[*A Key to this Edition is provided : for Teachers only, price 5s.*]

—— *A Latin Prose Primer.* By the same Author.
[Extra fcap. 8vo, 2s. 6d.

King and **Cookson.** *The Principles of Sound and Inflexion, as illustrated in the Greek and Latin Languages.* By J. E. KING, M.A., and CHRISTOPHER COOKSON, M.A. . . . . . . [8vo, 18s.

—— *An Introduction to the Comparative Grammar of Greek and Latin.* By the same Authors. . . . . . [Crown 8vo, 5s. 6d.

Papillon. *A Manual of Comparative Philology.* By T. L. PAPILLON, M.A. *Third Edition.* . . . . [Crown 8vo, 6s.

Caesar. *The Commentaries* (for Schools). With Notes and Maps. BY CHARLES E. MOBERLY, M.A.
The Gallic War. New Edition. Extra fcap. 8vo—
  Books I and II, 2s. ;   III-V, 2s. 6d. ;   VI-VIII, 3s. 6d.
  Books I-III, stiff covers, 2s.
The Civil War. Second Edition. . . . [Extra fcap. 8vo, 3s. 6d.

Catulli Veronensis *Carmina Selecta*, secundum recognitionem ROBINSON ELLIS, A.M. . . . . . [Extra fcap. 8vo, 3s. 6d.

Cicero. *Selection of Interesting and Descriptive Passages.* With Notes. By HENRY WALFORD, M.A. In three Parts. *Third Edition.*
[Extra fcap. 8vo, 4s. 6d.
  Part I.   *Anecdotes from Grecian and Roman History.* . (limp, 1s. 6d.
  Part II. *Omens and Dreams ; Beauties of Nature.* . . [„ 1s. 6d.
  Part III. *Rome's Rule of her Provinces.* . . . . [„ 1s. 6d.

—— *De Amicitia.* With Introduction and Notes. By ST. GEORGE STOCK, M.A. . . . . [Extra fcap. 8vo, 3s.

—— *De Senectute.* With Introduction and Notes. By LEONARD HUXLEY, B.A. *In one or two Parts.* . . . . [Extra fcap. 8vo, 2s.

—— *Pro Cluentio.* With Introduction and Notes. By W. RAMSAY, M.A. Edited by G. G. RAMSAY, M.A. *Second Edition.* [Extra fcap. 8vo, 3s. 6d.

—— *Pro Marcello, pro Ligario, pro Rege Deiotaro.* With Introduction and Notes. By W. Y. FAUSSET, M.A. . . . [Extra fcap. 8vo, 2s. 6d.

—— *Pro Milone.* With Notes, &c. By A. B. POYNTON, M.A.
[Extra fcap. 8vo, 2s. 6d.

—— *Pro Roscio.* With Introduction and Notes. By ST. GEORGE STOCK, M.A. . . . . [Extra fcap. 8vo, 3s. 6d.

—— *Select Orations* (for Schools). *In Verrem Actio Prima. De Imperio Gn. Pompeii. Pro Archia. Philippica IX.* With Introduction and Notes. By J. R. KING, M.A. *Second Edition.* . [Extra fcap. 8vo, 2s. 6d.

—— *In Q. Caecilium Divinatio* and *In C. Verrem Actio Prima.* With Introduction and Notes. By J. R. KING, M.A. [Extra fcap. 8vo, 1s. 6d.

Cicero. *Speeches against Catilina.* With Introduction and Notes. By E. A. UPCOTT, M.A. *Second Edition.* . . . [Extra fcap. 8vo, 2s. 6d.

—— *Philippic Orations.* With Notes, &c., by J. R. KING, M.A. *Second Edition.* . . . . [8vo, 10s. 6d.

—— *Selected Letters* (for Schools). With Notes. By C. E. PRICHARD, M.A., and E. R. BERNARD, M.A. *Second Edition.* [Extra fcap. 8vo, 3s.

—— *Select Letters.* With English Introductions, Notes, and Appendices. By ALBERT WATSON, M.A. *Third Edition.* . . [8vo, 18s.

—— *Select Letters.* Text. By the same Editor. *Second Edition.* [Extra fcap. 8vo, 4s.

Cornelius Nepos. With Notes. By OSCAR BROWNING, M.A. *Third Edition.* Revised by W. R. INGE, M.A. . . [Extra fcap. 8vo, 3s.

Early Roman Poetry. *Selected Fragments.* With Introduction and Notes. By W. W. MERRY, D.D. . . . . . [Crown 8vo, 6s. 6d.

Horace. With a Commentary. Volume I. *The Odes, Carmen Seculare,* and *Epodes.* By EDWARD C. WICKHAM, D.D. *New Edition.* [Extra fcap. 8vo, 6s.

—— *Odes,* Book I. By the same Editor. . . [Extra fcap. 8vo, 2s.

—— *Selected Odes.* With Notes for the use of a Fifth Form. By E. C. WICKHAM, D.D. . . . . [Extra fcap. 8vo, 2s.

Juvenal. *XIII Satires.* Edited, with Introduction, Notes, &c., by C. H. PEARSON, M.A., and H. A. STRONG, M.A. *Second Edition.* [Crown 8vo, 9s.

Livy. *Selections* (for Schools). With Notes and Maps. By H. LEE-WARNER, M.A. . . . . [Extra fcap. 8vo.
    Part I. *The Caudine Disaster.* . . . . . . [limp, 1s. 6d.
    Part II. *Hannibal's Campaign in Italy.* . . . [,, 1s. 6d.
    Part III. *The Macedonian War.* . . . . . [,, 1s. 6d.

—— *Book I.* With Introduction, Historical Examination, and Notes. By J. R. SEELEY, M.A. *Second Edition.* . . . . . . [8vo, 6s.

—— *Books V—VII.* With Introduction and Notes. By A. R. CLUER, B.A. *Second Edition.* Revised by P. E. MATHESON, M.A. [Extra fcap. 8vo, 5s. *Book V,* 2s. 6d. ; *Book VII,* 2s. By the same Editors.

—— *Books XXI—XXIII.* With Introduction, Notes, and Maps. By M. T. TATHAM, M.A. *Second Edition* . . . [Extra fcap. 8vo, 5s.

—— *Book XXI.* By the same Editor. . . [Extra fcap. 8vo, 2s. 6d.

—— *Book XXII.* By the same Editor. . . [Extra fcap. 8vo, 2s. 6d.

Ovid. *Selections* (for the use of Schools). With Introductions and Notes, and an Appendix on the Roman Calendar. By W. RAMSAY, M.A. Edited by G. G. RAMSAY, M.A. *Third Edition.* . [Extra fcap. 8vo, 5s. 6d.

—— *Tristia,* Book I. The Text revised, with an Introduction and Notes. By S. G. OWEN, B.A. . . . . [Extra fcap. 8vo, 3s. 6d.

—— *Tristia,* Book III. With Introduction and Notes. By the same Editor. . . . . [Extra fcap. 8vo, 2s.

Persius. *The Satires.* With Translation and Commentary by J. CONINGTON, M.A., edited by H. NETTLESHIP, M.A. . . [8vo, 8s. 6d.

Plautus. *Captivi.* With Introduction and Notes. By W. M. LINDSAY, M.A. . . . . [Extra fcap. 8vo, 2s. 6d.

—— *Trinummus.* With Notes and Introductions. (Intended for the Higher Forms of Public Schools.) By C. E. FREEMAN, M.A., and A. SLOMAN, M.A. . . . . . . [Extra fcap. 8vo, 3s.

Pliny. *Selected Letters* (for Schools). By C. E. PRICHARD, M.A., and E. R. BERNARD, M.A. *Third Edition.* . . . [Extra fcap. 8vo, 3s.

Quintilian. *Institutionis Oratoriae Liber X.* Edited by W. PETERSON, M.A. . . . . [Extra fcap. 8vo, 3s. 6d.

Sallust. *Bellum Catilinarium* and *Jugurthinum.* With Introduction and Notes, by W. W. CAPES, M.A. . . [Extra fcap. 8vo, 4s. 6d.

Tacitus. *The Annals.* Books I—IV. Edited, with Introduction and Notes for the use of Schools and Junior Students, by H. FURNEAUX, M.A.
                                                    [Extra fcap. 8vo, 5s.

—— *The Annals.* Book I. By the same Editor. . . [limp, 2s.

Terence. *Adelphi.* With Notes and Introductions. By A. SLOMAN, M.A. . . . . [Extra fcap. 8vo, 3s.

—— *Andria.* With Notes and Introductions. By C. E. FREEMAN, M.A., and A. SLOMAN, M.A. *Second Edition* . . [Extra fcap. 8vo, 3s.

—— *Phormio.* With Notes and Introductions. By A. SLOMAN, M.A. . . . . [Extra fcap. 8vo, 3s.

Tibullus and **Propertius.** *Selections.* Edited, with Introduction and Notes, by G. G. RAMSAY, M.A. *Second Edition.* . [Extra fcap. 8vo, 6s.

Virgil. With an Introduction and Notes. By T. L. PAPILLON, M.A., and A. E. HAIGH, M.A. . . . . [Crown 8vo, 12s.

—— *Bucolics and Georgics.* By the same Editors. [Crown 8vo, 3s. 6d.

—— *Aeneid.* With Introduction and Notes, by the same Editors. In Four Parts. . . . . [Crown 8vo, 3s. each.

—— *The Text, including the Minor Works.*
                          [On writing-paper, 5s.; on India paper, 6s.

—— *Bucolics.* With Introduction and Notes, by C. S. JERRAM, M.A.
                                                    [Extra fcap. 8vo, 2s. 6d.

—— *Georgics.* Books I, II. By the same Editor. [Extra fcap. 8vo, 2s. 6d.

—— *Georgics.* Books III, IV. By the same Editor. [Extra fcap. 8vo, 2s. 6d.

—— *Aeneid I.* With Introduction and Notes, by the same Editor.
                                              [Extra fcap. 8vo, limp, 1s. 6d.

—— *Aeneid IX.* Edited, with Introduction and Notes, by A. E. HAIGH, M.A. . . . [Extra fcap. 8vo, limp, 1s. 6d. In two Parts, 2s.

London: HENRY FROWDE,
OXFORD UNIVERSITY PRESS WAREHOUSE, AMEN CORNER.
Edinburgh: 12 FREDERICK STREET.